Press **one** for English

Press one for English

LANGUAGE POLICY,
PUBLIC OPINION,
AND AMERICAN IDENTITY

Deborah J. Schildkraut

PRINCETON UNIVERSITY PRESS

PRINCETON AND OXFORD

Copyright © 2005 by Princeton University Press

Published by Princeton University Press, 41 William Street, Princeton, New Jersey 08540

In the United Kingdom: Princeton University Press, 3 Market Place, Woodstock, Oxfordshire OX20 1SY

Library of Congress Cataloging-in-Publication

Schildkraut, Deborah Jill, 1973–
    Press "one" for English : language policy, public opinion, and American identity / Deborah Schildkraut.
        p.   cm.
    Based on author's thesis (doctoral)—Princeton University, 2000.
    Includes bibliographical references and index.
    ISBN 0-691-11814-0 (cloth : alk. paper)
    1. Language policy—United States.   2. English language—Political aspects—United States.   3. Public opinion—United States.   4. Group identity—United States.   5. English-only movement.   I. Title.

    P119.32.U6S34   2005
    306.44′973—dc22   2004054932

British Library Cataloging-in-Publication Data is available

This book has been composed in Goudy

Printed on acid-free paper. ∞

www.pupress.princeton.edu

Printed in the United States of America

10   9   8   7   6   5   4   3   2   1

Contents

Figure and Tables

Acknowledgments

IT GOES WITHOUT SAYING that the help of many people enabled me not only to complete this book but also to have interesting things to say in it. It is with great pleasure that I have the opportunity to thank them now. This book started out as my doctoral dissertation at Princeton University, where I had the good fortune to work with Larry Bartels, Jennifer Hochschild, and Tali Mendelberg. Each of them provided indispensable help at numerous stages. Anything that I've done well in this book can most likely be traced directly to one of them. I'm especially grateful that they've continued to offer research and career guidance generously, even though my formal status as their student ended years ago. While at Princeton, I also benefited from the help of Fred Greenstein, Jeff Lewis, and Karen Stenner. Doug Arnold and his dedication to Princeton's American Politics Research Seminar were valued resources as I fleshed out my ideas and began the analysis. The participants in that seminar always provided the right combination of criticism and support. Particular thanks are due to Sandy Gordon and Greg Huber, who seem to have a limitless amount of time and energy to devote to making sense of my ramblings. It is difficult to overstate how much I have appreciated their friendship, advice, and magical ability to restore my confidence just when I need it. A fellowship from the Woodrow Wilson Society of Fellows and a grant from the Center for Arts and Cultural Policy Studies—both at Princeton and under the able guidance of Stanley Katz—also deserve mention, for they gave me a year of freedom to devote my full attention to this project.

The book was completed while I was a member of the faculty at Oberlin College. I thank the entire politics department there for creating the collegial and supportive environment that enabled me to get the project done. Ben Schiff and Sonia Kruks were essential in helping me learn how to navigate the book-publishing process. And a sabbatical provided by Oberlin College gave me the time I needed to complete the final revisions.

Roberta Sigel, Michael Delli Carpini, and Montague Kern provided extremely useful guidance on all aspects of focus group research, especially when the project was in its earliest stages. The time and energy they were willing to spend with someone they had never met was extraordinary and helped set an example of the type of scholar I try to be. Special thanks are also due to Jeff Berry, who has been a mentor and friend for years, and who helped me get my start in this business. Various sections of the book have benefited from valuable critiques from conference panelists too numerous to name, and from anonymous reviewers for—and editors at—*Political Psychology*, *Political Behavior*, and Princeton University Press. Sections of the book were previously published in "American Identity and Attitudes Toward Official-English Policies," in *Political Psychology* (September 2003) and are reprinted here with permission. I am also very grateful for the hard work of the staff at Princeton University Press, particularly Chuck Myers, Jennifer Nippins, and Brigitte Pelner. Additional thanks are due to Joan Torkildson and Sylvia Coates.

Kristen Wall, Cesar Rosado, Jayne Bialkowski, Mildred Kalmus, and Monica Selinger each provided skillful and invaluable assistance while I was conducting the focus groups and content analysis. I am fully aware of how unusual it is for a graduate student to have such an amazing team at her disposal. Much of that team could not have been assembled, of course, without adequate funding. The National Science Foundation provided a dissertation improvement award (#9807968), and Jennifer Hochschild was able to provide funding through a grant from the Spencer Foundation.

This funding also made it possible for me to recruit the people who ultimately became the participants in the focus groups. I am very appreciative of their generosity with their time and willingness to share their personal thoughts and experiences with me. Anyone who has jaded views about the political sophistication of the American public should sit in on some focus groups. The depth and complexity that emerges when people are not forced to place their opinions in a box and are actually given time to sort out and articulate their views is both refreshing and remarkable.

Several family members and friends have always been able to provide necessary diversions and generally do the things that good friends are supposed to do. I am happy to thank Melanie Schneider, Danique Van Dongen, Jennifer Palumbo, Andrew Krull, John Smee, Daniel Markey, Ulrike Eggert, Majid Ezzati, Kasia Hagemajer Allen, Richard Allen, Sean Corner, Amber Miller, Amanda Dickins, Tomoharu Nishino, Irena Ivanovska, Anna Gade, Ellen Stroud, Pablo Mitchell, the Hollands (Peter, Donna, Aaron, and Arielle), the Princeton poker group, and the Oberlin Feve group. I'd also like to thank my friends at Oberlin who let me buy them beer in exchange for helping me come up with the book's title. In the end, the idea was my own, but I couldn't have gotten there without them.

By the time I met R. J. Russell, much of this book had already been written, yet it's fair to say that he's responsible for getting me through the final hurdles. I am constantly awed by his ability to sense what I'm going through and to provide exactly what I need to help get me through it. There isn't enough space or time to do justice to how much he means to me.

Finally, I wish to acknowledge my family. My brothers Rob and Dave both serve as inspirations, and my parents are simply without equals. Their bottomless reservoir of love and support never ceases to amaze me. Of all of the wonderful gifts I have been given in my life, my family has always been my most prized possession. It is to the four of them that I dedicate this book.

Press ⬤one for English

CHAPTER ONE

Introduction

In 1996, Wayland H. Cooley, the tax assessor of Madison County, Alabama, was sued for refusing to grant a tax credit—a local benefit that is supposed to be given to people who live in the homes that they own rather than renting them out—to a Korean-American family and to other minorities. He defended his action by arguing that even with a translator, he could not be sure if their oath of residency was accurate. He also maintained that his refusal to grant the credit was in accord with the state's constitution, which declares that English is the official state language. The case was eventually settled in November of 1999, with Cooley agreeing to grant the tax credits as long as the applicants brought translators (Sack 1999; Associated Press 1999).

Nearby, in suburban Atlanta, some Hispanic store owners were fined for violating an ordinance that requires signs to be at least 75 percent English. In defense of making words like *supermercado* be changed to *supermarket*, Sergeant H. Smith, a local police officer, said, "The 'super' is English. But I don't know what 'mercado' means. If an American was out there driving by, he wouldn't know what that was" (Branigin 1999). The case is working its way through the judicial system, with the store owners charging that the ordinance violates their freedom of speech (Lezin 1999b). As in Alabama, English is the official language in Georgia.

Regardless of whether one finds the actions and comments of Cooley and Smith to be offensive, justified, or simply entertaining, it is certain that conflicts such as these are becoming more and more common in the United States. The ethnic composition of the population has undergone dramatic changes over the past thirty years. From the mid-1960s to the mid-1990s, levels of immigration rose steadily, as did the proportion of immigrants arriving from Latin American and Asian countries. The government estimates that the foreign-born now make up 11.5 percent of the population, up from 5 percent in 1970 (Camarota 1999; Schmidley 2003). Several public policy issues have gained prominence in response to these demographic changes, including bilingual education, immigration laws, border enforcement, official-English laws, and the provision of public services to immigrants.

All levels of government, from the U.S. Congress and the Supreme Court to the assemblies of places like Evergreen Park, Illinois, and Englewood Cliffs, New Jersey, have been faced with the challenge of developing appropriate policies to help immigrants adapt and become full members of the community.

In 1996, for example, four Chicago suburbs, including Evergreen Park, voted to make English their official town language. Supporters claimed that the measures were intended to encourage immigrants to learn English and, as one mayor argued, to ensure that they would become better citizens and be able to do more than "sweep floors [and] work in places like McDonald's" (Cotliar 1996). But not everyone saw such admirable intent. Critics charged that the declaration was a form of immigrant bashing and would only promote discrimination and alienation. Also in the mid-1990s, six towns in Bergen County, New Jersey, including Englewood Cliffs, passed ordinances requiring storefront signs in foreign languages to have words in English. Some of those towns have since repealed their ordinances to avoid lawsuits, though supporters still assert the integrity of their concerns: promoting communication among residents and protecting public safety by ensuring that firefighters and emergency crews can locate where they need to be (Geller 1997). As these examples illustrate, policies that deal with language have become both common and contentious, and debates about how to respond to the presence of non-English-speaking residents and citizens, including debates about whether to make English the official language, have become an important feature of American political discourse.

Official-English legislation consistently enjoys widespread support among the American people. In 1998, for example, Alaska voters approved an initiative to make English the official state language with 70 percent of the vote (Clark 1998). Also in 1998, California voters opted to end bilingual education programs by passing Proposition 227 with 61 percent of the vote (Terry 1998). Since then, Arizona and Massachusetts have done the same. In the 1994 General Social Survey (GSS), 60 percent of the respondents supported making English the official language of the country, and other surveys throughout the 1990s show similar figures. This high level of public support for restrictive language policies remains substantial across the traditional political and social cleavages along which competing interests in America normally divide. Hispanics and liberals tend to be the only groups whose support for official-English is under 50 percent, but even among these groups, support is often above 25 percent.

With figures such as these, the question that begs to be answered is, why do so many people support restrictive language policies? The high levels of public support become even more curious when we take into account some key elements of the role of the English language in American society. First, for all practical purposes, English already is the de facto official language of the United States. Second, most non-English speakers are aware of the need to learn English if they hope to "make it" in mainstream American life. It is also becoming more and more essential to learn English if one hopes to "make it" anywhere in the world. Third, most immigrants and their children want to and do learn English (Stevens 1994; Portes and Rumbaut 2001) and think that the United States should expect immigrants to learn English (Public Agenda 2003). In short, strong incentives to learn English already exist, and by and large, those incentives work (Schmidt 2000). Moreover, there is no evidence to suggest that making English the official language would add to the incentive structure or make it easier for people to learn English.

Because a logical connection between learning English and official-English laws appears to be lacking, accounts of support for official-English laws have tended to focus on two other motivations, both of which simply involve the desire to make immigrants feel unwelcome. The first motivation is economic security. The argument here is that people become more willing to close borders and deny services to immigrants when they perceive that either the nation or their own family is economically vulnerable. Conventional wisdom holds that people blame immigrants when they fear for their economic security. By this reasoning, official-English is just a way to send a message that "America is for Americans" and that we should look after our own before expending our efforts on others. I show in later chapters that evidence for this economic security argument is less than sound despite the intuitive appeal of its hypotheses.

The second motivation is racism, or more precisely, anti-immigrant sentiments targeted specifically at Latinos and Asians (e.g., Perea 1997). The United States has always had citizens who do not know English, yet official-English battles are largely a recent phenomenon. That the changing face of immigration coincides with an increase in debates about language is, some fear, no coincidence at all. For instance, opponents of Atlanta's ordinance requiring signs to be 75 percent English point out that the policy has not been enforced at French and Italian restaurants the same way it has at Latino markets. Noting the potential absurdity of the ordinance, the Mexican consul general in Atlanta remarked that true enforcement would require El Taco Veloz, a restaurant chain in the area, to change its name to "Speedy Cornflour Pancake" (Lezin 1999a). Enforcement has not been taken to this extreme but rather has been more selective, leading many to feel that the motivation behind enforcement is not really about language but instead about sending a message to a particular group of people that they are not welcome.

In another example, Carbon County, Pennsylvania, passed an official-English resolution in 1997 with the support of a county commissioner who said, "We have to gear everything around Spanish. That doesn't make a whole lot of sense to me" (Ayers 1997). Yet Carbon County has very few non-English speakers and did not print any bilingual materials before the resolution was passed. The county did request one hundred voter registration guides in Spanish from the state in 1996, but two years later, all one hundred were still sitting in a file cabinet due to lack of demand (Ayers 1998). When a county commissioner justifies an official-English law through complaints about accommodating non-English speakers when in fact the county has never found itself negatively impacted by such accommodation, one cannot help but wonder if anything other than anti-immigrant sentiments are at work. I show throughout the analysis that such sentiments help to explain some, but not all, of the public support for restrictive language policies.

But there is also a third possible explanation for why so many Americans support official-English laws, one that has surfaced primarily in academic circles. It concerns language itself more directly than the previous explanations and focuses on conceptions of American national identity. Scholars have derived this explanation from the idea that national symbols, values, norms, and myths shape how people interpret the social and political world and help them make sense of policy debates. For some, this process will still involve a degree of racism, but for many, the ideals that are considered to make America unique are seen as endangered without a single public language.[1] Likewise, other people feel that American values and ideals will be threatened if official-English is mandated. A wide range of American ideals, including individualism, economic opportunity, participatory democracy, openness to immigration, and tolerance, are all implicated in debates about language use. People seek to protect the images of American identity that they cherish; for some this leads to support for official-English laws, whereas for others it leads to opposition.

Americans have always been somewhat obsessed with ideas about "what it means to be an American" and with whether certain practices and beliefs emulate "the American way of life." This obsession, which seems to have gained prominence in recent years, centers on values, myths, and norms that dictate the conceptual boundaries of national identity. Some of these norms and values are ideological, others cultural. But regardless of whether the norms people associate with national identity are attitudinal or ascriptive in nature, they all have the potential to be activated when people think about the appropriate role of government in addressing political issues. In other words, this third explanation for why official-English enjoys such widespread support maintains that how people think the government should respond to ethnic change will be affected by their understanding of what it means to be an American and by their expectations about whether the proposed governmental action—or inaction—will sustain or threaten the American way of life. Many people see ethnic change as a threat to the American way of life (for a variety of reasons—some ideological and some ascriptive) and, consequently, as a threat to their own sense of self. It is this perceived threat that leads to support for official-English.

An appealing aspect of this argument is that it allows scholars to study opposition to restrictive policies rather than forcing them to rely on the assump-

[1] Support for official-English as a means to preserve the integrity of American identity assumes that official-English laws will actually promote the learning of English. This assumption reappears among the participants in my study and in pro-official-English rhetoric despite its questionable accuracy.

tion that opposition results from an absence of the factors that drive support. For example, American society is popularly defined by an unparalleled amount of freedom. For some people, making English the official language could be seen as a violation of certain freedoms and thus pose a threat to what America is supposed to stand for. This motivation is missed by studies that assume opposition to official-English results from simply a lack of nativist sentiments. Certain ideas about what being American means can lead to one policy preference, while other ideas about what being American means can lead to the opposite preference. Regardless of the resulting policy view, the desire to protect one's sense of national identity drives his or her opinions on the issue.[2] There is a growing amount of evidence to support the argument that the way people define being American is an important influence on how they feel about political issues. There is disagreement, however, over what exactly people think it means to be an American and over which national norms and values should be included in the analysis. In this book, I add to the evidence that national identity shapes attitudes, and I address in great detail the competing images people hold about what being American means. I argue that these competing images constitute distinct conceptions of American identity and that all of them need to be incorporated into analyses of public support for, and opposition to, ethnicity-related policies such as official-English.

AMERICAN IDENTITY AND OFFICIAL-ENGLISH

In response to the increasing prominence of debates about language and ethnicity, more and more political scientists have begun to examine several aspects of this issue area. Some scholars have tried to understand why certain states have chosen to declare English the official state language (e.g., Hero 1998; Tatalovich 1995; Gamble 1997; Schildkraut 2001), while others study how Congress and the courts address language and immigration issues (e.g., Baron 1990; Gimpel and Edwards 1999; Schmid 2001) or how activists in language policy battles frame their positions (e.g., Perea 1997; Schmidt 2000; Schmid 2001). Another set of research examines public opinion and seeks to understand how Americans feel about issues that arise from ethnic change and why (e.g., Espenshade and Calhoun 1993; Espenshade and Hempstead 1996; Huddy and Sears 1995; Hood et al. 1997; Hood and Morris 1997; Vidanage and Sears 1995; Citrin, Reingold, and Green 1990; Citrin, Reingold, Walters, and Green 1990; Citrin et al. 1997; Citrin and Duff 1998; Frendreis and Tatalovich 1997; Citrin, Sears, Muste, and Wong 2001). On one level, these studies have provided avenues through which we can learn more about the

[2] Sapiro and Soss (1999) demonstrate similar claims about the role of symbolic politics and interpretation of events.

broader sets of issues surrounding state politics and the initiative process, congressional position taking and agenda setting, and opinion formation. On another level, they have helped to advance the study of ethnic politics and policy in the United States, a growing research tradition itself.

Following suit, my goals in this book are to contribute to our understanding of opinion formation on a general level and to provide an analysis of how Americans use their interpretations of American identity to come to terms with the specific and increasingly salient issue of language policy. I define and document four distinct conceptions of American identity and show how each one is implicated in debates about language use. The four conceptions are the universally accepted *liberal* tradition (America as a land of freedom and opportunity), the under-studied *civic republican* tradition (America as a participatory democracy with vibrant communities and dutiful citizens), the highly contested *ethnocultural* tradition (America as a nation of white Protestants), and the equally contested *incorporationist* tradition (America as a diverse "nation of immigrants"). I rely on focus groups with ordinary Americans and survey data to establish that these four traditions guide what people think it means to be American and to demonstrate how people rely on them when forming and explaining their views on different language policies, such as declaring English the official language and printing election ballots only in English. Throughout, I argue that these different conceptions of American identity are often at odds with one another and can be internally conflictual as well, and I show how these clashes between and within alternative ideas of what it means to be an American are an integral part of how people debate these salient political issues. People on both sides of the language issue have very strong and cherished notions of what being an American means, and both sides feel that their sense of American identity is at stake in these debates.

LINKING AMERICAN POLITICAL THOUGHT AND PUBLIC OPINION RESEARCH

One central aim of this book is to expand the range of concerns that have been used to explain the widespread support for official-English legislation by showing how multiple conceptions of American national identity shape opinions about language policies. I argue that people's views about the role of the citizen in the polity—views that are guided by the tenets of civic republicanism—affect preferences at least as much as the other aspects of American national identity that have received more attention in public opinion research, namely liberalism and ethnoculturalism. American political culture is infused with the image of the participating citizen in a cohesive community in which deliberation and compromise contribute to a stable public life. The power of this image to affect policy preferences has not been addressed adequately in past attempts to explain how American identity shapes public opinion on language issues or on public policy more broadly. By incorporating this version of

American identity into the analysis and by using a combination of quantitative and qualitative approaches, I am able to increase our understanding of the role that national identity plays in debates about diversity and ethnic change.

Three of the four conceptions of American identity on which my analysis centers—liberalism, civic republicanism, and ethnoculturalism—are adopted from Rogers Smith's work on the history of citizenship laws in the United States (1988, 1993, 1997). Smith is not the only scholar to describe the political culture in the United States as derived from these traditions, but his explicit juxtaposition of them provides a systematic framework that can address some of the shortcomings that plague existing data and analyses. For example, this framework allows me to study the role of civic republicanism, an ideological tradition that has virtually been ignored by public opinion research.

Despite this advantage, however, Smith's analysis emphasizes the attitudes and behaviors of elite political actors only through the Progressive Era and may not accurately describe the contemporary beliefs of ordinary Americans. To address this possibility, I add a fourth conception of American identity to Smith's formulation—incorporationism—and it is derived from the immigrant legacy of the nation. Although many Americans identify the nation with particular ideological principles, they also recognize the unique role that immigration has played in the political and social development of the country. This role may not have been particularly relevant for Smith's project, but could prove to be an important addition here. Thus, another aim of the book is to provide structure to the very nebulous treatment that the image of the United States as a "nation of immigrants" has received in public opinion research and to evaluate its role as a conception of national identity.

In assessing opinion formation on the increasingly salient and contentious debates about language use, I unite theory-based treatments of American identity with opinion data. These two types of scholarship often address the same topics, but scholars in each field do not pay enough attention to what the other is doing. I maintain that the problem of inadequate survey design could be remedied if public opinion scholars did more to acknowledge the insights that work in American political thought offers. Theoretical and historical approaches have often done a more thorough job of exploring enduring national myths than survey-based analyses or studies of interest group activity. These works discuss the philosophical underpinnings of civic traditions, how these traditions have evolved over time, and how elite actors have employed them in the political arena. The behavior of elites and the opinions of citizens unquestionably have different sets of influences, but thorough accounts of elite-driven ideals need to be consulted when generating hypotheses about opinion formation among ordinary Americans and when designing methodological tools for testing them. Research shows that the public often takes cues from political elites about values, norms, and specific policy stances (e.g., Zaller 1992; Baumgartner and Jones 1993; Mendelberg 2001). These works demonstrate that the ways in which issues are framed and in which social norms are constructed often start from above and eventually make their way into the consciousness of the average citizen.[3] Studies of nationalism suggest that elite influence is particularly potent when it comes to defining the content of national identity (e.g., Anderson 1991; Brubaker 1996; Gellner 1983; Hobsbawm 1990; Snyder and Ballentine 1996). It is for these reasons that I look to work by scholars such as Rogers Smith, Michael Walzer, Louis Hartz, Gordon Wood, and John Higham for developing the model of American identity that I expect ordinary Americans to endorse. Whether the guidance these studies provide results in a more accurate model of how people conceive of American identity than the guidance provided solely by studies of public opinion and language policy activists is an empirical question. Existing surveys, however, do not ask the kinds of questions needed that would allow for such empirical investigation to take place. In the end, I conclude from focus group analysis that a model informed by political theory does indeed provide a more useful way to characterize how people think about American identity and to examine the influence that identity has on policy views than the models currently in use in public opinion research.

METHODOLOGICAL APPROACH

Focus groups serve as the main tool that enables this project to achieve its goals. Hence, another central aim of this book is to demonstrate the value of focus groups for studying opinion formation on ethnicity-related policies and for studying public opinion more generally. The focus groups allow me to explore questions that surveys have had difficulty addressing and allow participants to express their views in their own words without being constrained by a fixed set of choices or by my specific hypotheses. They offer depth and insight that allow me first to test whether my model provides an appropriate framework for understanding how regular Americans describe their national identity and then to study the connections people make between that identity and their particular policy preferences. The discourse that emerges from these group discussions provides unique and useful information on which aspects of the political culture are revered (or abhorred), how people define those aspects of the political culture and use them to justify policy preferences, and what the important similarities and differences are between the policy proposals being debated. Finally, my use of the focus groups makes methodological as well as substantive contributions. Protocols and standards for using this relatively new research tool are still being developed. My analysis adds to the

---

[3] Other studies suggest that elite behavior on certain issues follows from, rather than precedes, changes in public opinion (e.g., Page and Shapiro 1983), and still other works argue that the relationship between elite opinion, mass opinion, and policy outputs is reciprocal, or one of "opinion sharing" (e.g., Hill and Hinton-Andersson 1995). Understanding the conditions that affect the direction of the links between elite and mass beliefs is an ongoing research agenda.

growing list of ways that people have used this exciting method to gain important insights into opinion formation. The description and justification of my methodological choices should be of interest to the increasing number of scholars considering incorporating focus groups into their own research.

Using the theoretically derived model of American identity advances our knowledge of how people conceive of what it means to be an American, how conceptions of identity guide opinion formation, and how people apply their notions of national identity to the specific realm of language policy. Using the focus groups demonstrates the complex and contextual nature of how people feel about language issues. The focus groups provide insights into the very real struggle people go through in sorting out their competing values. People sense that language policy can be a window into the soul of the nation. The focus groups give them a chance to articulate what it is they want to see when they look through that window.

OPINIONS ABOUT LANGUAGE: BELOW THE SURFACE, GROWING STRONGER

My interest in this project originally grew out of a discomfort with existing studies that looked at how people feel about language issues and ethnic change. Certainly we can think of benefits of having everyone in a society speak the same language. For instance, a common public language facilitates political participation and fosters a public sphere where citizens can communicate and debate with one another over public policy in an efficient manner. Yet supporting official-English laws is often cast as irrational or nativist, though such condemnation is, I argue, premature. In a crude sense then, determining how much of this support is "bad" (i.e., driven by anti-minority affect or the belief that only people with certain cultural backgrounds can be American) and how much of it is "good" (i.e., wanting the benefits of having a common language used in the public sphere) is one of the underlying motivations of this project. People frequently rely on the questionable assumption that official-English laws will actually promote the learning of English. Why they think that is so is a question to be pursued elsewhere. But agreeing that all Americans should know English is not in and of itself a sign of sinister motives.

I was also drawn to this project simply because of the salience that language issues have in today's political landscape and what that salience reveals about the United States at the start of the twenty-first century. It is difficult pick up a major newspaper without seeing stories of diversity, population projections, or other conflicts and issues that arise from demographic change. Moreover, there has been much more legislative activity and many more court cases at all levels of government that deal with language over the past two decades.

Official-English may not be an issue that people think about regularly. Few issues are. But for the past several years, whenever I meet someone who asks me what I do, without fail, we end up in an animated discussion with the person arguing for his or her own view on language policies. The frequency and consistency of this reaction indicates that the issue strikes a chord despite not being considered one of the "most important problems facing the country today." It speaks to concerns that academics have focused on for a long time— attitude formation, prejudice, national identity, diversity—but it also speaks to concerns that provoke strong emotions among the rest of the American population.

The United States already has an incentive structure that promotes the learning of English, yet many people feel that this incentive structure is no longer working. As the country becomes even more diverse, examining whether they are right or wrong and what the implications are becomes more important. This study is about language policy in particular, but it is fundamentally linked to broader issues that deal with how the government of a democratic society addresses the presence of multiple ethnic and language groups. These dilemmas are not new, but they are increasingly prominent. Although the United States has been fortunate relative to most other countries in its ability to deal with ethnic and linguistic diversity, investigating the role of identity politics in the causes and consequences of language debates is imperative.

LANGUAGE POLICY IN THE UNITED STATES

Before delving into theories of opinion formation or the specific conceptions of American national identity and their power to shape how people interpret language policy debates, it is first necessary to have a basic knowledge of the current state of language policy in the United States. The following brief history of language politics in American society is not meant to be an authoritative account of the development of language laws in the United States. Rather, this review is meant to provide context to the debates explored throughout my analysis.[4]

LANGUAGE CONFLICT AT THE NATIONAL LEVEL

According to the 1997 *Political Handbook of the World*, the United States is one of 8 countries (out of 191 entries) that do not have an official language.[5] Many Americans are surprised when they are told that English is not the official language of the country. The questions that usually follow are valid ones: Why not? Why did the Framers not include a language provision when they wrote the Constitution? Why has one not been added since? English has without a doubt been the dominant language of public discourse in America since

[4] See Baron (1990), Schmidt (2000), and Schmid (2001) for more detailed accounts of language policy debates and court decisions.

[5] The other seven countries are Great Britain, Somalia, Eritrea, Ethiopia, Pakistan, Costa Rica, and Bosnia-Herzegovina (Banks et al. 1997).

the establishment of the colonies. This dominance has been unchallenged for so long that many people assume that the English language has official status.

Two arguments have been offered to explain why the founders did not make English the official language when they wrote the Constitution. The first posits that the founding fathers did not think language was or would be an issue. It is argued that they felt that all men of importance (that is, white Anglo-Saxon Protestants) spoke English and that English would eventually spread to become the only language of the land (King 1997; Schmid 2001). Those men who were considered citizens at the founding were ethnically homogeneous, and the cultural and ethnic homogeneity of the American people in future generations was assumed (Gleason 1980). As John Jay (Hamilton, Madison, and Jay 1961 [1787–1788]) famously wrote in Federalist #2: "With equal pleasure I have as often taken notice that Providence has been pleased to give this one connected country to one united people—a people descended from the same ancestors, speaking the same language, professing the same religion, attached to the same principles of government, very similar in their manners and customs. . . ." In short, they saw no reason to designate English as the official language when all people who were considered to be true Americans already spoke it.

The second argument asserts that language use was indeed an issue, but fears that a language provision would thwart the ability to form a union won the day and such a provision was left out. Many official and unofficial political documents of the time were printed in German and French in addition to English. The ability to spread information to the different ethnic groups living in the colonies was seen as essential in building support for and loyalty to the new nation (Piatt 1990). Being open to several languages both made the new nation more attractive to immigrants and allowed for the spread of democratic ideas (Heath 1992; Marshall 1986). Benjamin Rush, a member of the Continental Congress, for example, was against language regulations and felt that education, in any language, was crucial for the survival of a democratic government. Those Americans who did not speak English, he argued, should have opportunities for intellectual development and political involvement. Such opportunities were necessary if the new nation was going to endure. Others agreed with him and felt that mandating this cultural norm did not fit with the sentiments in the Declaration (Heath 1992).

Opposing Rush were John Adams and Noah Webster, both of whom supported the idea of a common language as a means to social and political progress. Webster even opposed regional accents because of their tendency to create divisions (Crawford 1992; Simpson 1986). He argued that multiple languages and dialects would only separate people and make them less willing and able to cooperate in a common political enterprise. At a time when union and independence were so tenuous, establishing a single public language was seen by some as necessary for the creation of the nation itself (Baron 1990). Adams even proposed the establishment of a national academy for language but was unable to garner enough congressional support for its approval (Edwards 1985).

The first known congressional vote concerning language occurred in 1795. The first language bill of that year would have allowed Congress to print its laws both in German and in English. It was rejected, but debate continued and led to a second proposal that same year. This second bill required that all federal statutes be printed in English only. The bill passed and was signed by George Washington. The story behind these votes has been transformed over the years into the myth that the United States came within one vote of declaring German the official language (Baron 1990).

Over the next 150 years, the ethnic composition of the American population continued to evolve, and congressional debates about immigration policy became common. Debates about language, however, were largely confined to the states and localities. The federal government did not return to the issue of language until the post–World War II era when immigration laws and trends entered their current phase.

Strict quotas on the number of immigrants allowed to enter the United States from different nations were in place for much of the twentieth century. In 1965, Congress passed the Immigration and Nationality Act amendments, which amended the McCarran-Walter Immigration and Nationality Act of 1952. The 1952 act eliminated racial barriers to naturalization but left immigration quotas in place. The 1965 amendments finally dropped the country-specific quotas and shifted the focus toward family reunification (Mills 1994; Edmonston and Passel 1994). Since then, the overall number of immigrants legally entering the country each year has increased dramatically. In the 1960s, the United States saw an annual average of 332,000 immigrants entering the country. In the 1990s, the annual average was 991,000.[6] Another important change in immigration trends is that the countries from which most immigrants arrive have shifted away from Europe and toward Asia and Latin America. According to the U.S. Immigration and Naturalization Service (INS), immigration from Asia, Latin America, and the Caribbean has come to account for over 70 percent of all legal immigration to the United States, whereas in the 1950s and early 1960s, it accounted for only 47 percent.[7]

[6] In recent years, the overall number of legal immigrants admitted per year has declined somewhat. The INS attributes this decrease to a substantial rise in the number of pending "adjustment of status applications." Applying for an adjustment of status is the process through which "aliens" living in the United States attempt to get legal permanent residence. The INS estimates that the mid-1990s would have seen between 350,000 and 450,000 more legal immigrants had the pending applications been processed. The INS also estimates that the 1990s saw about 275,000 undocumented immigrants entering the country per year (U.S. Department of Justice 1999). Note: As of March 1, 2003, the INS was replaced by the Bureau of Citizenship and Immigration Services (BCIS) and is now under the jurisdiction of the Department of Homeland Security.

[7] U.S. Immigration and Naturalization Service 1999.

   This major—and rather rapid—change in the demographic makeup of people living in the United States, combined with an added boost from the civil rights movement, led Congress to pass two pieces of legislation that required political and social institutions to be more responsive to the needs of language minorities. The first language provision passed in this era was the 1968 Bilingual Education Act, which provided funding for bilingual education programs across the country. It set broad guidelines for programs to be eligible for funds but stopped short of prescribing how such programs should be implemented (Schmid 2001). In 1974, the Supreme Court ruled in *Lau v. Nichols* that schools that did not provide the opportunity for non-English-speaking students to "participate meaningfully" in the classroom were violating the 1964 Civil Rights Act, and that the failure to meet the educational needs of these students is discrimination based on national origin. The burden was placed on state boards of education and local schools to develop programs that would meet those needs (Citrin 1990).

   The second piece of legislation came in 1975 when language provisions were added to the Voting Rights Act of 1965 (VRA). These amendments required election officials to provide bilingual voting assistance in communities where 5 percent or more of the citizens speak a language that is not English (Thernstrom 1980). In 1992, these provisions were extended for another fifteen years and were amended to require bilingual assistance in communities where at least ten thousand citizens in a jurisdiction speak a language that is not English even if they do not constitute 5 percent of the jurisdiction's population. This and other provisions of the VRA come up for reauthorization in 2007.

   The passage of these laws has not allowed supporters to rest on their laurels. Instead, they have faced continual challenges since the 1980s from policy makers, organizations, and citizens who favor more restrictive policies. In 1981, Senator S. I. Hayakawa (R-CA) introduced a bill to amend the Constitution to declare English the official language of the United States, and similar bills for either amendments or statutes have appeared in every Congress since then. These bills have often died in committee, but in 1996, the Bill Emerson English Language Empowerment Act passed in the House of Representatives by a 259–169 vote. It died in the Senate and has consistently been reintroduced (Ricento 1998). If the act had become law, it would have declared English the official language of the U.S. government, required that all "representatives" of the federal government conduct business in English, required all naturalization ceremonies to be conducted in English, and repealed the bilingual voting requirements of the VRA. It also curiously stated that "no person shall be denied services, assistance, or facilities, directly or indirectly provided by the Federal Government solely because the person communicates in English."[8]

----

[8] See http://thomas.loc.gov for the full text of the bill.

Two official-English bills have been introduced in the House of Representatives of the current Congress (108th), and both have been sent to committee. One, the National Language Act of 2003 (H.R. 931), states: "Unless specifically stated in applicable law, no person has a right, entitlement, or claim to have the Government of the United States or any of its officials or representatives act, communicate, perform or provide services, or provide materials in any language other than English."[9] It would repeal the Bilingual Education Act, terminate the Office of Bilingual Education and Minority Languages Affairs (OBEMLA), require all naturalization ceremonies to be conducted in English, and repeal the bilingual voting requirements of the VRA. As of this writing, the bill has forty cosponsors. To date, such efforts to pass restrictive language laws have been unsuccessful at the federal level. Yet the efforts continue unabated. The states, however, have enjoyed much more success in this area.

LANGUAGE CONFLICT AT THE STATE LEVEL

The needs of language minorities have always been both met with and frustrated by state and local policies more so than with national ones. Many states used to allow public schooling in the languages of ethnic minorities and printed official state proceedings in multiple languages (Baron 1990). The first state to declare English the official language was Louisiana, and it did so in its 1812 constitution with the hope of securing its admission to the Union (Foote 1942).[10] After Louisiana, there was little state-level activity until 1920, when Nebraska amended its constitution to declare English its official language. In a wave of anti-German paranoia, this period saw many states legislate that only English could be used in public schools. By 1923, thirty-four states had passed laws prohibiting public—and in some cases private—schools from using languages other than English (Marshall 1986). The Supreme Court ruled in *Meyer v. Nebraska* (1923) that such laws violated the due process clause and were unconstitutional. States still control the form and extent to which educational and other services are provided in other languages, but they do so largely under federal mandate.

Corresponding to the federal limits on immigration, state-level language policy activity waned during the middle part of the twentieth century and resurfaced in the 1980s. As of this writing, twenty-eight states have declared English the official state language. Of these twenty-eight declarations, twenty-three have been since 1980 and eleven have been since 1990.[11] Figure 1.1 displays a map of the United States highlighting all twenty-eight states that have

[9] See http://thomas.loc.gov for the full text of the bill.

[10] Some controversy exists over whether English is in fact the official language of Louisiana, with proponents of official-English interpreting early nineteenth-century documents one way and opponents interpreting them another. The interpretation I use was provided to me by a reference librarian at the Louisiana State Library who relayed a 1942 analysis via telephone.

[11] The following websites provide useful information about official-English legislation: English-First at www.englishfirst.org/efstates.htm; U.S. English, Inc. at www.us-english.org/inc/official/states.asp; and James Crawford at http://ourworld.compuserve.com/homepages/jwcrawford/langleg

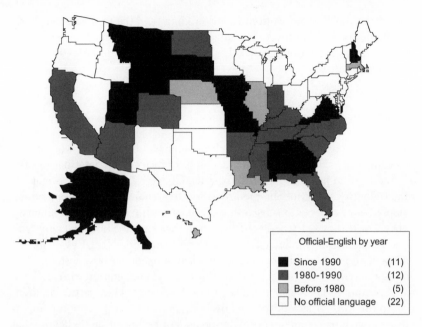

Fig. 1.1 States that have made English official.

declared English official.[12] Most states with English as the official language are clustered in the South and in the plains with a few outliers in the Northeast and the West. At least fifteen of the remaining twenty-two states have debated making English official over the past decade,[13] leaving—at most—only seven states that have not publicly considered official-English legislation in recent

---

.htm#stateleg. Note that the state of Hawaii has declared both English and Native Hawaiian to be official state languages. Also note that Massachusetts' official-English declaration came about through a state supreme court ruling in 1975 (*Commonwealth v. Olivio*) rather than through explicit legislative activity. The commonwealth has since attempted to make English official through statutory as well as case law. As with Louisiana, some controversy exists over whether the English language has official status in the state, with U.S. English maintaining it does (telephone conversation with George Capacinsky, the organization's government director and director of technology, Jan. 24, 2001) and James Crawford, former Washington editor of *Education Week* and independent writer and lecturer on language policy, maintaining that it does not (e-mail exchange, Jan. 25, 2001). In the absence of concrete guidance over classification, I decided to include both Massachusetts and Louisiana among the states that have official-English laws, and I welcome more arguments and evidence in either direction.

[12] Arizona's official-English law was declared unconstitutional in 1999 (Greenhouse 1999) and Alaska's was declared unconstitutional in 2002. Supporters of Alaska's law have appealed to the Alaska Supreme Court; arguments were heard in June 2003 (Pemberton 2003). Thus, as of this writing, only twenty-six of the twenty-eight states (including HI, LA, and MA) effectively have English as the official state language.

[13] CT, ID, KS, ME, MD, MN, NJ, NY, OH, OK, PA, RI, WA, WI, and WV have all recently debated making English official but have not (yet) passed any laws or constitutional amendments on this issue.

years.[14] And as the stories from Madison County, Atlanta, Evergreen Park, and Englewood Cliffs illustrate, language use has continued to be a contentious issue on a more local level as well, causing a stir in cities and towns across the country.

PLAN OF THE BOOK

The book is organized such that each chapter builds upon the work of the preceding one, culminating with an analysis of focus group data that ties the arguments from previous chapters together. Chapter 2 makes the case for national identity as a symbolic predisposition that shapes preferences, and develops a set of expectations regarding this relationship in the area of language policy. For this task, I rely on the literature that explains how and why symbolic predispositions influence attitudes and behaviors. Next I evaluate the claims of empirical public opinion research that examines how abstract ideas affect preferences on issues related to ethnicity and immigration with regard to the expectations laid out in the first part of the chapter. I pay particular attention to the work of Jack Citrin and his colleagues, who emphasize the importance of two broad components of national identity: liberalism (believing that a set of liberal democratic norms are the basis for American national identity) and ethnoculturalism (believing that certain cultural characteristics, such as race or religion, determine who is and who is not an American). While these abstract notions of national identity clearly matter, I argue that focusing on these two conceptions of American identity provides only a limited understanding of the relationship between identity and opinion, for two reasons. First, it omits other widely cherished notions of American identity from the analysis, in particular civic republicanism and incorporationism. Second, it does not recognize the internal conflicts within each of the theoretical constructs, which can and do influence preferences in opposite directions.

In chapter 3, I define the liberal, civic republican, ethnocultural, and incorporationist conceptions of American identity and describe their historical and contemporary relevance in American society. I also look at research on the rhetoric and motivations of activists in language policy debates to examine the extent to which the conceptions of American identity in my model are employed and if so, how. This chapter brings together theory-based treatments of American identity with concrete accounts of policy battles; together, these literatures enhance the set of expectations regarding how ordinary Americans might invoke national norms and values when explaining their views on language issues.

In chapter 4, I use data from the 1996 GSS to demonstrate that the ways in

[14] Those seven are DE, MI, NV, NM, OR, TX, and VT. Note, however, that the Texas legislature considered, and rejected, an official-English bill in the 1980s (Tatalovich 1995).

which notions of American identity influence opinions toward immigrants and immigration policy are more complex than a unidimensional construct can capture. I show that at least two distinct components of American identity can be constructed from the limited range of items that appear on the survey and that these components each have a powerful influence on attitudes. The two components represent an ascriptive or ethnocultural definition of being American (e.g., that true Americans were born in the United States) and a more fluid or "adoptable" definition (e.g., that true Americans have American citizenship). I find that the former makes people more likely to harbor anti-immigrant sentiments than the latter, but that an adherence to either conception makes a person more willing to impose immigration restrictions. I also find that the impact of ethnocultural views is mediated through anti-immigrant sentiments, while the impact of assimilationist views on policy preferences is more direct. While these two constructs are still too broad to fully appreciate the relationship between identity and opinions, they confirm the need to separate the different conceptions of American identity rather than join them together in a single "Americanism" scale. The findings in this chapter also demonstrate that not all support for restrictive policies is driven by anti-immigrant sentiments, but rather that some support derives from other, less exclusive, ideas about national identity.

In chapter 5, I turn to the content analysis of the fourteen focus groups that I conducted in New Jersey in 1998. Before analyzing how conceptions of identity shape attitudes, I first need to confirm the appropriateness of the constructs being used. Thus, the goal of this chapter is to examine the extent to which my model of American identity accurately reflects how citizens think about and discuss what being an American means. I find that describing American identity in terms of Smith's model provides a useful, though incomplete, framework for analyzing opinions about American national identity. His tripartite setup describes ideal types that are not always neatly delineated at the individual level. People not only adhere to different aspects of each, but also often simultaneously express sentiments derived from each one. I also find frequent criticism of the ethnocultural tendencies of American political culture. This criticism, combined with frequently expressed descriptions of American society as one in which people maintain and celebrate their ethnic differences, suggests that a fourth tradition should be added to Smith's trilogy, one that grows out of America's legacy of immigration. This incorporationist conception of American citizenship is indeed quite prevalent among the participants in my study.

Chapter 6 uses the focus group discussions to show how people justify attitudes on official-English laws and proposals for English-only ballots with the symbolic conceptions of American identity. I find that the four conceptions of national identity provide a common means of discourse for talking about language conflicts and ethnic change, but that none of them is consistently associated with either support for or opposition to these policies. Liberal discourse, for example, is used to justify support for making English the official language when people emphasize the belief that a command of English is essential for economic self-sufficiency and success and when they value the distinction between private and public spheres of life. On the other hand, liberal opposition to this policy focuses on civil rights and freedom of expression. In another example, the civic republican conception of national identity leads to support for restrictive language policies when people think the United States is too "balkanized" and needs a common language to help prevent further "balkanization." It also promotes official-English laws when people want to protect the quality of political participation. Participants in the study argue that allowing non-English speakers to be involved in the project of self-governance violates the sacred civic republican image of citizens making informed choices to promote the public good. On the other hand, civic republican concerns lead to opposition to restrictive policies when people value participation—both in terms of quality and *quantity*—and fear that the policies will exclude language minorities from being able to take part. Similar patterns exist regarding ethnoculturalism and incorporationism as well.

Chapter 7 continues my analysis of the relationship between identity and policy preferences by showing how the combination of different conceptions of American identity (conceptual hybridization) shapes support for, and opposition to, these language policies. I also show that the interplay between identity and opinion will vary from issue to issue. It is not surprising that this might be true across issue domains (e.g., immigration vs. school vouchers), but I find that it is also true within a single issue domain (e.g., declaring English the official language vs. printing election ballots only in English vs. bilingual education). The degree of abstraction, the number of policy alternatives, and the clarity of policy options all affect which aspects of identity will matter and whether identity will matter at all. For example, symbols of national identity are more likely to be invoked when the issue at hand is itself abstract and has few policy alternatives, as in the case of declaring English the official language, and less likely when the issue is more complex, as in the case of bilingual education. Even though both issues concern the incorporation of language minorities into the polity, concerns about identity drive preferences on the former more so than on the latter.

I conclude the book with chapter 8, in which I review my arguments, summarize my main findings and discuss their implications, and suggest avenues for future research. When all is said and done, I show that the idea of national identity is an extremely important component of debates about language and ethnicity. People on both sides of the debate, those who support official-English laws and those who oppose them, have very complex images of what being American means. These images are often learned early in life, they are deeply held, and they are also seen to be at risk. On both sides, people fear that many political and cultural norms will be violated if the "wrong" side of the debate prevails.

Above all, I show that civic republicanism, a doctrine of active and responsible citizenship that emphasizes the public good and political participation, is seen as a central aspect of what it means to be an American and plays a large role in how people justify their views on restrictive language policies. That civic republicanism is both cherished by Americans and influential in shaping their preferences, however, does not mean that there is consensus on the language issue. Both supporters and opponents of official-English legislation invoke civic republican ideals and feel that their preferred policy outcome will enable us to live up to them. My hope is that this complex pattern will be explored further in future research, and I offer a variety of theoretical and methodological suggestions in this regard.

The analysis in this book provides insights into how political symbols in general and images of American national identity in particular influence policy preferences. It introduces innovations that will spark debates about both core concepts and methodology. I expect, for example, that some readers will take issue with my articulation of the incorporationist conception of American identity, while others will be skeptical about conclusions drawn from focus groups. Yet these innovations break us out of existing constraints and are necessary for achieving a richer comprehension of the various dynamics that guide opinion formation on salient ethnicity-related policies. Our understanding of the contours and substance of the ideals underlying views about how the state should respond to ethnic change is still evolving. It is my hope that this book will advance that understanding and that it will stimulate the kinds of conceptual and methodological arguments that are needed for this evolution to progress.

Debates about the language(s) in which interactions between citizens and government should be in the United States are on the rise and will most likely be an element of national and local political dialogue for quite some time, especially as the ethnic composition of the American polity continues to change. The Census Bureau projects that by 2020 the U.S. population will be 64 percent white non-Hispanic, 16 percent Hispanic, 13 percent African-American, and 6 percent Asian. By 2050, it will be roughly 53 percent white non-Hispanic, 25 percent Hispanic, 13 percent African-American, and 8 percent Asian.[15] These projections underscore the growing importance of this issue and of understanding the political dynamics that drive these debates.

On one level, my analysis is about the relationship between identity and opinion, a relationship that warrants analysis across a variety of policy domains and should interest scholars of public opinion and political psychology.

[15] Population projections can be obtained from the U.S. Census Bureau's website at www.census.gov.

On another level, it emphasizes a set of concerns that are specific to debates about language, immigration, and ethnicity. The challenge of simultaneously upholding liberal democratic norms, facilitating and encouraging political participation, and incorporating new members into the dominant society has always been, and will continue to be, an important feature of American politics. In studying the relationship between ethnic change and conceptions of American identity, I uncover the fears and desires that need to be addressed as lawmakers try to design policies that both promote the common good and protect the rights of all citizens.

CHAPTER TWO

Symbolic Politics

THEORY AND EVIDENCE

> No matter what part of the world we or our ancestors come from, we all came to America for the same reason. We are here in search of the freedoms and opportunities that make our country great. We are here in search of a better life for themselves and their families. In short, we are here because we want to be Americans. The English language is part of the fabric that keeps us together.
>
> —Rep. Peter Torkildsen (R-MA), in support of H.R. 123, the English Language Empowerment Act, *Congressional Record*, 142, no. 116, part 2 (August 1, 1996): H9749.

> Everyone in this Nation wants the same things—security and opportunities for themselves and their children. This legislation is unnecessary, discriminatory, and would deny opportunities to everyone who is perceived to be different. . . . I urge my colleagues to vote against this distinctly un-American legislation.
>
> —Rep. Nancy Pelosi (D-CA), in opposition to the English Language Empowerment Act, *Congressional Record*, 142, no. 116, part 2 (August 1, 1996): H9741.

AS THE PREVIOUS QUOTES from Representatives Torkildsen and Pelosi illustrate, the debate about whether to make English the official language of the United States is often couched in terms that refer to ideas about what it means to be American or about what the United States stands for. Whether the arguments favor or oppose official-English proposals, the stakes are often seen to be the same: people fear that the very idea of the United States will be threatened if the other side gets its way. How can this be? Can both sides legitimately claim to be the guardian of American identity? Or are both sides simply exaggerating and using grand emotional rhetoric to debate an inconsequential proposal?

Political scientists, anthropologists, and historians have long recognized the ability of intangible and abstract concerns to influence the terms of political debate, define the relevant conflicts within a society, and confer more tangible rewards such as status or power. These intangible and abstract concerns constitute political symbols and create a political reality. In this chapter, I argue that conceptions of American identity are such political symbols. They help people locate themselves within the polity and are often intricately tied to an individual's sense of self. Moreover, conceptions of American identity shape debates about ethnic change and influence the needs and desires of American citizens as far as public policy is concerned. To make this claim, I first review social science literature that explains the importance of symbols and myths in guiding political discourse. I pay particular attention to the work of Murray Edelman (1985 [1964], 1971), Charles Elder and Roger Cobb (1983), and David Sears (1993), who argue that political symbols are functional and powerful because they fulfill individual needs. They also argue that a politically relevant and potent symbol can be interpreted quite differently by different members of a society and yet still be accepted as representing cherished values and norms. While there is consensus over some of the basic elements of American identity, those elements do not always have a uniform interpretation. In the issue area under investigation here, this means that whether one supports or opposes regulating language use will be determined in large part by one's emphasis on the different components of the complex entity known as American identity.

The second part of this chapter contains a review of empirical investigations into the role that such symbolic predispositions play in shaping views toward language and immigration policies. The goal of this review is to see whether the theoretical claims raised in the first part of the chapter are tested adequately by existing scholarship and to draw some preliminary conclusions about the relationship between identity and opinions in this issue area. Taken together, the findings of previous research suggest that conceptions of American identity are indeed a central component in determining policy preferences. But I take issue with their use of narrow measures of American identity and argue that they overlook some important ideas about what many citizens think being American means. Further, they do not test whether people within a given society interpret certain symbols differently or how such differing interpretations influence attitudes.

Throughout, I argue that we should be focusing on abstract concerns of national identity rather than on more self-interested concerns, such as whether a person feels economically vulnerable, if we want to understand why restrictive language proposals consistently get so much support (although I also examine this claim empirically in this and later chapters). I also maintain that we need to adopt theoretical constructs from studies of political theory and American intellectual history about the nature of American identity and incorporate them into analyses of public opinion. The conceptions of national identity that I propose we emphasize are liberalism, civic republicanism, ethnoculturalism, and incorporationism, all of which are described in detail in chapter 3. The idea of being American consists of more than the liberal notion that all people are inherently equal or the ethnocultural idea that all

Americans should look and sound alike. But before I can make this case, I first need to convince the reader that abstract concerns about national identity should be the focal point of this analysis at all, and that is the main goal of this chapter.

OF SYMBOLS AND MYTHS

WHAT ARE SYMBOLS?

Elder and Cobb (1983) define a symbol as "any object used by human beings to index meanings that are not inherent in, nor discernible from, the object itself" (28). They are socially constructed and develop when objects (broadly defined) are endowed with socially significant meaning. They are used in a society to communicate and represent complex ideas and concepts (Firth 1973). Making and referring to symbols is a normal and constant human activity. Political symbols are a subset of socially relevant symbols and are perceived to have political significance. Edelman writes they are a mechanism through which people determine what they want, what is possible, what to fear, and who they are (Edelman 1985). Attachments to political symbols result in a set of attitudes that are referred to as "symbolic predispositions" that are learned early in life, reinforced throughout one's life, "invested with emotional meaning," and "central to one's self-concept" (Citrin, Reingold, and Green 1990, 1125). Elder and Cobb write, "By definition, significant political symbols serve as common focal points for people's orientations toward politics. Those orientations constitute an important link between the individual and the larger polity, binding him to some, while distinguishing him from others" (143).

Elder and Cobb explain that political symbols are "associated with the political community [and] are likely to be the objects of the broadest and most enduring attachments" (36). There is generally a high degree of consensus regarding the importance of such symbols to political life, and they tend to be more influential over lower order ideas rather than vice versa (Sears 1993). For example, my understanding of or attachment to liberalism might affect whether I would be willing to grant free speech rights to Nazis who want to march through Skokie, Illinois, rather than the other way around.

FUNCTIONS OF SYMBOLS

So how can political symbols, such as conceptions of what being American means, wield such influence in a society? Simply put, symbols are functional, and by using them, individuals become better able to navigate the political and social world. In a complex world where people often lack control over their surroundings, they are drawn to symbols to help them understand and derive meaning from their environment. Needs, hopes, and anxieties provoke a quest for simplicity, conformity, and security. Political symbols can be used to make the complex seem simple and can provide prescriptions for bringing order to a disorderly world.

Elder and Cobb describe three specific reasons why people seek out and utilize symbols. The first is the need for "psychic economy." People are cognitive misers, and symbols help to simplify and organize the constant parade of political information and actors.[1] The second reason is the need for communication. Symbols provide common references and make political discourse possible. The third reason is that they affirm identities. Part of the simplification process is the creation of an "us" and a "them." Elder and Cobb write that symbols "index different social identifications and summarize different patterns of tastes, moralities, and general lifestyles" (122). This indexing serves to delineate the relevant group identities in society through the establishment of norms in a variety of realms. In other words, for a variety of psychic needs, individuals rely on symbols to help them make sense of the world and to provide guidance regarding their own preferences and behavior. When people are asked for their opinions on matters of public policy, their symbolic predispositions guide them through the process of arriving at and articulating an answer.

Conceptions of American identity, or images people have about "what it means to be an American," provide one set of the kind of symbolic predispositions that fulfill the functional needs just described. They are learned early in life, are reinforced throughout one's life, enable psychic economy, constrain and facilitate political discussion, dictate behavioral norms, and, by definition, delineate identities. How exactly people define the content of the symbolic construct of "American identity" can vary across time and space, though certain features have remained constant. There are many ways to describe "what it means to be an American," yet most descriptions entail some sort of normative element. When a person says what he thinks being American means, his answer will likely involve describing what he thinks ideal citizens should be like, what he thinks the criteria for membership in the political community should be, what principles he thinks should be upheld, what he thinks the proper scope of government should be, and so on. When ordinary people are asked for their opinions on concrete policy matters, their own answers to these normative questions constrain the range of acceptable alternatives.

The specifics regarding what exactly people do think it means to be American are explored further in later chapters. For now, it suffices to point out that conceptions of American national identity that people hold are the kind of symbolic predispositions that scholars of symbolic politics expect to shape how people interpret their social and political surroundings. Different perspectives on American identity provide different normative guidance. It is therefore important to study distinct clusters of symbolic predispositions sepa-

[1] For more on individuals as cognitive misers, see Popkin (1991), Fiske and Taylor (1991), and Simon (1985).

rately, on their own terms, in order to understand how this particular set of predispositions shapes attitudes on the contentious policies that arise from ethnic change and how the nature of the policy itself enhances the power of some symbols over others.[2]

SYMBOLIC POLITICS

"Symbolic politics" is the name given to the theory that maintains that attitudes are shaped by long-standing symbolic predispositions rather than by economic cost-benefit analyses over tangible goods. Empirical symbolic politics research usually compares the influence of attachments to political symbols, such as party identification or ethnic stereotypes, with measures of self-interest as determinants of policy preferences. Self-interest, in this line of research, generally refers to tangible concerns only, such as perceived economic vulnerability or having family members that might be affected by a particular policy (e.g., having school-age children would be tested as a predictor of opinions about school busing programs). The theory, as articulated by scholars like Sears, sees the individual as largely inattentive to politics and often driven by emotion rather than cognition. Despite this inattentiveness, there are predictable ways in which emotions affect attitudes and behavior. Long-standing predispositions, or attachments to certain symbols, are at the root of this predictability. Responses to political issues are not based on cold calculations of costs and benefits, but they are not random either.

Sears (1993) downplays the role of motivation, arguing that the interaction between symbols and attitudes is affective and automatic rather than cognitive and reasoned. The affective tags people attach to symbols and myths are acquired through conditioning as one grows up, not through psychic needs as they arise. He writes that "people are emotionally invested in their values and attitudes and challenges to them stimulate emotional responses. But there is no assumption that other needs are involved" (136). Yet motivation is central to the notion of defending values and attitudes when they are challenged.

[2] Throughout the book, I refer to conceptions of American identity interchangeably as symbols and as "civic myths." I do not doubt that there are interesting debates to be had about the distinctions between symbols and myths, but such distinctions are not essential here. Edelman (1985) writes that myths are used to communicate communal beliefs and that they are unquestioned, widely accepted, and have real social consequences (4). And Elder and Cobb (1983) write that myths "represent prepackaged symbolic orientations that are simply internalized" (54). To be sure, there are some differences between symbols and myths. For instance, one could make the case that a symbol is the "object" attributed with meaning whereas a myth consists of the meaning attributed to it, or that myths tend to be more substantive than symbols, which tend to be more affective. But throughout their work, Elder and Cobb refer to "equal opportunity" and "communism" as symbols, yet these ideas are "objects" only in the loosest sense of the term. I am more interested in the similarities between symbols and myths, namely, that they both encapsulate important ideas and values that solidify groups of people, limit the range of ideas that are communicated and debated in public discourse, and are internalized through social learning. That these similarities are the focal point of my interest, I believe, justifies using the terms interchangeably.

And unlike Edelman and Elder and Cobb, Sears does not delve into the question of why people rely on symbols in the first place. Yet the answer to the question of "why symbols?" is where the functionality and motivations enter the process.

The notion of threat is a slippery one in this research agenda. If opinions are shaped by affective attachments to symbols, then threats are seen as irrelevant. If opinions are shaped by tangible goods, then threats to those goods drive attitudes in a traditional cost-benefit manner. Yet people can sense that the values and norms encapsulated by symbols are being challenged, in which case both symbolic predispositions and threats are driving the process, which brings motivation back into the picture. For example, if my conception of American identity consists of an attachment to the idea of universal suffrage, I might oppose making English the official language for fear that it would preclude many new citizens from being able to take part in the political process. Likewise, if my conception of American identity is tied to the idea that all true Americans speak English, then I might support making English the official language for fear that an unregulated proliferation of languages will make true Americans an endangered species. In either case, my sense of what being American means is challenged and my desire to preserve it shapes my policy preference.

Edelman writes that "the stakes are intangible, of course, not in the sense that the benefits involved are insignificant but rather in the sense that the reality of the threat is itself unverifiable and the subject of dispute" (69). He then adds: "Whatever seems real to a group of people is real in its consequences regardless of how absurd, hallucinatory, or shocking it may look to others in different situations or at other times. Multiple realities are inherent in politics and so are the rationalizations that justify particular interpretations of the political scene" (199). In other words, symbols and threats are not incompatible, and it is impossible to take threat out of the picture in a symbolic politics story. Whether the perceived threats are real or not and whether the object being threatened is abstract or tangible is irrelevant to the individual who perceives the threat. As long as people feel challenged and want to defend or protect whatever it is that is under the gun, then threat is a part of the process. The only distinction necessary to observe in the symbolic politics story is between the tangible, such as income or direct impact on family members, and the symbolic, such as beliefs about "true Americans."[3]

Implications

The theory discussed thus far provides us with a set of general expectations about how conceptions of American identity should relate to language policy

[3] Complicating matters further, Kinder and Sanders (1996) have shown that symbolic predispositions can lead to perceptions of threat on more tangible concerns in the absence of any concrete basis for feeling threatened. This finding is addressed in more detail in chapter 7.

preferences. The first, and most obvious, expectation is that symbols that communicate information about what being an American means should be significant predictors of preferences in empirical analyses.[4] As Edelman writes: "The natural assumption is that men see political events and institutions and then react to what they see, explaining their reasons for doing so. Careful observation reveals, however, that a 'given' world is a fiction. Men perceive and only then see. In one respect after another, it appears that the vantage point for a perception becomes the key to mass behavior" (185). In other words, to understand how people evaluate political events, actors, or policies, we need to look at what their vantage point is and what general predispositions are shaping the reality that they perceive. Whether existing research demonstrates that conceptions of American identity are the relevant sorts of vantage points to examine in the domain of language and immigration policy is investigated in the next section of this chapter.

A second expectation is that not all symbols or myths will be interpreted in the same way or lead to the same policy preference. A central theme of Elder and Cobb's argument is that if a given symbol is to take on a functional role in society, there must be a consensus that the symbol is important, but it is not necessary that people derive shared meaning from that symbol. People can agree that a particular symbol embodies critical societal norms and values, but they can interpret it quite differently. Divergent interpretations can lead to divergent preferences even when people agree on the overall importance of the value in question. Elder and Cobb write: "The meaning of the message is heavily colored by the significance to the receiver of the symbols involved and his or her own interpretation of their meaning. The same symbol may communicate different things to different people. . . . This heterogeneity of interpretation is likely to go unrecognized, however, because all are reacting to the same objective stimuli and tend to assume that the meaning they find there is intrinsic to the symbols involved and thus common to all" (10). Chavez (2001) articulates this argument using the example of a traffic signal. A yellow light has been arbitrarily assigned to signal the transition from "go" to "stop" and is universally recognized as such in American society. Yet the meaning that some people derive from that symbol is to slow down, while the meaning that other people derive from that symbol is to speed up (35). Returning to the voting example, two different individuals can agree that allowing citizens to take part in the political process is a central component of American identity, yet rely on that idea to arrive at opposing preferences. One person may feel that regulating language use is an affront to a participatory democracy, while another may feel that a common language is necessary in order for

---

[4] The particular hypotheses about which aspects of American identity will lead to support for restrictive policies and which ones will lead to opposition will be addressed in later chapters. At this point, the arguments discussed only suggest that symbolic conceptions of American identity should have a part to play in the opinion formation process.

members of the polity to take part in the common pursuit of self-governance. These multiple interpretations, Chavez argues, "may be magnified in multi-cultural societies" because of the vastly different individual experiences that people bring to the table (36).

Similarly, "there may be considerable substantive agreement on what a symbol means but discordant affective feelings toward it" (Elder and Cobb, 135). This might be the case with ethnoculturalism, a conception of American identity that maintains that Americans are white Christians of northern European ancestry. The norms encapsulated in this myth are pretty well-known and straightforward, as are their implications for language policy preferences, yet people can disagree quite strongly about their virtues.

A third expectation is that some political issues will be couched in symbolic terms more so than others and that the relevant symbolic predispositions will vary with issue type. As Sears (1993) writes, "The particular symbols contained in an attitude object determine which predisposition it evokes" (21). This phenomenon should hold true across issue domains, but could also be true across different policy types within a single domain. For example, we might expect conceptions of national identity to be more influential in opinion formation about immigration and language policy than about campaign finance reform. Likewise, we might expect conceptions of identity to matter more on a broad policy question, such as whether immigration should be increased or decreased, than on a more specific or complex one, such as whether the government should increase or decrease the number of H1-B visas it grants per year. Depending on the policy in question, we might expect different symbolic predispositions to come into play, or we might expect symbolic predispositions not to matter at all.

In sum, the way people define being American should influence their attitudes on language policy proposals. Agreeing that a given symbol is an important part of American identity, however, will not necessarily lead to a consistent policy preference across individuals, and not all symbols will matter to the same degree across different policy types. Testing whether or not this is the case is a challenge that symbolic politics researchers face. The next step then is to review their findings to date to see whether the theories and expectations just described are confirmed and to locate the areas needing further investigation.

EMPIRICAL TESTS OF SYMBOLIC POLITICS AND ETHNIC CHANGE

RESEARCH AND FINDINGS

Over the past two decades or so, several attempts have been made to examine the relationship between symbolic predispositions and issues concerning ethnic change. I devote the remainder of this chapter to reviewing the approaches, measurements, and findings of these projects, keeping the following questions in mind: How well does the empirical work examine the theoretical arguments discussed earlier? Do these studies include symbolic predispositions about American identity in their models, and are these predispositions more potent predictors of preferences than concerns about tangible goods? Do consensual symbols of national identity have uniform interpretations among the mass public? Does the impact of identity vary by issue type (i.e., does it matter if the dependent variable is language policy or immigration policy)?[5]

This review is not meant to suggest that national identity is the only symbolic predisposition that has been examined in public opinion research or that may affect attitudes. Other attachments that are learned early in life, reinforced through later learning, and delineate politically relevant groups, such as partisan identification, political ideology, or racial prejudice, have indeed been studied extensively and have been found to routinely and significantly influence the opinion formation process in many policy areas, including immigration.[6] Rather, my intent is to isolate what existing scholarship has to say about this particular symbolic predisposition. National identity satisfies the definition of symbols employed by social scientists and fulfills the functions of political symbols, yet its role in opinion formation is not understood as well as these other predispositions. It is with the goal of ultimately filling some of the gaps in our knowledge of how American identity shapes attitudes that this assessment of existing scholarship is conducted.

I group studies examining opinions about language and immigration policy into three categories: those that do not include conceptions of American identity; those that include conceptions of American identity in a way that is either too vague or too narrow; and those that feature conceptions of American identity as central and complex independent variables. Studies in the first category tend to focus on measures of self-interest and on standard social and political cleavages in American society, such as partisan identification, as predictors of policy preferences (Hood and Morris 1997; Espenshade and Hempstead 1996; Citrin et al. 1997; Fetzer 2000). Though these studies ignore symbolic conceptions of American identity, their findings are useful for they all show that measures of personal economic conditions are weak influences on individual desires to decrease immigration levels or deny government benefits to immigrants. Sociotropic concerns (i.e., fears about the national economic situation rather than about one's personal economic situation) are stronger

[5] Symbolic politics research has targeted a variety of issue areas, including race relations, cigarette taxes, and gun control (Green and Gerken 1989; Sears et al. 2000; Wolpert and Gimpel 1998). Looking across a variety of issues can give us a good sense of when symbolic predispositions are more likely to matter in the opinion formation process. The project at hand, however, is concerned with how such predispositions matter in a particular policy area, namely language policy. The current examination, therefore, only focuses on research in this issue area. Studies of attitudes on immigration are also included because both issues are concerned with ethnic change and because few studies look exclusively at language policy preferences.

[6] See Sears (1993) for a review.

predictors of opinion (in some, but not all, studies), as are fears that more immigrants will lead to increased taxes, higher crime rates, and fewer jobs for American citizens. These sorts of concerns about the national economy and about the impact immigrants have on the society at large are not fully tangible—they do not capture an individual's sense that his or her personal well-being is under direct attack—nor are they symbolic—they do not explicitly or directly tap into long-standing beliefs about what being American means.[7]

Citrin et al. (1997), a group of scholars with research in this first category, have an interesting finding worth highlighting. Rather than measuring job insecurity with only subjective questions or with an unemployment indicator variable, they distinguish between high- and low-threat blue-collar occupations. A high-threat blue-collar occupation is defined as "one in which the number of immigrant workers as a proportion of all immigrant workers is greater than the equivalent figure for native workers" (864). They find that this distinction does not affect attitudes on whether immigrants should be allowed to receive public benefits, such as food stamps and Medicaid, but that it does affect attitudes toward the overall level of immigration. Those respondents in high-threat jobs are more likely to favor immigration restrictions, leading the authors to conclude that "the economic threat posed by immigrants may only be felt in specific locales and job categories that are not adequately sampled in a national survey" (876).

Studies in the second category include measures of symbolic predispositions about national identity in their examinations of attitudes about bilingual education and immigration policy, but the measures they use are either too vague or too narrow to address many of the questions raised earlier (Espenshade and Calhoun 1993; Huddy and Sears 1995; Vidanage and Sears 1995). The findings from this set of studies confirm that economic concerns are weak predictors of public opinion and suggest that the role of symbolic conceptions of identity in the opinion formation process is worth pursuing. But their measures of American identity do not allow one to conclude much more than that. For example, Espenshade and Calhoun (1993) use a survey question that asks if the respondent thinks speaking English is an important component of American identity as their sole measure to test whether symbolic politics theories should be included in this type of analysis. They find this measure to be significant, yet it is not clear which conception of American identity is being captured by the notion that speaking English is an important characteristic for Americans to have. If I agree that speaking English is important, does it mean

[7] Perceiving that immigrants will have a negative impact on society may indeed be driven by symbolic concerns, such as long-standing anti-minority beliefs, though this possibility is not tested in the studies cited. Instead, these items are treated as independent causal variables. It is important to note that the studies reviewed here concentrate on the views of white, non-Hispanic Americans. See Hood et al. (1997) for an examination of Hispanic-American views on immigration. Their findings largely conform to the findings of the studies described here.

that I adhere to a narrow cultural definition of American identity, or does it mean that I see a common language (be it English or any other) as necessary if a nation can ever hope to function peacefully and efficiently?

Similarly, Vidanage and Sears (1995) use a survey item that asks respondents if they tend to think of themselves primarily as American or as a member of an ethnic group when thinking about social and political issues to capture the role of American identity in shaping attitudes toward immigration policy. They also include measures of symbolic racism—the combination of anti-minority or anti-immigrant affect and the belief that immigrants violate American norms such as individualism and the work ethic.[8] They find that both types of measures are significant predictors of attitudes, yet like Espenshade and Calhoun, can offer only limited insight into what it is about American identity that drives preferences. Thinking of oneself as American matters, but it is not clear what "thinking of oneself as American" means. Moreover, measures of symbolic racism emphasize the "American" norms of individualism and the work ethic while ignoring other conceptions of American identity.

Huddy and Sears (1995) also rely on measures of symbolic racism, in their case to study how symbolic predispositions affect attitudes toward bilingual education. Yet the authors go an extra step in commenting on the elusive relationship between symbolic predispositions and threat. They test for the role of educational, linguistic, and economic threat, distinguishing between subjective and objective measures, and find that both types of measures can predict opposition to bilingual education programs. Then they show that white respondents who harbor anti-Latino affect (as measured by feeling thermometers) are more likely to perceive economic and educational threats and are more likely to agree with symbolic racism measures. They conclude that symbolic racism and realistic conflict theories "may be less mutually exclusive than we had assumed at the outset" (142). As with the other two studies in this category, Huddy and Sears's findings show that symbolic predispositions matter, but they do not contribute to our understanding of the role that attachments to broad civic myths such as liberalism, civic republicanism, or ethnoculturalism play in shaping attitudes toward language policy. They do suggest in their conclusion, however, that scholars should consider testing whether opposition to bilingual education is fueled by perceived threats to national identity.

The final category of research contains studies that are more concerned with tackling different aspects of American national identity and accounting for how they shape attitudes in this issue area (Citrin, Reingold, and Green 1990; Citrin and Duff 1998; Citrin, Wong, and Duff 2001; Frendreis and Tat-

---

[8] Measured with questions such as, "The Irish, Italians, Jews and many other minorities overcame prejudice and worked their way up. Hispanics/Asians should work their way up without any special favors" (for more on symbolic racism, see Sears et al. 2000).

alovich 1997; Citrin, Sears, Muste, and Wong 2001). Jack Citrin and his various colleagues have been particularly committed to pursuing this line of research. To varying degrees, all studies in this category try to account for a variety of symbolic predispositions about American identity. All find that conceptions of national identity are strong predictors of immigration and language policy preferences, while personal and sociotropic economic concerns are not.[9]

The earliest of these studies, by Citrin, Reingold, and Green (1990), relies on a summated rating scale that the authors call "Americanism" to examine the role of American identity in shaping whether respondents oppose bilingual education and would be willing to deny voting rights to non-English speakers. This scale is the sum of the respondent's answers to whether certain characteristics are important in making someone a true American.[10] An important drawback of this scale is that it combines disparate symbolic attachments into a single measure, but the mere presence of these disparate attachments in an empirical analysis is still an advance. The findings allow the authors to conclude that "symbolic challenges to the status of English and to the status of the dominant culture in general inevitably arouse hostility among the majority" (1149). They also write that they expect this "attitudinal construct" to become more salient over the years as immigrant groups continue to have a growing impact in American society.

Eight years later, Citrin and Duff (1998) take a step away from the "Americanism" scale, allowing for different conceptions of American identity to influence immigration policy preferences (also see Citrin, Wong, and Duff 2001). Using a battery of "true American" questions from the 1996 General Social Survey (GSS), along with other questions about national pride, they construct measures of patriotism, nationalism, assimilationism, and nativism.[11] They refer to patriotism and nationalism as measures of national pride and to assimilationism and nativism as measures of national identity. All four constructs make a person more likely to favor decreasing immigration levels and to think that immigrants have a negative cultural impact on the United States. An important finding to note about this study is that different conceptions of national identity influence preferences in the same direction. Whether a person feels that being born in America (nativist) or that simply having American citizenship (assimilationist) is essential in making someone a true American, she will favor restricting immigration. Yet, due to the design of the GSS, Citrin and Duff are limited in what they can say about the nature

[9] Citrin and Duff (1998) do not report results for their control variables, one of which was income. Citrin, Sears, Muste, and Wong (2001) do not include economic measures among their controls.

[10] The characteristics are believing in God, voting in elections, speaking and writing English, trying to get ahead on one's own efforts, treating people of all races and backgrounds equally, and defending America when it is criticized. Data are from a 1988 California Poll. Also see Citrin, Reingold, Walters, and Green (1990) for a similar analysis.

[11] This battery is discussed at length and analyzed in detail in chapter 4.

of American identity. They write: "Even more work is needed to measure alternative conceptions of what constitutes America's unique identity. . . . Most importantly, the 1996 GSS and previous efforts do not provide adequately for what might be termed the liberal conception of American identity, in which egalitarianism and tolerance are deemed the most significant virtues" (24).

In the third study in this group, Frendreis and Tatalovich (1997) use the 1992 National Election Study (NES) to examine support for official-English legislation. Rather than create "Americanism" or "nativism" scales, they use individual survey items as independent variables to represent alternative conceptions of American identity. Specifically, they include two items from a "true American" battery similar to those used by Citrin (whether treating people of all races and backgrounds equally and whether speaking English are important) and an item that asks if people prefer the idea of the melting pot or the maintenance of distinct cultures and traditions. They find that two of the three identity measures—speaking English and support for the melting pot—are significant predictors, while the more liberal measure of equal treatment is not. They conclude that not all support for official-English is insidious, that some support is grounded in concerns about English being "an important element of a necessary common attachment to American ideals," while other support is simply nativist (364). They also conclude that "English-only may prove to be part of an issue domain that cuts across normal cleavage lines and coincides instead with individuals' conceptions of American ideals and the relevance of a national identity to the national life" (365).

Using the 1994 GSS, Citrin, Sears, Muste, and Wong (2001) focus on how people reconcile their desire for a unified national identity with their appreciation of America's ethnic diversity. They examine how one's view on whether American identity should stress "the one" or "the many" shapes views on immigration and language policy. Like Vidanage and Sears, one measure they use asks if people think of themselves primarily in ethnic or "American" terms when it comes to thinking about political issues. Another measure asks people if they think it is better for the country if members of ethnic groups "blend into the larger society" or "maintain their distinct cultures" (260). This latter measure turns out to be more potent than the former; like Frendreis and Tatalovich, they find that people who favor "blending" are more likely than others to support restrictive language policies. The same is true for people with higher levels of racial hostility and who engage in ethnic stereotyping.[12]

EVALUATION

To assess where these studies leave us, I return to the theoretical concerns and expectations raised in the previous section and see what we can say about them after having reviewed the existing literature. First, can these studies say whether symbols of national identity are more potent predictors of preferences

[12] Their dependent variable is a composite index of responses to multiple language policy questions.

than concerns about tangible goods? Clearly, the answer is yes. Even in the first set of studies, which lack measures of national identity, economic concerns matter only erratically, and sociotropic measures tend to matter more than pocketbook measures. Survey items in the final two sets of studies that capture attachments to national identity, be they vague, narrow, simple, or complex, are consistently significant in shaping preferences.

Second, do consensual symbols of national identity have uniform interpretations among the mass public? This one is more difficult to answer, for the question was never addressed directly. One pattern of note is that attachments to conceptions of national identity almost always influence opinion in the same direction; they tend to make people more in favor of restricting immigration laws or of regulating language use. Whether this pattern says anything about uniform interpretation is unclear. Another finding of note is that some images of national identity are simply more consensual than others. For example, Citrin and Duff show that more respondents adhere to an assimilationist conception of national identity than to a nativist one. In general, though, none of the studies seek to answer whether a given symbol, such as free speech or the New England town meeting, means different things to different people or whether divergent interpretations of a given symbol lead to divergent policy preferences.

Third, does the impact of identity vary by issue type? The answer here seems to be "sort of." Conceptions of identity, when included in the model, always matter, and the policies examined range from restricting immigration, denying government benefits to immigrants, bilingual education, making English the official language, and denying voting rights to non-English speakers. Yet Citrin, Reingold, and Green (1990) show that this influence is stronger on whether people think non-English speakers should have voting rights than it is on views about bilingual education programs. And Citrin, Sears, Muste, and Wong (2001) find that a preference for immigrants blending into the larger society affects attitudes about language policy more than it affects attitudes about immigration policy. But no two studies test for the influence of American identity in the same way, and so it is difficult to say whether the same conception of identity will exert the same type of influence across different policies. Measures of symbolic racism do influence attitudes on both restricting immigration levels and opposing bilingual education, and anti-minority affect influences attitudes on all of the policies studied. Moreover, measures of identity often, but not always, retain their significance across issues when opinions on two different policies are examined within a single study.

One possible lead for answering this question comes from Frendreis and Tatalovich, who include one liberal measure in their set of items aimed at capturing the influence of national identity—namely, whether treating people of all races and backgrounds equally is an important part of being American. They find that this measure does not affect whether a person favors an official-

English law while support for speaking English as an important part of being American does. Although the significance of the "speaking English" measure does not tell us much, the nonsignificance of the liberal measure does. Over 90 percent of the 1992 NES sample said that treating people of all races and backgrounds equally is either extremely or very important in making someone a true American, indicating that liberal ideas about equal treatment and opportunity unquestionably form an important civic myth in the United States. Yet this civic myth appears to have nothing to do with opinions on language laws, which suggests that not all aspects of what it means to be an American matter in the same way in this issue domain, a finding that is worth pursuing further in this research agenda.[13]

In sum, the existing literature as a whole does a good job of establishing that conceptions of American identity matter in the opinion formation process in the area of ethnic change, but does not do as good a job of establishing which conceptions matter or when they are more likely to do so. This research agenda would be better equipped to test theoretical claims if survey items were more closely matched to theories of American identity, which can be found in studies of American political thought and intellectual history. The 1992 NES and the 1996 GSS made a step in the right direction with their batteries of questions about important characteristics for Americans to have, but as I show in chapter 4, these batteries are still not sufficient.

CONCLUSION

In 1994, the GSS asked respondents if they consider themselves "just American" or members of particular ethnic, racial, or nationality groups when thinking about national and social issues. Over 90 percent said they consider themselves "just American" on most or all issues. Of that 90 percent, 66 percent support making English the official language of the United States, 40 percent think election ballots should be printed only in English, and 38 percent oppose bilingual education. The correlation between thinking of oneself primarily as an American and each of these language policies is around 0.08. The pattern is similar among the 86 percent who says they are extremely or very proud to be an American. What these figures show is that emotional and cognitive attachments to the idea of being an American are widespread yet as a whole do not coincide with a particular language policy preference. But that is exactly what some of the research described earlier claims is the case. Scholars argue that an attachment to American identity, or "Americanism," is a strong predictor of whether a person favors making English the official language and cutting back levels of immigration. They are able to make this case because

[13] It may also simply be too difficult to get precise estimates of the impact of liberalism when so much of the sample is clustered at one end of the response set.

their measures of American identity generally focus on a particular subset of symbolic predispositions associated with American identity. It is my argument that the picture they present would be more compelling and more complex if they were able to incorporate a broader range of predispositions that are associated with American national identity. Through such incorporation, the theoretical arguments on the role of symbols in the political process advanced by Edelman and Elder and Cobb could be tested more adequately.

Theoretical work on the role of symbols in American politics points to two assertions that still need to be examined empirically. The first is that we should not necessarily expect a given symbol of American identity to be interpreted the same way by all members in a polity, even if they agree that the symbol is an important part of their national identity. The second is that we should not necessarily expect a given symbol of American identity to evoke the same response in all members of the polity. That symbols matter has been demonstrated; whether these two additional assertions can be added to the corpus of knowledge in this area has not.

Additional considerations about the relationship between identity and opinions are also worth considering. One is that real-world events will affect not only which policy issues are salient but also which components of American identity become associated with those policies. Symbolic predispositions have power, but they only come into play because of real-world conditions that provide the context for their meaning. For example, official-English has become more salient in recent years, and symbolic predispositions are strong predictors of how people feel about it. But the issue probably would not have become salient had there not been real and dramatic demographic changes over the past few decades. Further, whether political leaders, interest groups, and the media discuss ethnic change in symbolic terms will also affect the relationship between identity and opinions at the mass level. Representatives Torkildsen and Pelosi, quoted at the start of this chapter, are hardly unique in publicly defending their position on official-English legislation by invoking American civic myths like freedom and opportunity. Surely, such associations are going to influence the opinion formation process among the mass public.

Another consideration is the extent to which conceptions of national identity are dynamic or static. As Elder and Cobb write, "Over time, a symbol may take on new meanings, and new or different symbols may assume its previous role" (82). The symbol of Christopher Columbus provides an excellent example of how civic myths can change in both their interpretation and their salience. For years, Columbus was a source of national pride, symbolizing heroism and bravery, and was hailed as the discoverer of a New World that eventually came to be the United States of America. In recent years, however, many have challenged this depiction and have sought to remind their fellow Americans that the "discovery" of the New World was a precursor to genocide. Rather than serving as a proud figure in American history, Columbus is now often seen as a glorified pirate whose successors raped and pillaged and began the African slave trade (Vobejda 1992). In addition to the usual celebratory parades, many cities now find themselves hosting alternative protest parades as well, particularly since 1992 when the nation observed the five hundredth anniversary of Columbus's historic voyage. As one demonstrative headline at the time declared, "Columbus and the Sailing-the-Ocean Blues; Hero to Zero: Why the Quincentenary Went Bust." The first line of that article stated, "For the second time in 500 years, Columbus has hit the rocks" (Garreau 1992). Few national myths have something as convenient as an anniversary to spark the public reevaluation of their merits. More often, such change is gradual, even glacial. Clearly, this is not something that cross-sectional surveys can address, but changes in civic myths over time do occur, and public opinion scholars should keep an eye out for such change if they want their survey instruments to stay relevant.

Edelman writes that to understand how symbols affect elites and masses, "it is necessary to consider some general characteristics of symbols and the conditions that explain their appearance and meanings" (4). Elder and Cobb add that "to understand what is communicated to whom, it is necessary to inquire into the symbols that characterize [the] political culture. Of interest is not only the nature of the symbols themselves but also the way they are used and how people relate to them" (9). These two quotes get to the heart of the weaknesses with existing data and analyses and to the challenges that still lie ahead. In the next chapter, I address the first part of Elder and Cobb's assertion. Taking a step away from public opinion research, I look to historical and philosophical analyses of American political culture to explore the general characteristics of the symbols and myths that together constitute American identity. In later chapters, I comment further on the inadequacy of existing sources of data and use focus groups to study the questions that still remain. This more qualitative approach allows me to address the second part of Elder and Cobb's assertion. When ordinary citizens define American identity and talk about language policy with a group of their peers and in their own vocabulary, I am able to examine how myths and symbols are used, how people relate to them, and how they are invoked to justify language policy preferences.

CHAPTER THREE

Theories of American Identity

IN HIS EXTENSIVE STUDY of how ideas about American identity have shaped citizenship laws in the United States, Smith (1997) defines a "civic myth" as "a myth used to explain why persons form a people, usually indicating how a political community originated, who is eligible for membership, who is not and why, and what the community's values and aims are" (33). He then describes how three civic myths in particular—liberalism, civic republicanism, and ethnoculturalism—have collectively directed the legal and judicial politics of citizenship from colonial days through the Progressive Era. He argues that all three have at different times, and often simultaneously, shaped elite efforts to decide who can be a member of the American community and dictated to that community what its values and aims are. Smith's analysis has received a lot of attention from scholars of American identity not only because of its sheer size and detail, but also because it takes our history of racism and exclusion out of the skeleton closet and elevates it to the status of a national civic myth on par with liberalism and civic republicanism; his work is noteworthy for its explicit juxtaposition of these three alternatives. Smith establishes that these three traditions have shaped how American citizenship has been defined over the years. The symbolic politics argument is that this type of cultural commodity should shape opinions, and so Smith's work is a natural fit with the project at hand. His analysis has greatly influenced my research design, but once his trilogy of ideals is adopted, I turn to several other studies of American political thought to add to the analysis. Despite its utility, however, Smith's framework fails to capture an important and popular conception people have of what being American means, and so I add a fourth conception to my model. I label this conception "incorporationism" and it is derived from the notion of the United States as a nation of immigrants.

Over the past several years, studies of American identity like Smith's have reached beyond philosophical and historical circles. As "identity politics" have gained political salience, scholars of public opinion in particular have become interested in incorporating civic myths about national identity into their studies of how people arrive at public policy preferences. Immigration and language policy are good cases for examining how concerns about identity play a role in this process. These issues, by their very nature, are fundamentally about deciding who Americans are and are of particular contemporary importance. Yet if the studies described in the previous chapter provide sound evidence that immigration and language policy preferences are driven, in part, by a collective national identity, what else needs to be done? I maintain that the findings from these studies are like a broad brush stroke—they tell us what is important, but they do not provide much detail; they confirm the importance of identity, but do not take us any further than that. Understanding public opinion on identity politics has been so elusive because we have continued to use broad brush strokes. In other words, we know that identity matters in opinion formation, especially on issues that deal with race and ethnicity, but we know little about how it matters. We do not know whether aspects of American identity have uniform interpretations or what role differing interpretations play as people wrestle with important social phenomena such as immigration and ethnic change. Nor do we know when conceptions of American identity are more or less likely to be influential. A stark gap in this research agenda is our lack of knowledge about which aspects of America's civic myths matter and when. Filling that gap will be beneficial both for public opinion research and for our approach to this pressing policy concern.

The goal of this chapter, then, is to develop a cognitive map that will help us to navigate the American mind. Using analyses of elite-centered discourse and behavior as a guide, I delineate the different civic myths, or conceptions of American identity, that regular Americans are likely to use to help them decide what they value in a polity and who they think can and cannot be a part of it. These analyses of elite constructions of national identity provide essential guidance in trying to understand how language policy is framed and how the public comes to understand what the policy debates are about. Scholars of public opinion and of language politics acknowledge that debates about language are fundamentally about competing myths of national identity. Turning to literature on the content and contours of those competing myths is thus necessary in order to come up with a model that pushes our understanding of this phenomenon beyond the limits of where existing public opinion research has been able to go. The myths described here are ideal types and, as Smith and others have argued, are often blended in practice. But an examination of these ideal types is a useful and necessary exercise in order to ultimately provide a rich and enlightening study of how "what it means to be an American" shapes policy preferences. In the end, we will be armed with a theoretically driven framework that lays out a structured picture of how people are likely to think about being American. The accuracy of this cognitive map is tested in later chapters and is then used to further our understanding of the relationship between conceptions of national identity and language policy preferences.

LIBERALISM: THE PRIVILEGED CITIZEN

I begin with liberalism because it is the least challenged among the conceptions of American identity under investigation here. By "least challenged" I mean that few people would argue against the proposition that liberal principles have played an important role in the development of American political consciousness. First, a brief description of what is meant by the term is in order. As is well-known, the tenets of liberalism grew out of the Enlightenment and present a philosophy grounded in beliefs about universal rights. Although the term has evolved over time, it has certain key features that have been rather stable. As a political doctrine, it dictates that the private lives of individuals should be free from arbitrary government intervention and that the rule of law is paramount in protecting this freedom. The emphasis on the private rights of individuals and the privileges of citizenship translates into a reverence for tolerance, individualism, privacy, and civil rights and liberties. It also leads to a preference for minimal government and a free market economy where people are able to pursue their individual desires and private gain (Kingdon 1999). Above all, the liberal philosophy asserts that people are fundamentally equal and that all of these things—liberty, freedom, opportunity, and so on—should be applied to all simply by virtue of being human. Moreover, liberalism is hostile to the notion of group rights, contending that people should be treated equally *as individuals* before the law.[1]

It hardly needs to be said that liberalism has had a profound influence on the development of political culture in the United States and that it continues to do so. From an early age, we are bombarded with liberal discourse and imagery. One cannot avoid hearing the United States described as the land of the free, and all children are taught to cherish the Declaration of Independence's famous proclamation of the self-evident truth that all men are created equal. The American Dream—the myth that anyone in America can pursue economic success through hard work and individual drive—grows out of the liberal tradition and has been a powerful motivating force that continues to inspire (Hochschild 1995). As a testament to the continuing power of the dream, the CBS Evening News with Dan Rather recently had a weekly feature called "The American Dream," which told the heartfelt stories of successful yet hardworking people, most of whom have had to overcome adversities of one kind or another. Rather's inaugural segment began with the following introduction:

> The American Dream: The idea and the ideal are an important part of who and what we are, and it's at the very heart of our history. It's more than two centuries old and still going strong. Tonight, the CBS Evening News begins an every-Wednesday report about the men, women and children striving for the American Dream, making a difference and inspiring the rest of us.[2]

---

[1] See Held (1996), chapter 3, for a more detailed discussion.

[2] The transcript from this September 22, 1999, broadcast can be found on LexisNexis. Rather also put the stories from these segments into a book called *The American Dream: Stories from the Heart of Our Nation* (2001).

Whether the emphasis is on our rights to free speech and assembly or just to be left alone so we can make money, an adoration of liberalism is, and has always been, everywhere in America.

Several prominent observers of American politics have written that American identity is defined primarily, or even solely, by liberalism. Most notable among these are Louis Hartz (1955) and Gunnar Myrdal (1944). Hartz writes that Americans are irrationally liberal at the expense of all other possibilities. He calls his classic work a "single factor" analysis of American political thought and argues that this "factor" of liberalism is the dominant lens through which American politics, history, and character should be analyzed. The argument that liberalism dominates the American landscape has since become known as the "Hartzian thesis."

Preceding Hartz by a decade, Myrdal writes that American identity is based not on culture but on an explicit set of ideals known as the American Creed and that whites and blacks alike believe in its principles of rule of law, freedom, and equality. Others have added that America is unique in that its entire identity is derived from a common set of laws and liberal ideological beliefs, unlike other nations whose identities are based more on a shared history, language, or ancestry. Adding his take on the matter, Samuel Huntington (1981) writes that internal conflict in the United States has never been about challenging the liberal paradigm but about broadening its scope. I call this the "me too" phenomenon, where conflicts like those of the civil rights and women's movements are in essence an affirmation of liberal principles and call for making the liberal ideal more of a reality.

Even some of the critics who challenge the Hartzian thesis have acknowledged the staying power that liberal ideas have had in the United States. In fact, much of the criticism of Hartz's work has not argued that liberalism is not a *central* and *important* factor in American political thought, but rather challenged its *dominance* over alternative ideological perspectives. As Richard Ellis writes (1993), the recognition that American identity has included other elements, such as civic republicanism, does not destroy the Hartzian thesis because these other elements never displaced liberalism. Daniel Rodgers (1992) writes that scholars who challenged Hartz, like Gordon Wood and J.G.A. Pocock, did not doubt that "liberalism ultimately swept up the nation's economic, political, and cultural life. [Their] project was to stay the hand of the Hartzian moment, not to deny it" (24). And William Sullivan (1982) admits that civic republicanism has been "so long under the shadow of liberal individualism" (xiii) in the American mind.

Contemporary survey data validate the claim that liberalism plays a powerful role in American politics. When people are asked about what they believe in and what they think Americans should be like, liberal ideas come out strong. Jack Citrin and colleagues (1994) report findings from a 1991 California Poll that asked respondents to name what, if anything, makes America different from other countries. Forty-four percent of the people who said that there were indeed unique "American" characteristics mentioned freedoms of one kind or another, and 34 percent mentioned qualities related to individualism. In a 1988 California Poll, 74 percent of the respondents said that trying to get ahead on one's own efforts is very important in making someone a true American; 88 percent said the same about treating people of all races and backgrounds equally (Citrin, Reingold, and Green 1990).

The identification of American-ness with liberal principles exists outside of California as well. In the 1992 NES, 80 percent of the respondents said that getting ahead on one's own efforts is extremely or very important in making someone a true American, and 92 percent said the same about treating people of all races and backgrounds equally. In a survey called "Looking for America," conducted by Princeton Survey Research Associates for Wisconsin Public Television (1997), respondents were asked whether they agree that several items make the United States different from all other countries. Eighty-nine percent agreed that freedom of speech does, 86 percent agreed that freedom of religion does, 79 percent agreed that the opportunity for a poor person to get ahead by working hard does, and 75 percent agreed that a belief in self-reliance does.[3] These data lend credence to McClosky and Zaller's observation (1984) that "liberty is more deeply embedded in the nation's system of values than any of the others" (18), and they should give pause to any critic of the Hartzian thesis.

CIVIC REPUBLICANISM: THE RESPONSIBLE CITIZEN

Earlier I referred to a set of such critics whose aim was not to unseat the role of liberalism in contemporary America but rather to highlight the importance of an alternative doctrine in the early years of the Republic. This strand of research has been termed the "republican hypothesis" or the "republican synthesis" and consists of reinterpretations of revolutionary thought starting in the late 1960s. The most notable scholars in this group are Wood (1969), Pocock (1975), and Bernard Bailyn (1967). In describing this corpus, Lance Banning (1986) writes: "The major novelty and most important contribution of revisionary work has not been to deny that Revolutionary Americans were Lockean and liberal, but to demonstrate that liberal ideas were only part of their inheritance. . . . Among the most important implications of this work is the suggestion that nineteenth-century America did not begin with and may never have achieved a liberal consensus" (13).

And even a critic of the revisionist work, Joyce Appleby (1986), concedes this contribution. In a response to Banning, she writes: "The significance of

[3] The data set and codebook for this survey, USPSRA1997-COLUMBUS, were obtained from the Roper Center for Public Opinion Research at the University of Connecticut.

the recent republican revision has been the discovery that many eighteenth-century Americans thought within a classical republican frame of reference. For me, the importance of this fact is that it enables us to see that liberalism did not sprawl unimpeded across the flat intellectual landscape of American abundance, as Louis Hartz maintained" (26). It seems that despite liberalism's continued prominence in America, many would agree that there have been other influences on political culture in the United States that do not fit within a liberal framework. Thirty years after the beginning of the revisionist era, Smith (1997), an avowed liberal, does not even question the importance of civic republicanism in the history of American political thought. He takes it for granted, focusing his efforts on establishing ethnoculturalism as a rival to both liberalism *and* civic republicanism in the set of ideals that have guided American citizenship laws.

The simplest way to think about civic republicanism is to note that it focuses on the responsibilities, as opposed to the rights and privileges, of citizenship and that it highlights the importance of participation in public life for its intrinsic value. In a civic republican society, citizens strive to be virtuous and become so by identifying their own well-being with that of the community (Bellah et al. 1985). Civic republicans challenge the liberal belief that the public good is the sum of individual satisfactions. They argue that the public good is more than that, and that it is derived from social connections that are forged through community interaction. This tradition steps away from liberalism's autonomous individual and recognizes that individual lives are intertwined (Conover et al. 1991; Barber 1984). Robert Putnam (1995, 2000) has recently described the importance of social interaction and civic engagement in society. He refers to such engagement as "social capital," and argues that involvement and trust reinforce one another and that both are instrumental in the ability of a community to achieve shared ends.

Civic republicanism is, at its root, an ideology about active citizenship. In the ideal form, individual citizens value the collective good over personal private gain (Held 1996). Civic republicanism in the United States has not been practiced to this extreme, but has instead emphasized that the public good should be valued *as much as* private pursuits. Indeed, an active and involved public is often seen as more of an instrumental good, essential for protecting the health and stability of the very system that allows people to pursue their individual desires (Fishkin 1995). The identification of one's own good with the common good is seen as a necessary component of a self-regulating decentralized political system (Epstein 1984). In this sense, liberalism and civic republicanism can be quite compatible. But Banning (1986) warns us to keep in mind important differences between the two. The former is based on thinking of the individual as being the possessor of inherent individual rights, conceives of the state as protector of these rights, and postulates that individuals are driven by self-interest. Civic republicanism, on the other hand, introduces a concern for the community and contends that individual pursuits alone cannot enable the survival of a democratic society. Smith concurs (1988): "In contrast to Locke's focus on liberty as freedom from state interference with individual private pursuits, the distinctive element common to the diverse strains of republican thought is an emphasis on achieving institutions and practices that make collective self-governance in pursuit of a common good possible for the community as a whole" (231).

The prescriptions of civic republicanism, then, are to be knowledgeable about and involved in public life and to structure institutions in a way that enables such involvement. This involvement can range from the simple and purely political, such as voting, to the more time-consuming and quasi-political, such as belonging to an organization that promotes the use of public parks. When public welfare is seen as inseparable from private welfare, a sense of personal attachment to the national community develops. This personal attachment often takes the form of pride, or patriotism, which in turn reinforces one's commitment to the common good. Hence, patriotism is also a mark of civic republicanism, for it makes people more willing to act upon their concerns regarding the good of the nation (e.g., Walzer 1983). Tocqueville (1972 [1835]), for example, observed strong patriotic feelings among the many people he encountered on his trip to the United States in the 1830s, and he wondered how Americans could have developed so strong a love of country in such a short period of time. The reason, he concluded, was because "everyone, in his sphere, takes an active part in the government of society" (243). In other words, pride and participation are central and linked in the civic republican ideal.

One issue that begs to be addressed is whether civic republicanism's presence in American political thought is a thing of the past. Does it still play a role in shaping how elites and masses think about American identity? Some, like Wood and Pocock, conceded that civic republicanism eventually faded and gave way to liberalism. Yet Smith's research documents that civic republicanism remained an important force in shaping ideas about citizenship at least through the Progressive Era. And signs in contemporary America point to the continuing relevance of the republican call for informed and involved citizens who work together to solve common problems. Although Americans often fall short of the civic republican ideal, as evidenced by low voter turnout rates, its prescriptions are still valued and continue to dictate how Americans think they should act, even if they fail to do so in practice. In fact, the frequently heard lamentations over citizen apathy, low voter turnout rates, or the federal government making decisions that are seen as best left to lower levels of government bolster the claim that Americans continue to value the duties of citizenship and are fearful that individual self-interest or a reliance on "Washington insiders" will eclipse essential alternatives.

An example of civic republicanism's continued relevance in American politics is the 1997 "Summit for America's Future," held in Philadelphia by Colin Powell and then-president Bill Clinton. The stated goals of the summit involved securing a better future for at-risk youths, and the participants touted volunteerism as an important tool for achieving this end. Whether this summit actually resulted in higher levels of civic engagement has been a matter of debate, but the event received a lot of favorable press coverage at the time. The perceived importance of the message was so strong that it brought Clinton and Powell together with former presidents Gerald Ford, Jimmy Carter, and George Bush (Thompson 1997), a gathering that is rarely seen outside of funerals for world leaders. Though people may not have become more involved in the long run, the important thing to note is that they think they should, and they think they should because they are Americans and an active public life is seen as distinctly American. For example, in talking about the challenge of bringing Americans out of their living rooms and into the streets to help make communities safer, Powell said, "We can do it. We can do it because we are Americans" (Frolik 1997). Clinton added: "I want the children here, starting next week and all over America, if you're asked in school, what does it mean to be a good citizen, I want the answer to be, 'Well, to be a good citizen, you have to obey the law, you've got to go to work or be in school, you've got to pay your taxes and, oh, yes, you have to serve in your community to help make it a better place' " (McGrory 1997). The event sparked similar summits in cities across the country, and for years Powell led efforts to promote more volunteerism among Americans of all ages. And Presidents Bush Sr. and Carter have highlighted volunteerism during and after their tenure in office with the Points of Light Foundation and Habitat for Humanity, respectively. Both organizations encourage and sponsor volunteer projects across the country.

The continuing link between American society and an active public life is also documented by Theda Skocpol and colleagues in their "civic engagement project" (1999). In this project, Skocpol monitors the membership figures of national organizations over time and finds that several can still claim to have at least 1 percent of the American population as members, including Greenpeace, Mothers Against Drunk Driving, and the PTA. The nature of membership has changed over time, and the consequences of those changes are still being debated. But we are still, as Tocqueville observed, a nation of joiners. Over 150 years ago, he wrote, "Americans of all ages, all conditions, and all dispositions constantly form associations" (1975 [1840], 106). Americans at the dawn of the twenty-first century continue to belong.

From 1990 to 1994, the General Social Survey (GSS) asked respondents about their group memberships. Each respondent was asked: "Now we would like to know something about the groups or organizations to which individuals belong. Here is a list of various organizations. Could you tell me whether or not you are a member of each type" (Davis and Smith 1997)? The list of groups in the battery is as follows: fraternal, service, veterans, political, labor union, sports, youth, school service, hobby, fraternity/sorority, nationality/ethnic, literary or art, professional society, church-affiliated, or some other type of group. Providing further evidence that Americans devote time and energy to efforts outside of their individual pursuit of the American Dream, 69 percent of the respondents reported that they belong to at least one of these types of organizations (see Putnam 2000; Hibbing and Theiss-Morse 2002; and chapter 5 for more on the debate about the extent to which Americans emulate the civic republican ideal).

Yet relying on survey data to substantiate claims about the extent to which the tenets of civic republicanism exist in the American mind is a difficult task. Most surveys fail to ask respondents about their beliefs about civic republican concerns. They have questions designed to examine if Americans are good civic republicans (i.e., if they participate in politics, if they are informed, if they belong to associations, if they are patriotic), but they do not ask if people *value* the ideal, regardless of what the reality may be. The dearth of survey questions relevant to civic republicanism goes to the heart of my claim that public opinion scholars have failed to devote appropriate attention to the theoretical underpinnings of "Americanism" when designing questionnaires. Only a handful of questions can help us out in this respect. A 1998 New Jersey poll conducted by Gregory Huber and myself showed that 88 percent of respondents said that "feeling American" is either somewhat or very important in making someone a true American, 87 percent said that voting in elections is either somewhat or very important, and 88 percent said the same about participating in community life.[4] And in the 1996 GSS, 88 percent of the respondents said that "feeling American" is either very or somewhat important in making someone a true American. I argue that "feeling American" can be loosely interpreted as a civic republican measure, for it concerns the cultivation of an emotional attachment to the national community. Such emotional attachments are necessary if people are to value the collectivity as much as the individual, as is required by the tenets of civic republicanism.

New research by Elizabeth Theiss-Morse offers, to my knowledge, some of the only national data on whether Americans subscribe to beliefs about active citizenship. Her 2002 survey includes a battery of questions that asks people if they believe they have particular obligations to the government and to the American people. She finds that many people do indeed endorse the civic republican call to promote the public good. She finds, for example, that 75 percent of Americans say they have an obligation to help out if there is a crisis or disaster in the nation, 77 percent say they have an obligation to pay taxes, 62

[4] The 1998 New Jersey Poll is a statewide telephone survey that asked respondents for their views about language policy, the potential effects of making English the official language, and the impact of immigration on the United States and New Jersey (n = 296). Feeling American: 55 percent said very important; 33 percent somewhat. Voting: 61 percent said very important; 26 percent somewhat. Participating: 37 percent said very important; 51 percent somewhat. Data and codebook are available upon request.

percent say they have an obligation to fight in a war for the United States, 47 percent say they have an obligation to volunteer in their communities, 44 percent say they have an obligation to ensure a basic standard of living for their fellow Americans, and 36 percent say they have an obligation to donate money to charities.[5] She found that patriotic feelings are strongly related to attachments to one's fellow Americans and to thinking that being an American is an important part of one's identity. In turn, people who feel such attachments are more likely than others to believe that they have the aforementioned obligations to other Americans and to the government (Theiss-Morse 2003b). The exact dynamics between love of country and love of one's fellow citizens are still being untangled. The evidence thus far supports a picture of mutual reinforcement between patriotism, affinity for one's fellow Americans, and the belief that one has an obligation to promote the public good (regardless of whether one actually fulfills those obligations).

Although liberalism may be the civic myth that comes most easily to mind when we think of American identity, it is clear from this brief survey of intellectual history and contemporary behavior that the principles of civic republicanism have also constituted an important civic myth in the United States. From Tocqueville's observations about associational life in America to Lincoln's famous description of our government as "of the people, by the people, and for the people," and to Clinton's charge that being a good American citizen means being involved in community life, Americans have always been reminded that the health of their society rests on the active involvement of its people and on the maintenance of a common sense of national purpose.

ETHNOCULTURALISM: THE WHITE CITIZEN

The one non-liberal feature of American society that opinion scholars *have* paid attention to is the tendency of white Americans to hold ascriptive beliefs about American identity. Since the mid-1980s, surveys have routinely asked questions such as whether believing in God or being a Christian is important in making someone a true American and whether immigrants who preserve the cultural traditions of their homeland are harmful to the country. Further, survey items designed to capture the extent and nature of racial prejudice among the mass public have been asked since the survey industry was born. Public opinion scholars have long recognized the enduring power of undemocratic and discriminatory thoughts and behaviors in American society and have not needed to rely on scholars of American political thought for guidance on this front.[6] In fact, they have largely been *unable* to do so; studies of

[5] These frequency statistics are not yet published; Elizabeth Theiss-Morse provided them through personal communication.

[6] See Sears et al. (2000) for detailed accounts of earlier research.

elite philosophy and decision making have been woefully inadequate in terms of recognizing the ethnocultural tradition in America.

In short, ethnoculturalism is the belief that certain ascriptive or immutable characteristics dictate who can and cannot be an American citizen. Smith (1997) writes that ethnoculturalism is an "intellectual and political tradition conceiving of America in inegalitarian, racial, patriarchal, and religious terms" and that it has "long been as much a part of American life as the liberal and republican doctrines" that other scholars have stressed (3). In other words, it is the belief that only white male Protestants of northern European ancestry are the true Americans. This tradition has also been called "ascriptivism" and "ascriptive Americanism." Smith argues that it has been a powerful civic myth in the United States, and he demonstrates that "American law [has] long been shot through with forms of second-class citizenship, denying personal liberties and opportunities for political participation to most of the adult population on the basis of race, ethnicity, gender, and even religion" (2).

Ethnoculturalism, then, focuses on the "nation" whereas liberalism and civic republicanism focus on the "state." A nation is commonly understood to be a group of people that share a set of characteristics (often cultural ones) and that believes it should be self-governing. A state, on the other hand, is a set of political institutions that makes governance possible. The relationship between nations and states is both complex and contested (e.g., Gellner 1983; Hobsbawm 1990; Hutchinson and Smith 1994; Miller 1995). Yet regardless of the differences between these two concepts, myths about both the nation and the state can perform similar functions when it comes to deciding what it means to be a member of the community. They both dictate values, acceptable norms of behavior, and guidelines for delineating membership. Thus, while it is important to note differences among civic myths in the extent to which they emphasize the nation or the state, their common status as civic myths and the implications that derive from their mythic status are more important for the analysis at hand.

One need not look far for evidence of Smith's claim that ethnoculturalism is indeed a full-fledged civic myth. The institution of slavery alone could be enough to convince. Add the denial of women's suffrage, the internment of thousands of Americans of Japanese descent during World War II, and the near extinction of indigenous peoples—just to name a few—and it becomes hard to deny that ascriptive beliefs about racial and gender hierarchies have been as prevalent in American politics as beliefs about the freedom of speech. Smith writes that these and other practices that grew out of the ethnocultural tradition "manifested passionate beliefs that America was by rights a white nation, a Protestant nation, a nation in which true Americans were native-born men with Anglo-Saxon ancestors" (3).

Despite the prevalence of illiberal and undemocratic practices throughout American history, the ethnocultural tradition in America has long been relegated to the world of aberration and described as a deviation from America's true liberal nature. For example, in 1963, Seymour Martin Lipset wrote *The First New Nation*, a book about the tensions between individualism and equality in the American ethos. Lipset was writing during the heart of the civil rights movement, yet his emphasis is squarely on liberalism. He does not mention "exceptions" until well into the book when he writes: "American egalitarianism is, of course, for white men only. The treatment of the Negro makes a mockery of this value now as it has in the past. . . . The contradiction between the American value system and the way in which the Negro has been treated has, if anything, forced many Americans to think even more harshly of the Negro than they might if they lived in a more explicitly ascriptive culture . . . the poison of anti-Negro prejudice is a part of American culture, and almost all white Americans have it, to a greater or lesser degree" (330). Despite this concession, whenever Lipset mentions racist practices, he describes them as being *against* American values and does not entertain the possibility that such practices might indeed be a part of what American identity is all about. For example, in his description of the 1924 immigration quotas, he writes: "Though it is possible to argue that the imposition of numerical restrictions on immigration was necessary with an end of an open land frontier, the fact remains that to have imposed particularistic ethnic and religious restrictions on immigration constituted a fundamental violation of traditional American values" (338). And Lipset is hardly alone in treating racial and ethnic oppression as deviant or as an afterthought (e.g., Kingdon 1999; Huntington 1981; Hartz 1955).[7]

Such oppression has been anything but deviant throughout America's past, yet as with civic republicanism, we must question whether and to what extent ethnoculturalism continues to play a role in shaping how Americans think and act. Clearly, it would be wrong to say that progress has not been made in terms of widening the scope with which liberal and civic republican principles are applied. Slavery has long been abolished, Jim Crow laws are a thing of the past, women and minorities now have the right to vote, and national origin quotas have been removed from immigration laws. McClosky and Zaller (1984) warn against "overstating the intensity of American ethnocentrism" (69), noting that many Americans opposed racist laws and behaviors even as they were being passed and practiced. They maintain that the degree of change we have witnessed in the twentieth century is a testament to the strength of egalitarianism and liberty relative to ethnoculturalism (as Myrdal would have expected). Additional evidence of ethnoculturalism's decline is the decrease over time in the public's willingness to express or endorse openly racist or sexist beliefs, as documented by public opinion polls (Schuman et al. 1997; Sears et al. 2000).

[7] See Stevens (1995), Mills (1997), and Higham (1963) for scholars other than Smith who argue and/or demonstrate that racism and prejudice form a core component of American identity.

Yet those same opinion polls still reveal that many people are willing to delineate American identity along ethnic or ascriptive lines. People may not say that blacks or women are inherently inferior to white men, but they do say that some people are just not able to be called "American" due to ascriptive characteristics. Though not as widespread as liberalism or civic republicanism, ethnoculturalism still gets a fair amount of support on public opinion surveys. For example, in the 1996 GSS, 55 percent of the respondents said that being a Christian is either somewhat or very important in making someone a true American, and 70 percent said the same about being born in America.[8] And 36 percent agree that "it is impossible for people who do not share American customs and traditions to become fully American" (Davis and Smith 1997). In the 1998 New Jersey Poll, 58 percent said that believing in God is either somewhat or very important in making someone a true American, and 45 percent said the same about being born in America. And in the 1992 NES, 68 percent said that believing in God was either extremely or very important in making someone a true American. Historian Philip Gleason (1980) once wrote that in order to be considered an American, a person need not possess certain cultural characteristics, that he or she must only believe in liberal principles like liberty and equality. Smith documents the fallacy of this statement in America's past, and these opinion data suggest that it still may not be true today.

Current practices indicate that ethnoculturalism still finds its way into official governmental activity and that the history of legislative and judicial bodies treating certain backgrounds more favorably than others persists. For example, legislative efforts in several states have pushed for laws requiring the Ten Commandments to be posted in public schools and in other public buildings (e.g., Ratcliffe 2002; Rein 2002; Simpson 2000). In late 1999, the U.S. Court of Appeals for the Second Circuit ruled that police officers in Oneonta, New York, did not violate the Constitution when they tried to stop and question every black man in town after a robbery victim told police that her attacker was black. The police efforts included contacting officials at the State University of New York College at Oneonta to obtain a list of all black students at the school (Newman 1999). In fact, "racial profiling" has become a household phrase in recent years to describe public and private practices designed specifically to target members of minority groups as crime suspects. On June 17, 2003, the Bush administration issued a policy barring federal law enforcement officers from engaging in racial profiling . . . except in cases related to terrorism (Lichtblau 2003).

---

[8] Ethnoculturalism, as articulated by Smith, is grounded primarily in race, religion, and gender and could allow for people born outside the United States to become thought of as American. However, nativity has long been barrier to true "American-ness." It refers to a characteristic that one cannot change and is widely accepted as something that people use to determine whether someone is a "real" American.

So why the continued prevalence of ascriptivist tendencies even though we "know better" and have made so much progress? Recent work by Conover and colleagues (1999) provides some guidance here. They argue that it is difficult to conceive of the concept of "citizen" without bringing ethnoculturalism into the picture, and they argue that this is true not just in the United States but in other societies as well. Citizenship, like any other group identity, entails distinguishing group members from nonmembers. As social identity theorists have demonstrated, the human tendency is to form in-groups and out-groups and to discriminate accordingly, whatever the group identity may be (Tajfel and Turner 1986). Psychologically, Conover argues, it is easy to make distinctions based on physical appearance, and thus, people do. The salience and meaning of group membership diminish when people are surrounded only by other members of their group. Thus, in order for the concept of "citizen" to make sense, people use their racial and ethnic communities as a proxy for their political community in determining boundaries. Conover finds that people simply do not "separate their understandings of what it means to be a member of the political community, a citizen, from what it means to be a member of their ethnocultural community" (27). Scholars of nationalism note that this tendency has often been encouraged by political leaders because it provides the necessary binding agent required to hold modern nation-states together (e.g., Brubaker 1996; Hobsbawm 1990; Schmidt 2000; Snyder and Ballentine 1996; Volkan 1994). Unfortunately, few remedies are recommended for counteracting this intractable phenomenon.

Ethnoculturalism is similar to what others have referred to as "nativism." Higham (1963), in his classic study of American nativism, defines nativism as "intense opposition to an internal minority on the ground of its foreign (i.e., 'un-American') connections" (4). Similarly, Perea (1997) defines it as "a preference for those deemed natives" along with a "simultaneous and intense opposition to those deemed strangers, foreigners" (1). Citrin, Wong, and Duff (2001) offer a more general definition, writing that nativism insists on cultural conformity and "gives an ethnocentric cast to American national identity" (77). In most formulations, nativism is explicitly anti-immigrant and antiforeign. In theory, nativists can be against immigrants from anywhere. In practice, however, America's most vehement nativist episodes have been aimed at immigrants that deviate most from dominant cultural and ethnic norms (Johnson 1997).

The two terms—nativism and ethnoculturalism—can be used interchangeably for most practical purposes; both speak to using specific cultural characteristics in determining who can and cannot belong to the national community. Yet I prefer using "ethnoculturalism" to "nativism" in this study for a conceptually important, yet admittedly subtle reason. In my view, nativism is a particular response to the demographic changes that result from immigration; its intensity varies with changes in the economy, in immigration patterns, and in international conflict. Ethnoculturalism, on the other hand, is more of a general guiding myth, or standing decision, about national identity. More specifically, nativism, strictly defined, is biased against people born outside of the United States and ebbs and flows with changes in context. Ethnoculturalism, strictly defined, is biased against people who do not fit into a dominant cultural type regardless of where they were born, and shapes how people imagine their national identity, even beyond the level of awareness. The automaticity with which people assume that a person with an accent is not an American is an example of the strength and depth of ethnoculturalism's day-to-day presence. In this sense, ethnoculturalism is a more appropriate term to use when considering not only the treatment of immigrants but also the treatment of American citizens who are not white, not Christian, and not possessive of unaccented English. Nativism, then, is a narrowly focused reaction to particular situations, whereas ethnoculturalism is an enduring and entrenched set of beliefs about the nature of American national identity. As more and more citizens deviate from the ascriptive ideal type, it will be increasingly important to study perceptions about nonwhite citizens in addition to—yet distinct from—perceptions about immigrants. This distinction is especially salient with regard to policies driven by post-9/11 security concerns. The ethnocultural willingness to deny citizens the full set of rights and opportunities that accompany formal citizenship is different from the nativist willingness to deny immigrants citizenship, or even entrance. This distinction is subtle, but one that I argue should not be ignored by conflating the two terms.

Although much progress has been made in terms of racial, religious, and gender equality in the United States, ethnoculturalism remains a core component of American identity and deserves to be recognized as such. The degree of change over the past several decades serves to remind us that identity is dynamic and that we need to update and reevaluate our analyses accordingly. That said, we cannot fully appreciate such changes until we also appreciate the entrenched and pervasive stature of ethnoculturalism in American politics. Likewise, we cannot make gains in understanding how identity shapes preferences if we do not acknowledge that ascriptive beliefs do not simply reside among those who have gone astray. Rather, they are a central part of what many people think being American is all about.

INCORPORATIONISM: THE IMMIGRANT CITIZEN

American identity is paradoxical if it is nothing else. Beliefs about the cultural characteristics that define American identity are not bound by the ethnocultural ideal of white Protestantism. In fact, ethnoculturalism shares space in the American psyche with a conception of national identity that cherishes cultural diversity. The symbolic image of immigrants coming to America to start a new life of freedom and opportunity is as cherished as the symbolic image of the Sons of Liberty tossing tea into Boston Harbor in the name of representative democracy. This immigrant-based tradition is not included in Smith's framework, yet should be considered in analyses about the relationship between American national identity and policy preferences, especially when the policies under investigation grow out of patterns of ethnic change.

The term I use to describe the immigrant-based conception of American identity is "incorporationism." It is not like struggles for racial equality, which have been liberal at root and have historically focused on the similarities between minorities and whites in terms of their rights to citizenship; it is not simply one more expression of the "me too" phenomenon. Further, it is not the belief that people should be left alone to either engage or ignore their ethnic background, whichever they prefer, on their own time—what Mary Waters (1990) calls "the ethnic option." The *individual* is *not* the central focus; our *immigrant legacy* and the resulting *cultural diversity* is. Nor is incorporationism really ethnoculturalism in drag. It does not pay lip service to the idea of the melting pot but in practice espouse a homogenous society in which all members look, sound, and worship alike, what Citrin et al. (1994) call "melting-as-cleansing." Finally, incorporationism does not favor the extreme scenario of complete cultural divisions or the promotion of a corporatist or consociational society; it does not call for placing ethnicity prior to citizenship. Although some proponents of what Citrin, Wong, and Duff (2001) have termed "hard" multiculturalism do indeed call for the state to provide ethnically based group rights, that particular perspective has never gained much currency beyond academic and activist circles; it has never achieved mythic status (also see Miller 1995; Ingram 2000; Schmidt 2000). Rather, as Zolberg and Woon write (1999), "extreme differentialism and extreme assimilationism are equally ruled out" (30) as political doctrines. The challenge of finding a balance between those two extremes is a matter of tangible political struggles; the incorporationist ideal, however, allows for both differentialism and assimilationism, each to some degree. In other words, in the incorporationist civic myth I add to Smith's typology, an Irish-American is neither solely Irish nor solely American. The commonality among citizens is the hyphenation. Everyone has a hyphen where the first term indicates an ethnicity that should, on some level, be preserved and cherished, and everyone shares the "American" half of his or her particular label with everyone else.

Horace Kallen (1924) was a proponent of a similar perspective, though he called it "cultural pluralism." He argued that living with "manyness" rather than forcing "oneness" is part of the American way of life. He was writing in response to the Americanization movement, which he criticized for trying to eliminate cultural differences. And he likened American society to an orchestra, arguing that harmony rather than unison should be the ultimate aim. Kallen's proposals did not get much formal political recognition in his time.

He was writing during the age of literacy tests for admission to the country, strict immigration quotas, the banning of foreign languages in public schools, and the Jim Crow South. But the essence of his arguments did not disappear and have since become even stronger in the wake of the social movements of the 1960s and the 1965 changes in immigration policy.

Michael Walzer (1996) stresses that immigration as a phenomenon and as an *experience* is an integral part of American identity. He writes, "The experience of leaving a homeland and coming to this new place is an almost universal 'American' experience' " (17). And as Bonnie Honig (2001) notes in her analysis of "foreign-founders," accounts of American exceptionalism are "inextricably intertwined with the myth of an immigrant America" (74). Recall Smith's definition (1997) of a civic myth: "a myth used to explain why persons form a people, usually indicating how a political community originated, who is eligible for membership, who is not and why, and what the community's values and aims are" (33). Incorporationism, as defined here, fits that bill. The persons form a people because of a shared immigrant experience; the political community originated from immigration; all immigrants are eligible for membership (in the ideal); and the values and aims it lays out for the nation are to welcome immigrants and forge a sense of national identity that retains and respects the manyness.[9]

There are two possible reasons why Smith does not include incorporationism in his work. First, identity is a dynamic concept, as is illustrated by the changes in the ethnocultural tradition over the years. To put it simply, things have changed. Smith's analysis focuses on the years between the colonial era and the Progressive Era, a time in which ideas about cultural diversity did not have much currency. Perhaps the civic myth of incorporationism is too much of a twentieth-century phenomenon to have shaped elite interpretations of American identity in earlier times. Higham (1993, 199), for example, documents the rise of multiculturalism and the politics of difference in the United States and describes it as a distinctly modern struggle, one that is still making only "halting" progress against the notion that white males form the core of American society. Hollinger (1995) writes of the "sheer triumph, in late-twentieth century America, of the doctrine that the United States ought to sustain rather than diminish a great variety of distinctive cultures carried by ethno-racial groups" (101). And Glazer, in the tellingly titled *We Are All Multiculturalists Now* (1997), says that "the increasing acceptance of pluralism as a central American value" is "one of the most striking changes of the recent past" (79).

A related reason why an immigrant-based conception of American identity is absent from Smith's work is linked to his main research question. Smith

---

[9] It should be noted that this myth refers to voluntary immigration only (i.e., it ignores the slave trade) and, as with other civic myths in America, discounts the experience of indigenous peoples.

himself points out that his is a "top-down" analysis because the voices from below have traditionally been left out of the lawmaking process. Since proponents of cultural pluralism have primarily come from outside of the halls of Congress and the courts, they have played little official role in deciding who can and cannot be an American. Smith writes (1997): "It would be seriously misleading to write as if the views of those who were ineligible to hold political office shaped American citizenship laws as much as the views of those who did possess such prerogatives. . . . It remains true that there is much more to the story of what American identity has meant to millions of people and how it has been shaped than I encompass here" (7). This "top-down" approach, then, might be sufficient for Smith's purposes, but it is not sufficient for mine. Incorporationism is exactly the kind of tradition Smith describes as being left out of his analysis. As Mendelberg notes (2001), cultural norms gain widespread acceptance and power when they are endorsed by elites, but new norms often emerge from social movements or protest efforts. The principles advanced by the activists in these efforts do not become "norms" until those in power promote them. The norm described by Hollinger—that we should celebrate rather than diminish diversity—grew out of social movements in the latter half of the twentieth century and did not achieve the civic status of the other traditions described thus far until relatively late in the game. Yet if it now indeed constitutes a full-fledged conception of American identity—if it shapes how millions of Americans think about being American—and if thoughts about being American shape policy preferences, then it needs to be included here.

Some readers may question why I do not use the term *multiculturalism* to describe this conception of national identity. As I argue in more detail in chapter 5, multiculturalism presents a specific interpretation of the incorporationist civic myth. *Incorporationism*, on the other hand, is an underused term with no specific prescription regarding the appropriate level of assimilation. Beliefs about the proper role and extent of assimilation for the idealized immigrant, I will demonstrate, play a role in how people interpret this civic myth; they do not define it. The struggle to balance "many" and "one" has been with us for over two centuries; arriving at a solution continues to elude us. People at all points on the political spectrum, from all backgrounds, and at all levels of political power genuinely believe that new arrivals should adopt American customs and traditions while also preserving aspects of their pre-American existence. Figuring out how to do that is no easy task, but the incorporationist ideal allows us to have it all; it envisions the United States as a place that welcomes immigrants and that manages to have both many and one. We are both an orchestra and "diverse cultural streams acquiring a common identity" (Citrin, Sears, Muste, and Wong 2001, 251; aka "melting-as-blending," Citrin et al. 1994). We fight over how to make this amorphous image more concrete, but we celebrate that image and view it as distinctly American.

As with all of the other civic myths, disjunctures between the ideal and the reality do not diminish the ideal's power to shape political consciousness. Just as liberal discourse and imagery are omnipresent in American life, so is the notion that America is a nation of immigrants. Just as the national anthem can form a lump in one's throat and send chills up one's spine, so can the famous lines of Emma Lazarus's "The New Colossus," the poem that graces the Statue of Liberty. We can all recite at least as much as "Give me your tired, your poor, / Your huddled masses yearning to breathe free," and when we do, the image of Lady Liberty herself, standing to welcome a boat full of hopeful newcomers as they approach Ellis Island, surely comes to mind. Historian Rudolf Vecoli (1994), describing the enduring symbolic power of the statue, writes: "Although the jet plane has replaced the steamship as the main means of transportation to the United States, and Los Angeles has replaced New York as the major port of entry, the Statue of Liberty retains its power to evoke the immigrant myth so central to the American identity" (59). It is part myth and part reality that without immigration, there is no America and without immigrants, there are no Americans.

Survey data suggest that many Americans endorse a general immigrant-based conception of American identity. In the 1997 "Looking for America" survey, 82 percent of the respondents agreed that "the blending of many different cultures into one culture" makes the United States different from all other countries ("melting-as-blending"). In the 1994 GSS, respondents were asked to place themselves on a seven-point scale where 1 meant that it would be better for America if different racial and ethnic groups maintain their distinct cultures, and where 7 meant that it would be better if the different groups would change so that they would blend into the larger society. Thirty-one percent of the sample scored between 1 and 3, favoring the maintenance of distinct cultural traditions; 37 percent scored between 5 and 7, favoring a more uniform population; and the remainder scored a 4, favoring a certain degree of variety along with a certain degree of homogeneity. As Citrin et al. (1994) write, "Many Americans may not consider maintaining one's ethnic heritage and blending into the larger society as mutually exclusive" (16). A similar question was asked on the 1996 GSS, and the distribution of opinion was more or less the same as it was in 1994.[10] Both of Citrin's studies from 2001 conclude that there is little support for the "hard" multiculturalism described earlier (across all ethnic backgrounds) but that there is widespread support for having both an ethnic identity and a common national identity; people do want it all. It is also interesting to note that 35 percent of the 1996 GSS sample had at least one grandparent that was not born in the United States. Coupled with the fact that the United States population is now almost 12 percent foreign-born, it is clear that the immigrant experience is still the recent or current reality for many families.

There is genuine ambivalence in the United States toward immigrants and

---

[10] The 1992 NES also had a similar distribution of opinion on this item.

immigration. Nativist episodes occur with regularity, and ethnoculturalism is an enduring feature of daily life. But Americans also relate to and romanticize the immigrant experience. As Honig (2001) puts it, xenophobia and xenophilia co-exist at both the societal and individual levels. Leo Chavez's (2001) study of seventy-six immigration-related covers from popular magazines from 1965 to 1999 provides a fascinating study of this persistent tension and ambivalence. One of his most interesting sets of findings involves the tone of the images (alarmist, neutral, or affirmative) and the calendar. In particular, he finds that only nineteen of the seventy-six covers were affirmative in tone but that 68 percent of those affirmative covers appeared in the month of July. *Time* magazine, for example, devoted its bicentennial issue of July 5, 1976, to profiling new immigrants and describing how they illustrate America's continued identity as "the Promised Land" (93). During the rest of the year, we can criticize immigration and warn of impending doom, but when we pay tribute to the nation on its birthday, we look to immigration as a way of celebrating who *we* are.

Some readers may wonder if ethnoculturalism and incorporationism are simply two poles of the same tradition, with nativist beliefs at one end, assimilationist beliefs in the middle, and "hard" multiculturalist beliefs at the other end. There is no doubt that ethnicity plays an essential role in shaping the contours of these two traditions and that many people are both xenophobes and xenophiles. But it is important to keep in mind that civic myths are fundamentally grounded in normative statements, such as: What should ideal citizens be like? What should the criteria for membership in the political community be? As such, each tradition should receive its own independent scrutiny; the ethnoculturalist makes very different normative claims from the incorporationist. The two are indeed related, but combining them into one tradition will not advance the larger goal of investigating how the normative force of each civic myth is employed in the formation of policy preferences.

To sum up, then, the incorporationist conception of American identity lacking from Smith's typology centers on the immigrant legacy of the nation, emphasizes the immigrant experience as a shared one, and sees American society as a multiethnic one that occupies a space somewhere in between the two extremes of cultural erasure and separatism. More radical voices calling for group rights exist, but there is little evidence that their calls enjoy much support. This incorporationist civic myth is a part of the American political landscape and should be taken into account by both theorists of American identity and public opinion scholars who strive to study the relationship between American identity and policy preferences.

Privileged, Responsible, White, Immigrant Citizens

Up until this point in the chapter, my main goal has been to discuss four civic myths that have served to shape what we think it means to be an American and to speculate about their staying power. The purpose of this exercise is to arrive ultimately at a set of identity constructs we can use to test whether these conceptions of American identity shape a particular set of policy views. In this vein, it is worthwhile to examine how these four traditions interact in addition to studying the ideal types. Smith and others have documented that conceptions of American identity are often blended in practice. Allowing the analysis to account for such hybridization might therefore provide further insights into the relationship between identity and attitudes.

Elements from multiple conceptions of American identity have often been expressed simultaneously. Several scholars have pointed out that battles over American identity have been waged not only across people and across different groups of people but within people as well, as they try to reconcile the competing influences on their perceptions. As Kammen (1972) writes in *People of Paradox*, "Conflicts *between* Americans have been visible for a very long time, but most of us are just beginning to perceive the conflicts *within* us individually" (296, emphasis in original). It is now widely recognized that cultural conflict is part of the American psyche. For example, in her analysis of attitudes about distributive justice, Hochschild (1981) describes a pervasive ambivalence among the people in her study. She points out that people often hold several important yet competing views but are rarely, if ever, called upon to sort them out. As a result, people are content in their ambivalence and are often unaware of it. A variety of scholars using a variety of research approaches have found that elements from different intellectual traditions are present in the minds of most Americans (e.g., Feldman and Zaller 1992; Chong 1993; and Kellstedt 2000). The internal competitions and collaborations among them are worthy of examination. In the paragraphs that follow, I describe some of the historical blending that has taken place among the traditions under investigation here.

The affinity between liberalism and civic republicanism was discussed earlier, and Smith's own use of phrases like "liberal democratic republic" and "liberal republican" (Hochschild 1998) is an indication of the tendency for these two traditions to appear simultaneously in American politics. For example, both the rule of law and popular participation in government are seen as necessary for the maintenance of America's unique democratic system. Both traditions grow out of a belief that people cannot be ruled without their consent, and both harbor a distrust of strong central governments. In *American Political Cultures*, Ellis (1993) points his readers to Jefferson and his followers for an example of a belief system that combines the liberal and civic republican ideals of individualism and participation. And he notes that the fusion of these ideals did not fade away with the Jeffersonians, adding that any satisfactory analysis of political culture in the United States still needs to examine the relationship between these two traditions.

The combination of principles from liberalism and ethnoculturalism is a bit more controversial. It involves both the belief in universal rights and the denial of those rights to certain classes of persons. Smith (1993) describes how this combination has often involved the promotion of elaborate theories of racial and gender hierarchy, and he points to social Darwinism as a particularly nefarious example. Perhaps the best-known instance of the hybridization of these two traditions is the Jim Crow doctrine of "separate but equal," judged to be constitutional in the 1896 Supreme Court case of *Plessy v. Ferguson* on the basis that it did not impose disadvantages on either race (Klinkner and Smith 1999; Wilson and DiIulio 1998). Although it is now, and perhaps always was, well-known that separate institutions for blacks and whites were never equal, the stated principles justifying this doctrine combined ethnocultural beliefs about racial superiority and liberal beliefs about rights and equal opportunity.

A more contemporary example corresponds to what public opinion scholars have termed "symbolic racism," which is defined as the combination of believing in the American values of individualism and the work ethic and feeling that minorities violate these cherished American norms.[11] Several studies have shown that symbolic racism shapes policy views in contemporary America, although its prevalence, influence, and even existence have been a source of intellectual debate for several years (e.g., Sears et al. 2000).

Some scholars argue that the conjoint expression of liberal and ethnocultural principles is not simply a historical accident but rather an inevitable outgrowth of liberalism itself (see Hochschild 1984). One common argument is that the unbridled pursuit of economic success leads to perpetual inequalities and that those at the top create rules that further entrench economic and political imbalance (Smith 1993; Berry 1998). Another asserts that a government whose existence and maintenance rests on majority rule and equality of opportunity inevitably results in an exclusive definition of who "the people" are.[12]

The principles of civic republicanism and ethnoculturalism can be jointly implemented and expressed as well. The founders, for example, feared that a participatory system of government could not survive across a vast territory and with a populace that was too diverse. The Anti-Federalists in particular, inspired by Montesquieu, feared too much reliance on a central government because they felt, as Ellis (1993) explains, "only in a small community, where one knew and sympathized with one's neighbors, could an individual be expected to prefer the common good over private interests" (15). Their arguments usually referred to general "interests" and not to race, gender, or religion in particular. But in practice, attempts to preserve a certain degree of homo-

---

[11] "Symbolic racism" has also been called "modern racism" and "racial resentment" (Kinder and Sanders 1996).

[12] See Stevens (1995) for citations. Also see Morgan (1975), who argues that the institution of slavery was central to the ability of southern whites in colonial America to revere and fight for liberty and equality.

geneity often fall back on such ascriptive characteristics as a proxy for "interests" (Conover, Searing, and Crewe 1999). And even in heterogeneous settings, social hierarchies such as race, class, and gender often prevent the outcomes of the face-to-face interactions required by the civic republican ideal from being met (Sanders 1997).

Moreover, when we envision a romanticized New England town meeting, the kind that Tocqueville so admired, the characters that come to mind are inevitably white men, and the scene resembles John Trumbull's classic painting of the signing of the Declaration of Independence. This revered civic republican image is so infused with ethnocultural characteristics that the linkage between the two in our minds is often beyond our awareness. As Kymlicka (1989) notes: "Eighteenth century New England town governments may well have had a great deal of legitimacy amongst their members in virtue of the effective pursuit of their shared ends. But that is at least partly because women, atheists, Indians, and the propertyless were all excluded from membership" (85). And Smith concurs (1988), noting that civic republican rhetoric has often been employed to justify political, social, and economic abuses over time (also see Schudson 1998).

Finally, the civic myth of incorporationism can be expressed in hybrid form as well. Incorporationism and liberalism have had a joint history in cases where the liberal interpretation of cultural pluralism has called for a hands-off approach. This perspective parallels the cherished separation of church and state, calling for a separation of culture and state. In this view, immigrants assimilate into American society as individuals and are able to take advantage of the same rights and opportunities as everyone else. Indeed, we romanticize the immigrant experience as a way of affirming the validity of the American Dream (Honig 2001).

Civic republicanism and incorporationism are expressed simultaneously when the argument is made that cultural assimilation is an obligation of citizenship. In this manifestation, assimilation is seen both as a process that makes up the American experience and as a necessary undertaking for maintaining the public good and national unity. This hybrid view of American citizenship was prevalent during the Americanization movement in the early part of the twentieth century. As Higham illustrates (1963), some aspects of the Americanization movement were driven by nationalist anxiety and the fear of too much "foreign influence" on American institutions, while other aspects were motivated by the love and charity of progressive urban organizations. What both strands of the movement had in common was the desire to encourage cultural assimilation and loyalty, and the belief that cultural assimilation was a civic duty. Higham describes how organizations such as the Daughters of the American Revolution "embarked on programs of patriotic education designed to indoctrinate the adult foreigner with loyalty to America" and make "aliens into good citizens" (236–37). Historical examples such as Americanization point to the compatibility of incorporationist reverence for the immigrant experience and civic republican concerns about patriotism and national unity. The extent to which Americans still explicitly link these concerns when they discuss what being American means remains to be seen.

The simultaneous expression of ethnoculturalism and incorporationism is perhaps more familiar and is best described as the belief that the melting encouraged by the melting pot means "cleansing" or erasing signs of a previous cultural existence. Welcoming immigrants and then requiring them to change is not really welcoming at all. For many, the symbol of the melting pot has, over time, been corrupted to suggest that new arrivals lose their cultural baggage and become more like the dominant culture. This "melting-as-cleansing" perspective combines a romantic image of the immigrant experience while simultaneously upholding a specific cultural type to which immigrants should aspire. Rather than seeing the cultures of new immigrants and citizens who have lived in the United States for generations blend *together*, this combination of traditions puts the onus of melting on the immigrants only.

The purpose of going over these conceptual hybrids is to acknowledge that Americans do not consistently subscribe to a particular tradition or civic myth. This is true not only across time and space, but within individual citizens as well. Together, the four traditions of liberalism, civic republicanism, ethnoculturalism, and incorporationism have served to guide how Americans decide what being an American means, yet inconsistency has rarely stood in the way of policy making and opinion formation. Despite the hybridization detailed here, I would warn against combining these traditions into a single construct called "Americanism." American identity is made up of different traditions, and each one needs to be taken into account on its own if we are to understand the interaction between identity and policy views. That said, as we move forward with a more accurate and theoretically driven account of how elites and masses might rely on American identity to think about issues like immigration and language policy, we do need to recognize that hybridization occurs. More important, we need to know what such hybridization entails so we can be prepared to look for it.

Civic Myths and Language Politics

The discussion thus far has examined general treatments of "what it means to be an American" in the pursuit of conceptual frameworks that might shape how people interpret debates about language conflicts. Before moving on to the empirical analysis, it would also be useful to examine scholarship on language politics in particular. The opinions I am most interested in studying are those of ordinary Americans. But many people out there are intimately involved in concrete policy battles over language policy. What do they think their efforts are about? Are their positions bolstered by views of what it means to be American? If so, what do they think it means to be American? Which, if any, conceptions of American identity appear to shape activist interpretations of language conflict? Do they correspond to the conceptions in my model, or are they different?

Scholars of linguistic politics indeed tend to agree that heated debates among activists on either side are often about competing visions of what it means to be American. As Schmidt (2000) explains, "Ultimately, the language policy debate in the United States is not about language as such but about what kind of political community we are and wish to be" (183). And Schmid (2001) writes, "In the American context, controversy over Official English and bilingualism is about competing models of Americanism" (10). What those competing models are is the subject of these, and other, studies. Looking at analyses of activist discourse, one finds elements of all of the traditions described in this chapter, although it seems that just about everyone uses different labels for similar concepts and that some address several traditions whereas others address only a few.

First, nearly all treatments of activist rhetoric note an ethnocultural, nativist, or racist aspect to language conflicts (e.g., Citrin, Sears, Muste, and Wong 2001; Citrin et al. 1994; Citrin, Wong, and Duff 2001; Espinosa-Aguilar 2001; González 2001; Perea 1997; Schmid 2001; Tatalovich 1995). They describe pro-official-English activists as being hostile and intolerant toward immigrants, as disparaging immigrants for allegedly refusing to assimilate ("melting-as-cleansing"), and as generally being driven by fears that the infusion of inferior cultures is threatening the American way of life. Schmidt (2000) is the one notable exception in this regard, charitably characterizing official-English proponents as "assimilationist." Toward the end of his book, however, he introduces two types of assimilationists: "liberal individualist assimilationists" and "communitarian nativist assimilationists" (191). He says activists in the latter camp "believe there are valid grounds for excluding from U.S. membership altogether those who are 'essentially' different from the dominant ethnolinguistic group" (254); he puts figures such as Peter Brimelow and Pat Buchanan in this category. In Schmidt's formulation, we see elements of liberalism, civic republicanism, *and* ethnoculturalism all being employed to characterize official-English supporters, and all being subsumed under the label "assimilationist." While it is entirely conceivable that all three of these conceptions of national identity provide values that lend support for restrictive language policies, it is not clear that a model fusing all three is more appropriate than a model examining each one on its own. In any case, the more important point to note here is that even though he does not analyze ethnoculturalism as a distinct element of language conflict, he still acknowledges that it plays a role for some official-English proponents.

The liberal tradition in America also features prominently in analyses of language conflict rhetoric, though it is not discussed in as many studies as nativism is. I've already noted that Schmidt characterizes some supporters of re-strictive policies as liberal; he writes that they think it is acceptable for people to maintain another language in their private lives but think that public life should be conducted in a single common language. Citrin, Sears, Muste, and Wong (2001) also note the public/private distinction that people employ to defend policies that promote commonality (also see Citrin, Wong, and Duff 2001; Citrin et al. 1994). Schmidt and Citrin also note that liberalism's pre-scription to treat people as individuals and to structure the state so as to em-phasize individual rights as opposed to group rights appears in pro-official-English rhetoric. Interestingly, Schmidt notes that *opponents* of restrictive policies also invoke liberal norms, but different ones from the proponents. Op-ponents characterize official-English as violating the liberal values of freedom of expression and equal protection. And Tatalovich (1995) notes that the American Civil Liberties Union (ACLU) aided opponents in several state-level battles against official-English. Thus, we see that activists on both sides of official-English battles invoke liberal claims when explaining their position.

As with survey-based analyses of policy preferences in this issue area, civic republicanism does not get much explicit attention in studies of language pol-icy activists, but that doesn't mean that civic republican concerns aren't pres-ent. As noted earlier, Schmidt refers to some supporters as "communitarian," and he describes the activists' goals as centering on national unity. He writes that for assimilationsists, "it is nothing less than national unity that is at stake—a subject that involves everyone in the country and thus goes to the heart of the common good" (163). He does not call these concerns civic republican, yet they clearly invoke the ideal of other-regarding citizens work-ing together toward goals that are more than just the sum of individual self-interested pursuits. Assimilationists fear that this ideal is threatened and look to official-English for protection. Opponents of official-English, Schmidt notes, counter this fear by pointing out that it is the language policies them-selves that foster conflict and destroy unity. Tatalovich (1995) likewise avoids labeling activist efforts as civic republican, but notes that two stated goals of an effort for English-only ballots in San Francisco were to "encourage national unity" and to "reduce the number of uninformed voters" (129). As with liber-alism, we see the same ideal—a harmonious national community of informed and involved citizens—being invoked by both sides to support their position.

Incorporationism, as I defined it previously, does not feature too promi-nently in studies of activist rhetoric. Instead, activists against restrictive poli-cies are described as being more likely to invoke "hard" multiculturalism; they look to the state for group rights and advocate "government efforts to preserve minority cultures" (Citrin, Wong, and Duff 2001, 77). Schmidt calls these anti-official-English activists "pluralists," and notes that they advocate "promotion-oriented" language rights, calling on government to "actively seek to maintain non-English languages and ethnolinguistic communities" (153). Yet even among these activists, none are cited as actually promoting ethnic separatism, and none argue *against* learning English. Schmidt himself ends up pitching a softer version of multiculturalism, one that is more in line with the incorporationist ideal I outlined earlier. He calls his perspective "pluralistic integration," which he defines as entailing a mix of integration on the one hand and ethnic integrity on the other. He credits Higham with coining the phrase and arguing that pluralistic integration "will not eliminate ethnic boundaries. But neither will it maintain them in tact. . . . Both integration and ethnic cohesion are recognized as worthy goals" (quoted in Schmidt, 225). The ideal, in other words, is the incorporationist vision of having it all.

Other studies of language activists do not delve too deeply into the multiculturalist perspective. Schmid's analysis, for example, focuses on supporters of official-English, as does Perea's edited volume on modern nativism. Tatalovich discusses the charges of racism and bigotry that opponents raise but does not indicate the presence of rhetoric calling for group rights in his detailed analysis of state-level conflicts. And Citrin notes that hard multiculturalism drives activist opponents but argues that the mass public prefers a more moderate position. Whether activist opponents really do call for separatism and/or group rights, or are just characterized that way by supporters of official-English, isn't always clear. From my review of the literature, it seems that some hard multiculturalist voices are out there, but only a few. And even the ones that are out there advocate group recognition rather than actual separatism. If my analysis of public opinion in later chapters finds that the public does indeed endorse hard multiculturalism, then I would need to revise my understanding of incorporationism. But if the public takes more of a middle position on diversity, wanting it all, then incorporationism would be an appropriate way of capturing that matrix of opinion, that enduring struggle to celebrate our differences and our immigrant legacy while also blending together to form a unique and dynamic American culture.

Even though these authors use different terminology than I do to describe how competing conceptions of American identity shape language conflicts, they confirm the prominence of the values and norms I describe as being long associated with "what it means to be an American." Those who have spent time analyzing the rhetoric of partisans in language debates characterize it as being infused with the discourse and imagery associated with the conceptions of American identity described in this chapter, the main exception being "hard" multiculturalism. Although this hard multiculturalism characterizes some activist rhetoric, it is not a true civic myth and is therefore unlikely to be a major influence over the views of ordinary Americans. Other than that, the studies of language conflicts evaluated here indicate that the civic myths described in this chapter, and their accompanying norms and values, shape activist discourse in complicated ways; for instance, in some cases we see the same broad tradition being employed by both sides. We have also seen that this field is struggling to come up with appropriate labels for the different clusters of principles guiding activist efforts.[13]

So what should we expect as we move on to the empirical analysis? Opponents among the activists are probably more extreme than opponents among ordinary Americans due to the narrow scope of hard multiculturalism's appeal. Supporters, on the other hand, might come across as more extreme among the mass public than among the activists. As noted earlier, acceptable norms of discourse about race and ethnicity have changed in this country. For many people, it is not socially acceptable to be overtly nativist, especially for public figures trying to gain support for legislation. As Espinosa-Aguilar (2001) writes, "Because we live in a world that considers xenophobia irrational, modern colonialists such as members of U.S. English know they must mask their agenda in language that does not appear racist" (275). If pro-official-English activists do use blatantly nativist rhetoric, they risk alienating potential supporters. But ordinary citizens are less bound by the constraints that public figures face. As far as the liberal and civic republican traditions (the two "state-centered" traditions) are concerned, their entrenched and relatively noncontroversial hold on the American mind suggests that there won't be much of a disjuncture between activist and mass attitudes. People on both sides of the issue are likely to invoke these traditions to support their views, although people on opposing sides might emphasize different specific aspects of each tradition.

Conclusion

Hochschild (2000) has written that like biologists, some social scientists are "lumpers" and others are "splitters." Lumpers put several ideas and concepts into fewer categories while splitters do the opposite; they take larger categories and break them down into their component parts. She argues that neither approach is inherently right and that the appropriate strategy depends on the research question at hand. My analysis is in the "splitter" camp, for I maintain that lumping liberalism, civic republicanism, ethnoculturalism, and incorporationism into a monolithic "Americanism" is not particularly useful for the type of analysis that I want to pursue.

The analysis in this chapter grows out of a frustration with some of the works described in chapter 2 that seek to explore the relationship between conceptions of American identity and attitudes toward policies addressing ethnic change, such as language and immigration. In these studies, either several survey items tapping into a wide range of concerns are put together in an

[13] Activists on either side of the issue are cited as invoking another justification in addition to those that relate to competing conceptions of American identity: the economy. Supporters decry the costs of providing multilingual services, and opponents maintain that being a multilingual society will enhance the country's standing in the global economy.

"Americanism scale," or one or two survey questions are used to serve as a proxy for American identity as a whole. One goal of this chapter has been to demonstrate that we might be missing much of the story if we use such "lumper" approaches to study how American identity shapes attitudes. If we want to understand how people use ideas about what it means to be an American to interpret social and political phenomena related to ethnic change, we should be including separate measures for the distinct yet powerful civic myths that pervade the American political landscape. The blame for the faults I find with the "lumper" approaches cannot be placed entirely on the authors. After all, it is difficult to test for the influence of a civic republican conception of American identity if the relevant survey questions are not asked. As Citrin, Wong, and Duff (2001) write, "It is important to conceive of national identity in a way that recognizes the possibility of several conceptions of 'American-ness' vying for popular support" (72). We haven't done that well enough yet.

In thinking about what role national identity plays in how people debate language policy and ethnic change, it is useful to look to enduring civic myths, such as those described by Smith, as well as at the discourse actually used by people on the ground fighting over concrete policy changes. Together, these literatures provide a picture of how elites over time and in current controversies conceive of American national identity. This examination has allowed me to document the static and dynamic components of that identity and the extent to which they are widely endorsed. And together, these literatures generate expectations about when the public will follow the lead of elites and when they will be either more moderate or more extreme. The terminology employed varies across studies; in fact, no two studies were found to use the same terminology in characterizing activists and their arguments even though each of the studies described essentially identical phenomena. I have tried to make the case in this chapter for the terminology and conceptual boundaries that I use throughout the remainder of the book. I have explained the ways in which my conceptual categories mesh with, and differ from, categories used by others and laid out the bases for my conceptual choices.

Smith ends the opening chapter of *Civic Ideals* by stating that the development of American citizenship laws becomes more comprehensible when the analysis takes account of the illiberal and undemocratic practices that were a constant element throughout the time period he studies. The equivalent statement for my research is that the story of public opinion about American identity and policy preferences is more comprehensible when our vision encompasses America's civic republican tradition and pays more attention to what political theorists have written on "what it means to be an American." It becomes even more comprehensible when we include newer civic myths that grow out of our immigrant legacy. To this point, I have only argued that I expect these assertions to be valid. Whether they are is an empirical matter, and testing whether they can be sustained is the subject for the remaining chapters.

CHAPTER FOUR

American Identity in Surveys

THE WAKE OF THE CHANGING DEMOGRAPHY in the United States is replete with debates about the societal, environmental, and economic effects that immigration is having in the United States. Interest groups on all sides of the issue have sprung to life, and concerns about what immigration means for the future of America have become common topics of discourse in the media and in lawmaking bodies. Accompanying these debates is media coverage of census estimates stating that whites will no longer be a majority in the United States by the end of the twenty-first century, if not sooner. Major newspapers have carried articles that describe these population changes as "roiling" and as resulting from immigrants "piling" into the United States (Cohn 2000; Belsie 1999).

Needless to say, scholars of public opinion have become increasingly concerned with understanding how people feel about these dramatic demographic changes and about issues that arise from them, such as bilingual education and immigration policy. As I described in chapter 2, competing theories about what causes people to be hostile toward immigrants and to favor stricter policies have been tested by several scholars with a variety of data sets. To simplify their findings, the dominant influences on attitudes appear to be conceptions of American identity, education, income, partisanship, ideology, and antiminority affect. Some of these factors, such as American identity and education, are consistently significant across studies, while others, such as partisanship and income, are more erratic (e.g., Citrin, Reingold, and Green 1990; Citrin et al. 1997; Espenshade and Calhoun 1993; Frendreis & Tatalovich 1997).

The focus of this book is on the first of these factors—conceptions of American identity and their ability to serve as integral components of the opinion formation process on issues relating to ethnicity and ethnic change. The studies described in chapter 2 provide convincing evidence that definitions of national identity can indeed shape preferences, but they are not able to go beyond that, to say much more about American identity itself or about which parts of this elusive entity are relevant in this issue area. My goal in this project is not simply to confirm the findings of previous studies that establish identity as an important causal variable, but to further our understanding of the relationship between identity and opinions by comparing the influence of alternative conceptions of what being American means and by showing which of these conceptions are more influential in the decision-making calculus. In this chapter, I begin the empirical work needed to achieve this goal. I demonstrate that American identity consists of more than one unidimensional construct, and I show how these constructs influence attitudes on issues related to language policy, namely perceptions of immigrants and preferences on immigration policy. More important, however, the analyses in this chapter serve to underscore the complexity of how people imagine American identity and the need to complement existing survey data with more in-depth approaches.

Measuring Identity and Policy Preferences

In this first cut at exploring the relationship between American identity and policy preferences, I use data from the 1996 GSS. The battery of GSS questions regarding American identity, administered to 1,367 respondents, is one of the longest of its kind, with seven items. The survey also includes many useful items about immigration and general feelings about America. Noncitizens were removed from the database, leaving a sample size of 1,237. The GSS does not ask respondents if they are of Hispanic or Asian origin, but it does ask people to name where their ancestors are from. Based on their answers, rough measures of ethnic categories can be established. In the end, the sample of respondents is 80 percent white (non-Hispanic), 14 percent black, 4.6 percent Hispanic, and 1 percent Asian.[1]

The core set of questions examined here is a battery that asks respondents to rate how important certain characteristics are in making someone a true American. Respondents are asked: "Some people say the following things are important for being truly American. Others say they are not important. How important do you think each of the following is?"

- to have been born in America
- to have lived in America for most of one's life
- to be a Christian
- to have American citizenship
- to respect America's political institutions and laws
- to feel American
- to be able to speak English

Respondents may answer: very important, fairly important, not very important, or not important at all (Davis and Smith 1997). The last item, whether it is important to be able to speak English, was dropped from the analysis because it is too closely related to the dependent variable under investigation.[2] Observed correlations among the remaining six items are presented in table 4.1.

---

[1] According to 1997 census estimates, the United States population in 1994 was approximately 74 percent white (non-Hispanic), 12.5 percent black, 9 percent Hispanic, 3.5 percent Asian, and 1 percent Native American (U.S. Bureau of the Census 1997).

[2] All analyses were also run with this item added to the inclusive measure of American identity. The substantive results do not change.

TABLE 4.1
Observed Correlations among American Identity Items

	Born in America	Lived in America	Be a Christian	Have U.S. citizenship	Respect U.S. government	Feel American
Born in America	1.00					
Lived in America	0.72	1.00				
Be a Christian	0.50	0.51	1.00			
Have U.S. citizenship	0.43	0.45	0.32	1.00		
Respect U.S. government	0.16	0.18	0.19	0.30	1.00	
Feel American	0.29	0.35	0.32	0.35	0.40	1.00

To this point in the book, the primary policy concern has been about language, not immigration. So why does this chapter focus on how American identity influences perceptions of immigrants and immigration policy preferences? The answer is simple. One of the occupational hazards in this line of work is being dependent on surveys designed by other people. In 1994, the GSS contained questions about language policy. It did not, however, include the battery of questions about American identity. In 1996, the survey sees the introduction of the American identity battery but does not have the questions about language policy, and no other survey contains sufficient questions about both American identity and language policy along with enough background information about the respondents. The 1992 National Election Study (NES) contains questions on both language policy and national identity, but its national identity battery is quite short and is even more poorly suited for the constructs under analysis in this project than the 1996 GSS.[3] Because of these factors and given the close relationship between immigration and language issues, the immigration questions are serving as a proxy for questions about language policy. There are differences between these issues, to be sure, but their common ties to the changing demographics of the American citizenry warrant the substitution. I discuss this substitution in more detail at the end of the chapter.

The limitations of the available data also explain why American identity is represented by only two conceptions (described next) rather that the four I describe in chapter 3. Ideally, the battery of questions regarding what it means

[3] The 1992 NES only asks about speaking English, believing in God, treating all people equally, and trying to get ahead on one's own. Several scholars, including myself, have tried to use the 1992 NES to investigate the impact of national identity on language policy views, and all end up with frustratingly vague results. For example, Frendreis and Tatalovich (1997) can only conclude that opinions on official-English are affected by attitudes related to "the broader issue of national identity" (367). Citrin et al. (1994) apologetically note that the American identity items "were not consciously developed to measure nationalist ideologies in a systematic way" (10).

to be American would have been designed to capture multiple ideological traditions. It would include some questions that tap into the liberal conception, with its emphasis on rights, tolerance, and economic freedom; other questions that tap into the civic republican conception, including items about participation, community cohesion, and self-governance; and still other questions designed to capture other conceptions of American identity. Here, the typology from chapter 3 cannot be tested explicitly for its accuracy, yet it still serves as a guide for constructing the model and interpreting the results. Despite this deficiency in the data, this analysis is still useful because it underscores the need to pursue the relationship between identity and policy preferences further and to incorporate alternative methodologies in doing so.

American Identity or American Identities?

Looking at the items in the American identity battery, one pattern becomes apparent. Three of the items ask if characteristics that are more or less fixed are important in making someone truly American (being born in the United States, being a Christian, and having lived in the United States for most of one's life), while the other three items deal with characteristics that are more fluid and can be acquired by anyone (being a citizen, respecting American institutions and laws, and feeling American). Although being a Christian and living in America for most of one's life are technically things anyone can do, these items appeal to an image that is in fact quite difficult, if not impossible, to acquire. Because of this pattern among the six items, I expect that only two conceptions will be justified upon further empirical analysis. Moreover, I expect that the two conceptions will shed more light on how notions of American identity influence the ways people interpret and evaluate immigration-related issues than a single measure does.

To be more specific, I expect that the first conception will tap into ethnocultural, or ascriptive concerns. The second conception is more difficult to label. Unlike the ethnocultural items, the three items here do not neatly map onto any of the conceptions of American identity described earlier. One could make the case that they measure a weak form of civic republicanism, since feeling American and having American citizenship are concerned with attachments, both legal and psychological, to the national community. However, "respecting American political institutions and laws" does not fit into that typology; one could argue that this item is more liberal, but the link there is not so straightforward either. For lack of a better term, I call this dimension *assimilationist Americanism*, or *assimilationism* for short. The term *assimilation* carries some historical baggage, and I do not mean for it to be confused with the notion of the melting pot, which is often criticized for requiring people to shed important cultural traditions. In this context, assimilationist Americanism is simply typified by the notion that mutable characteristics, such as believing in democracy or having American citizenship, define American national identity. The assimilationist believes that anyone can become truly American, provided that he or she adapts to particular norms. To be sure, this process requires a certain amount of assimilation before someone can be considered truly American, but unlike the ethnocultural conception, it does allow a person to become *more* American.

To determine if these two conceptions of American identity are supported by the data, I conducted an exploratory factor analysis (see appendix A). Based on the results, I adopted a two-factor model and created variables for the ethnocultural and assimilation factors using summated rating scales. A summated rating scale is exactly what it sounds like; it is a scale created by adding responses to several questions together. These scales then become variables like any other that can be used in empirical analysis. The six identity items are first coded so that a higher score means the respondent feels that the item in question is very important in making someone a true American. Next, the variables are rescaled to range from 0 to 1. Then, for each scale, responses to the relevant items are added together and divided by the total number of questions answered. For example, if a respondent answers all three questions on the ethnoculturalism scale, the coded values of his answers are added together and the total is divided by three ("not at all important" = 0; "very important" = 1). If he skips a question, such as whether being a Christian is important in making someone truly American, then his answers to the other two ethnocultural items are added and the total is divided by two. Finally, Cronbach's α, the scale reliability coefficient, is calculated for each scale. The ethnoculturalism scale has an α of 0.79, and the assimilationism scale has an α of 0.62.[4] These coefficients suggest that the ethnocultural scale is a more accurate measure of one underlying notion of what it means to be an American than the assimilationist scale, an observation confirmed by the factor analysis. But taken together, the factor analysis and reliability measures provide enough confidence that all six items should not be combined into a single "Americanism" scale.[5] The three ethnocultural items certainly belong together in their own measure; whether the same can be said of the assimilation items is not as clear. One should, perhaps, think of the assimilationism scale as a set of important "noncultural" concerns about what it means to be an American rather than as a theoretically coherent form of American identity in its own right.

Before examining whether these two scales influence attitudes toward immigrants and immigration policy, it is instructive to look at their distributions

[4] These coefficients are nearly identical to those found in Citrin and Duff (1998) and Citrin, Wong, and Duff (2001). The correlation between the two scales is 0.45 ($p < 0.001$).

[5] Cronbach's α for a scale made from all six items is 0.77—not as good as the ethnoculturalism scale but better than assimilationism.

TABLE 4.2
Distribution of Opinions about American Identity

Item	% Saying "Very Important"	Standard Deviation	N
Born in America	42.10	0.35	1202
Lived in America	45.20	0.31	1199
Be a Christian	39.23	0.40	1193
(Ethnoculturalism)	25.90*	0.31**	1220
Have U.S. citizenship	76.44	0.21	1214
Respect U.S. government	64.64	0.22	1199
Feel American	62.54	0.26	1204
(Assimilationism)	44.95*	0.18**	1219

Note: All items re-scored to be on a 0 to 1 scale.
* Percentage of respondents saying all questions they answered are very important.
** Standard deviation for the summated rating scale.

among respondents. I use two indicators to do this, both of which appear in table 4.2. The first column displays the percentage of the total sample saying that each item is "very important" in making someone truly American. The second column displays the standard deviation of the responses to each question. The top half of the table contains the items from the ethnoculturalism scale; the bottom half contains the items from the assimilationism scale.

Well over half of the sample feels quite strongly that the assimilationist items are essential characteristics of true Americans, while considerably fewer respondents feel the same way about the ethnocultural items. Over 17 percentage points separate the *most highly* supported ethnocultural item (having lived in America for most of one's life) and the *least* supported assimilationist item (feeling American). The standard deviations confirm that there is less consensus regarding the immutable prerequisites of American identity than there is about the more fluid ones. Observations are spread out over a wider range for the former than they are for the latter. This disparity carries over into the summated scales as well; the ethnoculturalism scale has a standard deviation of 0.30, while the assimilationism scale has a standard deviation of 0.18.

This pattern of distributions suggests that there may be an asymmetric relationship between these conceptions of American identity. In other words, people who agree that fixed characteristics define Americans most likely believe that more mutable characteristics are also important, while the reverse might not be the case. People who think that having a legal or psychological attachment to the United States is important might not also support a more narrowly conceived notion of what being American means. Perhaps this asymmetry confirms the observations of Smith, Kammen, and others who maintain that Americans are conflicted not only against one another, but individually as well (Kammen 1972; also see Hochschild 1981 and Feldman and

Zaller 1992). This pattern also provides a link between opinion research and debates among scholars of American political thought. That political and "noncultural" concerns are an important component of American identity is undeniable, as Hartz and others have argued. But a more exclusive definition of national identity exists as well, though it lacks the overwhelming consensus of its more inclusive counterpart.

Who Believes What

An obvious question to ask at this point is: what factors influence whether a person will adhere to assimilationist and/or ascriptive beliefs about American identity? Do traditional social and political cleavages in American society account for the patterns of support described earlier, or do these conceptions of identity resonate with people from all backgrounds? Do background characteristics, such as partisan identification, lead to support for both conceptions, or do they lead to opposite ends of the ethnocultural and assimilationist scales? In this section, I address these questions by exploring the social and political antecedents that determine which Americans are more likely to voice support for these conceptions of national identity.

The background characteristics under investigation are age, education, gender, self-placement on a liberal/conservative scale, whether the respondent was born in the United States, partisan affiliation, family income, the respondent's perception of his or her own economic situation, ethnicity, and whether the respondent speaks only English in the home (see appendix B for question wording and coding).[6] Some of these variables—age, education, gender, income, and ethnicity—are standard measures of important social differences in the United States. Others—partisan affiliation and ideology—capture traditional political cleavages that often influence policy preferences and opinions about the proper relationship between citizens and government. The remainder—economic perceptions, nativity, and speaking only English—consists of "threat variables." Previous research has shown that objective economic indicators, such as income, as well as subjective ones, such as the fear of an economic downturn, can influence attitudes on public policies when there is a cognitive link between the policy in question and one's economic security. But threats need not be economic. As scholars such as Luker (1984) and Huddy and Sears (1995) have shown, perceived threats to the world as one knows it, or to one's interests more broadly defined, can be powerful motivating forces in terms of public opinion and political behavior. I consider being born in the United States and speaking only English to be objective "threat" variables because a person who fits this description might perceive that her lifestyle and the ability to pursue her own ends are endangered by demographic change.

[6] The 1996 GSS did not ask respondents to assess national economic conditions.

The result could be an increased tendency to define American identity by particular fixed characteristics and to be hostile toward the newcomers who are blamed for causing the perceived threat. The simple inconvenience of not being able to communicate with a store owner or the more serious feeling of becoming culturally and linguistically isolated in one's own community would constitute such threats. These two survey items—being born in the United States and speaking only English—are included in the analysis to test whether these sorts of threats shape views on American identity and immigration.

I expect to find that being older, less educated, Republican, conservative, white, a "native" American (born in the United States), and speaking only English would make a person more likely to say that ascriptive characteristics are important in making someone truly American. Other studies have shown that some of these factors make a person more likely to endorse an ethnocultural conception of American identity, and the data here should confirm their findings (e.g., Citrin et al. 1994; Citrin and Duff 1998; Citrin, Wong, and Duff 2001). At this point, I do not speculate about economic concerns; the economic measures are included simply to specify the model and to allow their influence, if there is any, to be captured.

Given the strong consensus that exists on the assimilationist dimension, I am more agnostic about the effects of social and political antecedents on a person's adherence to this notion of American identity. This consensus simply leads me to expect fewer significant coefficients on the independent variables, which would indicate that most people, regardless of social or political background, support the items in this scale.

To test these hypotheses, I conducted two stepwise ordinary least squares (OLS) regressions with background characteristics as independent variables and the summated scales as dependent variables. The models also include among the independent variables an indicator variable for those respondents who refused to divulge their income. The steps in the model advance temporally, with the first step consisting only of factors that are predetermined, or fully exogenous to the model (e.g., age, education, ethnicity). In the second step, I add characteristics that are expected to influence attitudes but that could be determined, in part, by variables from the first step (e.g., partisan identification, ideology, and economic perceptions). This procedure is derived from the notion of a "funnel of causality" developed in The American Voter (1960) and allows me to capture whether the effects of temporally prior circumstances are mediated through subsequent characteristics.[7] Before running the analysis, all non-dichotomous independent variables were rescaled to have a range of 1 and a mean of 0. The results are presented in table 4.3. The coefficients for the

[7] A two-stage least squares procedure (2SLS) was also attempted in this analysis but was dropped in favor of the stepwise model. Due to the high consensus on the assimilationism scale and the limited number of relevant questions on the GSS, identification of the two-stage model proved to be problematic. For more on stepwise models in opinion and voting research, see Miller and Shanks (1996) or Krasno (1994).

TABLE 4.3
Social and Political Determinants of Opinions about American Identity

Independent Variable	Ethnoculturalism		Assimilationism	
	Model 1	Model 2	Model 1	Model 2
Age	0.132***	0.126**	0.147***	0.146***
	(0.052)	(0.055)	(0.036)	(0.037)
Education	−0.636***	−0.642***	−0.169***	−0.166***
	(0.079)	(0.079)	(0.047)	(0.047)
Male	−0.009	−0.024	−0.007	−0.016
	(0.020)	(0.020)	(0.013)	(0.013)
Born in U.S.	0.119**	0.127**	0.022	0.025
	(0.055)	(0.056)	(0.031)	(0.031)
Family income	−0.051	−0.041	0.014	0.022
	(0.044)	(0.046)	(0.027)	(0.028)
Refused to give income	0.034	0.055	0.007	0.012
	(0.052)	(0.053)	(0.030)	(0.030)
Speaks only English at home	−0.017	−0.022	−0.019	−0.020
	(0.034)	(0.036)	(0.021)	(0.022)
Black	0.158***	0.158***	−0.005	−0.012
	(0.023)	(0.028)	(0.019)	(0.022)
Hispanic	0.075*	0.064	−0.039	−0.039
	(0.045)	(0.049)	(0.029)	(0.031)
Asian	−0.096	−0.062	0.026	0.061
	(0.107)	(0.117)	(0.046)	(0.046)
Conservative	—	0.213***	—	0.115***
		(0.047)		(0.030)
Republican	—	−0.004	—	−0.008
		(0.035)		(0.021)
Economic perceptions	—	−0.012	—	−0.002
		(0.025)		(0.016)
Constant	0.520***	0.524***	0.860***	0.862***
	(0.057)	(0.058)	(0.032)	(0.032)
N	907	868	907	867
R^2	0.15	0.17	0.04	0.06
F	19.55	17.07	3.90	5.06

Note: Standard errors in parentheses. Dependent variables range from 0 to 1, where 1 = highest level of adherence.

* $p < .1$; ** $p < .05$; *** $p < .01$

models with the first set of demographic characteristics appear in the columns marked "Model 1." The coefficients for the models with political and economic variables added are in the columns marked "Model 2." Standard errors are in parentheses.

A few general patterns should be noted in table 4.3. First, as expected, it is more difficult to capture the influences on the assimilationism scale than the influences on the ethnoculturalism scale, as revealed by fewer significant coefficients and a much lower R^2. Second, adding the political and economic variables ("Model 2") does not change the influence of the temporally prior demographic characteristics. This is true for both dependent variables, which means that the impacts of factors like education and age are not mediated through partisan identification, ideology, or perceptions of economic vulnerability. Third, in neither case does economic vulnerability influence scores on the summated scales.

Turning now to more specific findings, the results show that age, education, ideology, nativity, and race are strong predictors of whether a person adheres to an ethnocultural definition of American identity. Going from eighteen to eighty-nine years old moves a person up the ethnoculturalism scale by 13 points, moving from an eighth grade education to a college education moves him down 26 points, being born in the United States moves him up 13 points, being black moves him up 16 points, and strong conservatives are 21 points higher than strong liberals. To put it another way, when all other variables are held constant at their means, a person with an eighth grade education would score 0.80 on the ethnoculturalism scale, whereas a person with a college degree would score 0.54.[8] Similarly, when all else is average, an eighteen-year-old will score 0.58, while an eighty-nine-year-old will score 0.71; and a strong conservative will score 0.73, while a strong liberal will score 0.52. A person born in the United States will score 0.63, while a person born outside the United States will score 0.50; and black and white respondents will score 0.79 and 0.63 respectively.[9]

Looking at the second set of models, the most obvious finding is that there are fewer influences on whether a person adheres to the assimilationist vision of American identity. As with ethnoculturalism, age, education, and ideology influence a person's score. The magnitude of that influence, however, is much smaller for education and ideology. When all other variables are held constant at their means, people with an eighth grade education will score 0.91 on the

[8] Values are calculated for white women who were born in the United States and who speak only English in the home. Both dependent variables range from 0 to 1.

[9] All models were also run on a sample that consisted only of whites and on a sample that consisted only of whites who were born in the United States. In these restricted models, the effects of one's age, level of education, and political ideology are stronger, but the substantive results and patterns across temporal steps do not change. In the models for "native" whites only, the constant increases roughly by the coefficient on the nativity indicator variable from the full models.

assimilationism scale, whereas people with college degrees will score 0.84, a difference of only 7 points. Strong conservatives and liberals will score 0.92 and 0.80, respectively, a difference of only 12 points.

In both sets of models, older respondents, conservatives, and those with less education are more willing to endorse both the exclusive and the inclusive conceptions of American identity than their younger, liberal, and more educated counterparts. This finding supports the claim that people can simultaneously adhere to more than one definition of national identity. One important difference between the two conceptions, however, is that people who were born in the United States are more likely than foreign-born citizens to support ethnoculturalism but not assimilationism.[10] The foreign born, residents and citizens combined, now comprise 11.5 percent of the U.S. population, and the Census Bureau predicts that number will rise.[11] Given these figures, this finding is no trivial matter. If current immigration rates continue as they are today and if immigration-related issues continue to be politicized, then nativity is likely to become and remain an important influence on the distribution of public opinion toward a variety of social and political issues.[12]

ATTITUDES TOWARD IMMIGRANTS AND IMMIGRATION POLICY

Deconstructing the components of national identity is not a particularly useful exercise unless those components can be applied to concrete situations and tell us something about everyday politics. The search for causal relationships between abstract ideas about identity and concrete political relations among citizens is grounded in the belief that these abstract ideas are in fact capable of affecting how people perceive—and perhaps behave in—the sociopolitical arena. Clearly, then, the next step in this analysis is to see how the two conceptions of American identity that the 1996 GSS measures influence attitudes on policies.

The analysis here proceeds in two stages. Continuing with the "funnel of causality" framework, the first stage involves testing for the influence of identity on attitudes toward immigrants. In this stage, I start with the two-step

[10] Another difference between the two models is that blacks are more likely than whites to support ethnoculturalism. This is an unanticipated finding, the implications of which are not immediately clear. Most African-Americans were born in the United States, have lived in the United States for most of their lives, and are Christians. Perhaps they agree with these items because they feel they are only describing themselves, even though they are still excluded from the ethnocultural ideal-type.

[11] Eight percent of the total sample is foreign-born. Half of the foreign-born respondents are not citizens and were not included in the analysis.

[12] All models were also run on a sample consisting of black, Hispanic, and Asian respondents. In these models, nativity was a strong predictor of whether respondents adhered to either ascriptive or assimilationist conceptions of American identity.

model from the previous section and include a third step that involves adding the two summated scales as independent variables. In the second stage, I turn to immigration policy. Using the same three steps from the first stage, I examine how notions of American identity influence preferences for immigration restrictions. This time, a fourth step is included in which the perceptions of immigrants are added as an independent variable. The logic to this procedure is that background characteristics and conceptions of American identity are expected to have direct effects on attitudes toward immigrants and immigration, yet the impact of background characteristics may be mediated through characteristics that are determined at later points in one's life. Similarly, conceptions of national identity and perceptions of immigrants are expected to influence policy preferences, but the effect of identity may be mediated though anti-immigrant sentiments.

In the first stage, the dependent variable is a summated rating scale that captures how the respondent views immigrants. Respondents were asked how strongly they agree or disagree that immigrants increase crime rates, take jobs from Americans, make America open to new ideas, and are good for the U.S. economy. The coding of the last two items is reversed so that a higher score on the scale reflects greater hostility toward immigrants. The resulting anti-immigrant scale ranges from 0 to 1 and has a Cronbach's α of 0.73 (mean = 0.49; standard deviation = 0.19).[13] As before, people who identify themselves as politically conservative, who were born in the United States, and have lower levels of education are expected to be more hostile toward immigrants than liberals, the foreign born, and people with more schooling. I expect ethnoculturalism to be a significant predictor of anti-immigrant sentiment, perhaps overwhelming or absorbing the effect of temporally prior characteristics. An adherence to a set of beliefs that denies certain people the ability to become full members of the polity is expected to lead to unfavorable views of those very individuals whose membership is being denied.

Just as predicting the influence of demographic characteristics on assimilationism was difficult, predicting the influence of assimilationism on attitudes toward immigrants is not simple either. On the one hand, this conception of American identity can evoke a distinctly romantic vision of immigrants coming to the United States and working hard to make a new life for themselves. Moreover, the assimilationist view might make people think of their own ancestors and result in a favorable image of the immigrant in America. On the other hand, people who adhere to this dimension might feel that immigrants *should* try to develop emotional attachments to the United States but that they do not. Further, the word *immigrant* means, by definition, that the person is not quite American yet. That word alone may cause a person who values assimilation to perceive unassimilated immigrants in a negative light.

[13] An exploratory factor model yields an eigenvalue of 1.52, and all variables have factor loadings greater than 0.55.

The results are presented in table 4.4. Models 1 and 2 show that age, education, nativity, ethnicity, and ideology influence perceptions of immigrants. The impacts of the significant variables in Model 1 are not diminished in Model 2. Respondents with less education, who are born in United States, and who consider themselves conservative are more hostile toward immigrants, and whites are more hostile than Hispanics and Asians. Reversing direction from the previous analysis, age now has a negative coefficient; being older makes a person less hostile toward immigrants. Finally, respondents who refuse to divulge their income are more hostile toward immigrants than other respondents, though this finding does not necessarily mean that income, as an objective measure of economic threat, is a significant factor here. Rather, there could be something about people who refuse to tell a pollster their income—perhaps some personality dimension that has nothing to do with income, such as lack of generalized trust—that also makes them more hostile toward immigrants. Of these characteristics, education has the most influence over the range of its observed value. When all other variables are held constant at their means, people with an eighth grade education score 0.62 on the anti-immigrant scale while those with a college degree score only 0.42.

Adding the ethnoculturalism and assimilationism scales among the independent variables ("Model 3") changes these results, though not dramatically. As expected, ethnoculturalism is a powerful force, behind only education and age in terms of the magnitude of its influence. It absorbs some of the influence of education, ideology, and nativity (but not of ethnicity or age), which means that these characteristics exhibit both indirect and direct effects on perceptions of immigrants. When all other variables are at their means, a person who scores 0 on the ethnoculturalism scale scores 0.37 on the anti-immigrant scale, whereas a person who scores 1 on ethnoculturalism scores 0.54. Conversely, assimilationism does not influence attitudes toward immigrants. This nonresult could reflect that assimilationism leads some people to look favorably upon immigrants and their struggles yet leads other people to disparage them for not having assimilated yet. It could also mean that assimilationist concerns are simply not invoked when people are asked to evaluate the impact of immigrants on American society. In any case, the important point to note is that the two dimensions of American identity operate differently here.

I turn now to the second stage of this section to see how conceptions of American identity influence support for restricting immigration. The dependent variable is the respondent's answer to a question about whether the number of immigrants entering the United States should be increased a lot, increased a little, kept the same, reduced a little, or reduced a lot. The variable is coded to range from 0 to 1; a higher score reflects a preference for restrictions. Sixty-six percent of the sample feel that immigration should be decreased either a lot or a little, 8 percent feel it should be increased either a lot or a little, and 26 percent feel it should be kept the same. My expectations

Table 4.4
Determinants of Anti-immigrant Attitudes

Independent Variable	Model 1	Model 2	Model 3
Age	−0.132***	−0.143***	−0.165***
	(0.034)	(0.035)	(0.035)
Education	−0.513***	−0.492***	−0.385***
	(0.047)	(0.048)	(0.049)
Male	0.001	−0.005	−0.001
	(0.012)	(0.012)	(0.012)
Born in U.S.	0.112***	0.122***	0.099***
	(0.031)	(0.032)	(0.030)
Family income	0.010	0.018	0.025
	(0.028)	(0.028)	(0.027)
Refused to give income	0.059*	0.076**	0.061*
	(0.031)	(0.033)	(0.033)
Speaks only English at home	0.002	−0.001	0.001
	(0.021)	(0.021)	(0.020)
Black	0.023	0.030*	0.002
	(0.016)	(0.018)	(0.018)
Hispanic	−0.047*	−0.038	−0.049*
	(0.025)	(0.026)	(0.027)
Asian	−0.108**	−0.098*	−0.089*
	(0.052)	(0.053)	(0.047)
Conservative	—	0.100***	0.064**
		(0.032)	(0.031)
Republican	—	0.005	0.005
		(0.023)	(0.022)
Economic perceptions	—	0.019	0.021
		(0.016)	(0.016)
Ethnocultural scale	—	—	0.165***
			(0.024)
Assimilation scale	—	—	0.011
			(0.038)
Constant	0.372***	0.364***	0.272***
	(0.035)	(0.035)	(0.044)
N	883	845	840
R^2	0.17	0.17	0.23
F	20.46	15.44	18.79

Note: Standard errors in parentheses. Dependent variable ranges from 0 to 1, where 1 = most hostility toward immigrants.

* $p < .1$; ** $p < .05$; *** $p < .01$

about the role of ethnoculturalism and assimilationism are the same as they were before, as are my expectations about the other variables included in the model. I add the anti-immigrant scale in the last step and expect it to lead to support for immigration restrictions.

The results from the four-step model are presented in table 4.5.[14] Looking first at Models 1 and 2, the usual suspects are significant. Education, nativity, and ideology all influence preferences in the expected direction, with education having the strongest effect over its observed range. For the first time, whether the respondent speaks only English at home matters too, though its effect is small and its significance is marginal. Whether respondents refuse to divulge their income, though influential in making them hostile toward immigrants, does not appear to make them more in favor of restricting immigration. The conceptions of American identity are added in Model 3, and both play a significant role in promoting support for restricting immigration. Once they are added to the model, the effects of education, nativity, speaking only English, and ideology are all reduced, though education still has the largest coefficient. Political ideology, on the other hand, loses its significance. As before, the effect of ethnicity is not diminished by the introduction of these variables, with blacks being less likely than whites to favor limiting immigration.

The column labeled "Model 4" contains the fully specified model with anti-immigrant sentiments added as an independent variable. As expected, anti-immigrant feelings are a strong predictor of preferences for immigration restrictions. When all other variables are held constant at their means, a person who scores 1 on the anti-immigrant scale will want immigration decreased a lot, while a person who scores 0 will want immigration levels kept the same. In this model, the effects of education and ideology essentially disappear, as does the effect of ethnoculturalism; both coefficients shrink in magnitude and lose their significance. The impacts of assimilationism and of speaking English in the home are more or less unaffected. An important note, however, is that even though these two measures are significant, moving from their lowest to their highest observed values does not change the *direction* of the preferred outcome. When all other variables are held constant, high and low assimilationists and those who speak only English or English plus another language all want immigration decreased; they only differ in whether they want it decreased a lot or a little.

That the two identity scales behave differently in this analysis helps to confirm that there is indeed more than one dimension of national identity embedded in the responses to the six survey questions. When the dependent variable is hostility toward immigrants, an adherence only to ethnoculturalism is invoked. When the dependent variable is immigration policy, both ethnocultural and assimilationist concerns influence attitudes, and they do so in the

---

[14] An ordered-probit specification yielded substantively identical results.

TABLE 4.5
Determinants of Immigration Policy Preferences

Independent Variable	Model 1	Model 2	Model 3	Model 4
Age	0.037	0.039	0.010	0.118***
	(0.050)	(0.053)	(0.053)	(0.047)
Education	−0.418***	−0.406***	−0.285***	0.001
	(0.076)	(0.078)	(0.078)	(0.073)
Male	−0.021	−0.035*	−0.030*	−0.026*
	(0.019)	(0.020)	(0.019)	(0.017)
Born in U.S.	0.098**	0.103**	0.080*	0.017
	(0.047)	(0.048)	(0.050)	(0.050)
Family income	0.025	0.043	0.046	0.027
	(0.042)	(0.043)	(0.041)	(0.038)
Refused to give income	0.036	0.056	0.039	−0.003
	(0.044)	(0.045)	(0.046)	(0.039)
Speaks only English at home	0.071*	0.074*	0.066*	0.068*
	(0.040)	(0.041)	(0.038)	(0.038)
Black	−0.081**	−0.073**	−0.085**	−0.085***
	(0.031)	(0.036)	(0.035)	(0.033)
Hispanic	−0.065	−0.051	−0.062	−0.017
	(0.042)	(0.045)	(0.048)	(0.041)
Asian	−0.095*	−0.021	−0.031	0.007
	(0.060)	(0.053)	(0.060)	(0.075)
Conservative	—	0.111**	0.067	0.023
		(0.051)	(0.048)	(0.046)
Republican	—	0.029	0.035	0.043
		(0.036)	(0.035)	(0.032)
Economic perceptions	—	0.020	0.022	0.009
		(0.025)	(0.024)	(0.022)
Ethnocultural scale	—	—	0.138***	0.036
			(0.037)	(0.032)
Assimilation scale	—	—	0.117*	0.108**
			(0.063)	(0.055)
Anti-immigrant scale	—	—	—	0.642***
				(0.048)

TABLE 4.5 (cont.)

Independent Variable	Model 1	Model 2	Model 3	Model 4
Constant	0.588***	0.584***	0.422***	0.236***
	(0.050)	(0.052)	(0.072)	(0.067)
N	782	753	750	750
R^2	0.07	0.08	0.12	0.29
F	8.15	8.37	8.57	21.14

Note: Standard errors in parentheses. Dependent variable ranges from 0 to 1, where 1 = decrease immigration a lot.

* $p < .1$; ** $p < .05$; *** $p < .01$

same direction. But when anti-immigrant sentiments are added to the model, the two conceptions of national identity react differently. Ethnoculturalism works through these more immediate feelings about immigrants, while assimilationism maintains its direct effect on policy preferences. An assimilationist view of the United States can lead to preferences for decreasing immigration, and it does so for reasons that apparently have nothing to do with how immigrants are judged.[15] If we think of the measure as a weak form of civic republicanism, then perhaps people who score high on this scale feel that changes brought about by immigration threaten the stability of the community by either hastening "balkanization" or otherwise making it difficult for the project of self-governance to be carried out effectively.

Insights and Limitations

Two main conclusions may be drawn from this chapter. First, Americans rely on more than one symbolic construct when asked to define what being American means. The two constructs identified here—ethnoculturalism and assimilationist Americanism—are not mutually exclusive and are widely accepted among the American public (the latter more widely than the former). Second, I have shown that attachments to these abstract ideas about American identity can have a powerful effect on how people evaluate immigrants and decide whether the United States should discontinue allowing immigrants to "pile" into the country. This effect persists when the influence of other traditional social and political characteristics is statistically controlled and is often more powerful than prior economic, ethnic, or political predispositions.

A lesser conclusion, but still worth mentioning, concerns the set of variables used to capture feelings of threat. Measures of economic vulnerability, subjec-

[15] The correlation between ethnoculturalism and anti-immigrant attitudes is 0.44; the correlation between assimilationism and anti-immigrant attitudes is 0.15.

tive and objective, do not register in any of the models, whereas the measures of "lifestyle" vulnerability are persistent influences on attitudes in this issue area. One "lifestyle" threat measure, nativity, is an important influence across the models and is ultimately absorbed by hostility toward immigrants. The other "lifestyle" threat measure, speaking only English in the home, maintains its influence on immigration preferences, even in the fully specified model.

Taken together, these results present an encouraging and useful step in the overall project, but the analysis is limited in several ways. First and foremost, the indicators of American identity included in the 1996 GSS and in similar surveys overlook important components of American political traditions. A more complete analysis of how notions of national identity influence opinions must contain measures of the symbols associated with liberalism, civic republicanism, and incorporationism. Liberal concerns of rights, tolerance, and economic freedom are completely ignored by the GSS battery, yet liberalism is undoubtedly an important factor for both how people define being American and how they interpret policy debates. Civic republicanism did have a small role to play in this analysis, since one of the key constructs deals with psychic attachments to the national community, but the civic republican tradition consists of more than that. It highlights the value of participation, voluntarism, and self-governance, and emphasizes the responsibilities of citizens in a democratic society, all of which are absent from the assimilationism scale. And the one quasi-incorporationist measure in the GSS, a seven-point scale with a preference for ethnic groups to "blend into the larger society" on one end and to "maintain their distinct cultures" on the other, does not accurately capture the range of possibilities in the incorporationist ideal because one pole advocates "melting-as-cleansing," a corruption of incorporationist imagery. Further, the assimilationism scale used in this chapter is rather crude. It is not necessarily a good measure of theoretical expectations about the sorts of things that people think being American means. The most that can be made of this measure is that it captures a set of "noncultural" concerns that anyone, regardless of ethnicity, gender, or religion, can acquire. This commonality among the items, however, does not lead to a tight theoretical construct.

Another limitation of this analysis vis-à-vis the larger project is the focus on immigration policy and attitudes toward immigrants rather than on language policy. Immigration can be thought of as a precursor to language conflicts; language issues would not arise if the demographic makeup of the population were static. But whether the findings and conclusions presented here carry over to the realm of language policy is still to be determined. Do multiple dimensions of national identity influence attitudes toward language policy or is only one dimension, perhaps ethnoculturalism, invoked by language debates? I suspect that an analysis with language policy as the dependent variable would yield similar, if not stronger, conclusions to the ones presented here. That I cannot say for sure (yet) is a limitation that warrants attention.

Frendreis and Tatalovich (1997), using language policy as the dependent variable with the 1992 NES, do in fact find significant predictors similar to those found here despite the weaknesses of the American identity items in that survey. In particular, they find that anti-immigrant sentiments and vague measures of national identity increase support for official-English. These factors predict support for both issues because immigration and language policy are indeed related. However, there are important differences between language and immigration policy that should be considered. Immigration policy, by definition, deals with noncitizens, whereas language policy affects the state's relationship to *citizens* in a way that immigration policy does not. As Schmidt (2000) explains, language policies that recognize multiple languages in the public sphere challenge personal and deeply felt notions of one's own standing as a member of the national community. In this respect, it could be argued that language policy is an "identity issue" more so than immigration policy. If that is indeed the case, then the findings presented in this chapter should only be stronger when language policy is the dependent variable. Unfortunately, existing survey data do not allow for this explicit comparison. Nevertheless, the extent to which language and immigration policies are synonymous should be investigated more fully.

A more important next step for my purposes, however, is to look at the common predictor of national identity more closely. It has been established that symbolic images of national identity shape preferences on both language and immigration policy, but, as the analysis in this chapter has made clear, existing survey data have been taken about as far as they can go in this regard. The rest of the book addresses the limitations of using available survey data to study these issues. In the chapters that follow, I turn to a more qualitative approach to examine relationships between identity and opinion regarding language policy. Using focus groups, I am able to shift the analysis back toward language conflicts, and I am able to incorporate the theoretical conceptions of American identity developed in chapter 3. The result is a more complete and substantive demonstration of the complex yet powerful role that images of American national identity play in the process of coming to terms with ethnic change and the public policies that arise from it.

CHAPTER FIVE

Defining American National Identity

Trying to define "what it means to be an American" is much like V. O. Key's (1963) famous description of trying to understand public opinion: "[It] is a task not unlike coming to grips with the Holy Ghost" (8). This apparently insurmountable difficulty, however, does not stop political scientists and observers of American politics and culture from trying. Some notable attempts have been made by people such as Michael Walzer (1996), Seymour Martin Lipset (1963), Rogers Smith (1997), and Michael Lind (1995), to name but a few. Most efforts at pinning down the Holy Ghost of American identity focus on elite behavior. They study the texts of political philosophers like James Madison and Alexis de Tocqueville, analyze laws and judicial decisions over time, and examine efforts by prominent national organizations, such as the Daughters of the American Revolution or the Know-Nothing Party, to demarcate and protect particular notions of American identity. Using such studies as a guide, I too undertake the daunting effort of understanding American identity, but I turn the searchlight away from elite actors and onto regular Americans. Arguments developed in elite-centered efforts provide the framework I need to begin to study how conceptions of American identity shape policy views, and they help me to develop arguments about how Americans come to grips with this elusive entity.

As the analysis in the previous chapter demonstrates, attempts to use survey data to measure how Americans define their national identity are useful, though often incomplete. In chapter 4, I used the 1996 GSS to show that two quite different notions of what it means to be an American—an ascriptive notion and an assimilationist or inclusive notion—are widely accepted and influence attitudes about immigration policy and perceptions of immigrants. But the survey was not designed with my research goals in mind and does not allow for anything more than a crude distinction between immutable and adoptable considerations to be made. What is needed at this juncture is a way to account for the several competing conceptions of American identity that people actually believe in and use to interpret their social and political surroundings. The goal of this chapter, then, is to examine whether the liberal, civic republican, ethnocultural, and incorporationist framework accurately reflects how citizens think about what being American means. This analysis bridges the gap between theoretical and empirical treatments of American identity and lays the groundwork for studying more precisely how notions of American identity are called upon in interpreting and debating public policy.

To examine whether these four traditions account for how citizens think about being American, I conducted a series of focus groups in New Jersey in 1998. By allowing citizens to describe their understandings of American identity in their own vocabulary with a group of their peers, I am able to gauge the extent to which the different traditions play a role in shaping attitudes. I am also able to discern if my four-pronged model provides an appropriate framework for studying public opinion about American identity.

Through a content analysis of the focus group transcripts, I show that Smith's liberal, civic republican, and ethnocultural conceptions of American identity are indeed prevalent in the minds of the participants. Operationalizing American identity with these three different notions of being American provides a rich and compelling approach for studying the relationship between identity and opinions. I also show, however, that this framework is incomplete in two respects. First, it cannot incorporate the distinct notion of America as a multiethnic society, an image that features prominently in the discussions. The idea that the United States is a place where different cultures thrive and mutually coexist or where different cultures influence each other to create a uniquely evolving national character is common and does not fit into liberal, civic republican, or ethnocultural notions of what it means to be an American. The second way Smith's framework is incomplete is that his three conceptions of American identity are ideal types, and their manifestations in social discourse are, perhaps not surprisingly, less rigidly demarcated. This lack of rigidity is revealed in the simultaneous expression of liberal, civic republican, ethnocultural, or incorporationist sentiments. I call these sentiments "hybrids" and show that people routinely combine elements of more than one ideological tradition.

In Search of the Holy Ghost

My goals in this chapter are to test the relative frequency of the four conceptions of American identity, to examine which aspects of each one are particularly important among the focus group members, and to look for patterns that do not fit within this framework. For example, when people describe what it means to be American, do they respond in a Hartzian fashion, reciting the tenets of Lockean liberalism, or do they respond with patriotic statements, expressing reverence for the objects and rituals that provide a sense of peoplehood? Does the ethnocultural legacy of the United States persist to the extent that people feel comfortable excluding minorities from their image of who Americans are, or have ethnocultural sentiments become more of an aberration? It is not my intention to label participants in the study as "liberals," "civic republicans," or "ethnoculturalists"; I expect to find that most people accept more than one tradition and will express a wide range of beliefs during a two-hour conversation. Rather, my aim is to discern patterns among the aspects of each tradition that are associated with American identity within the discussions as a whole.

LIBERALISM

To expect participants in the focus groups to discuss American identity within a liberal framework is not particularly controversial. As the "dominant paradigm" of American political thought, liberal imagery is familiar to all Americans and should feature prominently in the group interviews. It is hard to avoid hearing the United States described as the land of the free or the land of opportunity. The president is called "the leader of the free world," and colloquial liberal expressions such as "It's a free country" permeate popular discourse. Given the sacred and unchallenged hold that this sort of liberal imagery has in our society, the Hartzian thesis should be validated. This is not to say that liberalism will be the only conception of American identity to be discussed, but it should emerge as a widely accepted view of what people think it means to be American. In particular, people are likely to describe American identity as consisting of freedom, civil rights and liberties, and economic opportunity.

CIVIC REPUBLICANISM

Although the civic republican tradition does not provide as many catch-phrases as liberalism, it too is communicated quite explicitly as an important component of what it means to be American. The notion that ours is a government "of the people, by the people, for the people" is well-known and widely cherished. Tocqueville's endorsement of the New England township has provided a romanticized image to accompany the more abstract value of political participation. And symbols like the flag, intended to evoke an emotional attachment and devotion to the national community, are present in public spaces to an extent uncommon in most other democracies; this was true before 9/11, but is even more noteworthy now. As with liberalism, participants should be familiar with the language of civic republicanism, and civic republican discourse should be a popular tool for articulating definitions of American identity. It is likely that participants will endorse being informed and involved in public life, praise the self-governing nature of American politics, and cherish the ceremonies and rituals that sustain a sense of belonging.

ETHNOCULTURALISM

If liberalism and civic republicanism can be thought of as the official "party line" that the United States wants to project to its own citizens and to the rest of the world, then ethnoculturalism is the dirty secret the country tries to deny exists. Open endorsement of the ethnocultural ideal is more or less frowned upon today. It wasn't always, but today, by and large, we know better. Arguing that only white male Protestants can be truly American is considered the unspeakable stuff of racists. As such, one might expect focus group participants to not include this unspeakable stuff in their discussions of national identity. One certainly should not expect endorsement of the idea that only white male Protestants can be considered American to appear to the same degree as endorsement of liberal and civic republican themes. However, as the 1996 GSS illustrated, many people still hold narrow ascriptive beliefs about what Americans look and sound like, and it would not be surprising to see expressions of these beliefs. It is unlikely there will be many blatantly racist comments, but it is likely that people will see ethnic minorities primarily as members of ethnic groups and not as members of the larger national community. As Conover and colleagues argue (1999), the very purpose of national identity is to distinguish those who belong from those who do not, and in their understandings of citizenship, people often fall back on racial and ethnic categories to separate members from nonmembers. The ethnocultural history of the United States, though relegated to the official margins, will still make it possible for people to discuss American identity in racial, ethnic, and religious terms.

INCORPORATIONISM

In *What It Means to Be an American*, Michael Walzer (1996) writes that "the United States is not most importantly a union of states but of nations, races, and religions, all of them dispersed and inter-mixed, without ground of their own" (15). He later adds that "the people are Americans only by virtue of having come together. And whatever identity they had before becoming Americans, they retain (or, better, they are free to retain) afterward" (27). Walzer emphasizes an immigrant legacy and a plethora of cultural backgrounds as important components of the American character, but the recognition of such cultural diversity does not quite fit into any of Smith's categories. One could argue that it is liberal because the minimal government philosophy should allow for the private observance of cultural traditions. But the essence of Walzer's analysis is more than that; it hinges on the explicit recognition of an immigrant legacy, not on political structures that allow one's cultural heritage to thrive or whither on one's own time, as if it were a hobby or, as Waters (1990) calls it, an "ethnic option."

America is often described as a nation of immigrants, and this description should be present in the focus group discussions. The proper level of ethnic identity that Americans should retain and that the government should encourage has been debated since the founding, and as a nation, we have never been able to settle on an answer. Therefore, it is likely that participants will struggle with this issue as they attempt to define American identity. As with so many spectra in American politics, the range of acceptable alternatives is likely to be constrained. As I argued in chapter 3, neither complete assimilation nor complete ethnic separatism is popularly endorsed; it is unlikely that either of these two extremes will be voiced in the focus groups. Rather, it is likely that participants will endorse more moderate views. They will promote both ethnic diversity and cultural assimilation. Some people will emphasize the former, which I label "multiculturalism," while other people will emphasize the latter, which I label "melting pot assimilationism."

The term *multiculturalism* has been adopted in many circles over the past few decades and has taken on a variety of meanings. In this study, I use the term to refer to the type of society that the cultural pluralists of the early twentieth century envisioned (Kallen 1924; Hollinger 1995). In such a society, different ethnic groups peacefully coexist under a unified political system while maintaining much of their cultural distinctions. The presence of multiple ethnicities in the American population is seen as not merely a fact of life, but a virtue. It is to be celebrated and preserved. This perspective resists both deliberate and merely evolutionary processes of cultural homogenization. It is not just an acknowledgment that freedom in the United States allows people to nurture a cultural heritage if they so choose, to exercise their ethnic option. Rather, it is the notion that American identity is characterized precisely by the presence and flourishing of many distinct cultures. Manifestations of the multiculturalist tradition in popular discourse might consist of praise for the cultural diversity participants see around them and lamentations that people have lost touch with many of their own ancestral traditions. For reasons discussed in chapter 3, I do not, however, expect ordinary citizens to promote ethnic separatism or ethnic-specific group rights.

The second form of incorporationism, melting pot assimilationism, is perhaps the most dynamic view of American identity in this analysis. The term *melting pot* carries negative connotations for some, for it has often been criticized for requiring people to erase signs of a prior cultural existence and adapt to the dominant cultural norms. As employed in this analysis, however, the term is meant to describe the imagery as it was originally intended, or rather, as the metaphor actually suggests. In other words, it describes American identity as evolving over time as more and more cultures get added to the mix. Rather than espouse a "melting-as-cleansing" process, I expect people to endorse "melting-as-blending." As with multiculturalism, this perspective acknowledges the immigrant tradition in America, yet unlike multiculturalism, it emphasizes how the very concept of "American" changes as the population changes.

HYBRIDS

In her review of Smith's *Civic Ideals*, Jennifer Hochschild (1998) finds few faults. Of the faults that she mentions, one is Smith's use of terms like "liberal republican" and "liberal democratic republican" (322). One could argue that Smith conflates these two political traditions when he uses such terms, or one could argue that he simply reflects the tendency of most Americans to simultaneously describe, endorse, or invoke elements of more than one. As Smith himself writes (1993), "Though Americans have often struggled over contra-dictions among these traditions, almost all have tried to embrace what they saw as the best features of each" (550). If Smith is right, then we should expect participants in the focus groups to engage in the simultaneous expression of tenets from more than one tradition. And recall the analysis in chapter 4 that showed that many respondents in the 1996 GSS adhere to both the inclusive and the exclusive definitions of national identity embedded in that survey.[1] As will be discussed later, the unit of analysis in this chapter is the "completed thought," which usually translates to a sentence or two of dialogue. A thought is considered to be a hybrid—the simultaneous expression of more than one conception of national identity—if two (or more) conceptions are invoked within that single thought. This means that the amount of hybridization I find will most likely be a lower bound; it will not take into account that a person may endorse liberalism at one point in the conversation and then endorse eth-noculturalism later on. Thus, I expect to find a noticeable amount of hy-bridization but perhaps not as much as I would find in an individual-level analysis that examines what each participant says throughout the two-hour conversation.[2]

Data and Methods

FOCUS GROUPS

To explore patterns among alternative expressions of national identity and their relationship to policy preferences, I conducted a series of focus groups in New Jersey from April to December of 1998. A focus group, to borrow a defi-nition from Roberta Sigel (1996), is "a small group of people led through an open-ended, in-depth discussion of a given topic by a group moderator who, in a more or less nondirective manner, seeks to elicit responses from as many par-ticipants as possible but carefully avoids being judgmental, hoping thereby to elicit a variety of opinions and attitudes" (29). Although still not common in social science research, focus groups are becoming more accepted as a way to research and analyze public opinion. Since many skeptics still raise valid con-cerns about this methodology, I take time here to discuss in some detail the benefits and drawbacks of focus groups in general and my specific method-ological choices in particular.

Among the many reasons why one might opt for focus groups, perhaps the most basic is that more traditional methods (e.g., surveys) have failed to in-clude appropriate questions on the topic of interest, or have only asked the ap-

---

[1] The correlation between the two conceptions of American identity in the 1996 GSS is 0.45, and 20 percent of the respondents score the highest rating on both scales.

[2] At this point, there is no reason for me to speculate on which combinations will be most com-mon. All permutations are possible and expected.

propriate questions infrequently or without sufficient background questions. And even if the proper survey questions have been asked, another reason for using focus groups is that, as Hibbing and Theiss-Morse write (1995), "if we have learned nothing else from survey research it is that we must be very careful to avoid asking respondents to provide more than they are capable of providing" (39).

Previous surveys have rarely, if ever, included questions on language policy together with questions on alternative conceptions of national identity. Further, people are not regularly called upon to discuss American identity or the role of English in American society, and when they are asked to do so, they will most likely find the task difficult. Most Americans are socialized to have certain beliefs about what America stands for, and they carry these beliefs throughout their lives. But they are rarely asked to articulate what those beliefs are. A valuable feature of focus groups is that they give participants the opportunity to answer the questions of interest in their own words and to "think out loud" rather than constraining them to a structure imposed by a fixed set of survey responses. In short, using focus groups for this project provides data that are otherwise unavailable and yields insights that more traditional means of opinion analysis cannot. This is not to say that surveys on these matters are not valuable. Rather, it is often the case that more attention needs to be paid to designing survey questions, and both sources of data can complement each other by allowing different types of analyses for the same phenomenon.

As with any research method, focus groups have drawbacks. One is the lack of generalizability. Conclusions drawn from focus groups are not as generalizable as those drawn from a national sample because the sample size is small and recruitment rarely uses probability sampling. To avoid severe atypicality, researchers often conduct several focus groups (Hibbing and Theiss-Morse 1996). A related problem is that replication is not possible with focus group research. Replication, however, becomes less valuable if the method that allows it (e.g., surveys) has been unable to address the substantive questions of interest.

Another potential problem is that the comments of the most colorful and articulate respondents may draw undue attention (Morgan 1993; Krueger 1998). This concern can be addressed through comprehensive approaches, such as content analysis. By counting the frequency of concepts, words, or conversational patterns, all statements are included in the analysis, not just the most quotable. Some scholars warn against this type of quantification, or frequency counts (e.g., Morgan 1997, 60–62). One worry is that not every speaker has a chance to respond to the same set of issues (Sigel 1996). Each group emphasizes different aspects of the overall topic, and even within groups, some people do not get a chance to comment on certain facets of the debate. Thus, quantification might not provide a complete portrayal of the extent to which certain beliefs exist among the participants. In defense of quantification, Gamson (1992) writes:

> [The numbers] are intended to provide information on the robustness of any given result. They tell us whether what is said is consensual, appearing independently of the race and gender composition of the groups; whether it is a majority view in groups of different types or restricted to a particular type; whether it occurs in a minority of groups but is not a rarity or an idiosyncratic expression of a few unusual ones; or, whether it never appears at all. These are important differences even if one takes the exact numbers with a grain of salt. (191)

Sigel (1996) adds that quantification is more acceptable when a study involves many groups: "Rigorous quantification, as is done in the case of systematic content analysis, might be appropriate after investigators have observed many groups and have gained information on the prevalence of certain ideas in the public so they can develop an observational code" (41). Content analysis is also a reasonable approach when there are a priori expectations about what topics participants will raise. Although content analysis of transcripts may not capture every concept relevant to the issue under discussion, it does allow examination of whether theoretically grounded expectations are at work while also providing opportunities to discover unanticipated relationships.

The large number of groups involved in my study (fourteen) and my a priori expectations about the roles different conceptions of American identity will play in discussions about language policy make me confident that content analysis is an appropriate strategy to use here. I am interested in the spontaneously generated reasons for why people hold certain opinions on restrictive language policies. Frequency counts allow me to see which types of justifications come up most often and in which direction, and to see whether patterns vary systematically across different types of groups. Using a quantitative approach does not pretend to cover all possible influences on policy preferences, nor does it imply that people who do not voice a particular argument do not share the same feelings as those who do. It only reveals how many people voice particular concerns with respect to national identity and language legislation and how often they do so.

PROFILES

Participants were recruited from apolitical community organizations in the greater Mercer County area in New Jersey. The current president or organizer of each group was contacted and asked if members of the group would participate in exchange for a small financial donation to the organization. The final sample consists of fourteen groups in which participants within each group had a prior acquaintance with one another. To minimize pressures for social desirability, I wanted each group to be ethnically homogeneous and to consist only of U.S. citizens. In the end, three groups were entirely Hispanic, eight were entirely white (non-Hispanic), and the remaining three were ethnically heterogeneous;[3] all but two participants were citizens. There were five "hobby" clubs (e.g., cars, gardening, dance), three community service or charity organizations (one of which serves a local Hispanic community), three career-related organizations, a public-speaking group, a historical society, and a Chicano culture organization.

The mean number of participants per group is 8 (min. = 5; max. = 12) and the total number of persons interviewed is 108. A pre-discussion questionnaire was used to gather demographic information and baseline opinions on language policy. The sample is disproportionately female (69 percent) because many local community groups were for women only, and in some of the mixed-sex groups, only women agreed to participate.[4] Participants range in age from 18 to 74 years old (mean = 47), the mean household income is between $50,000 and $60,000, and most consider themselves to be middle-of-the-road politically. Twenty percent of the participants ($n = 21$) are Hispanic: 8 Mexican, 7 Puerto Rican, 2 Dominican, 1 Cuban, 1 Ecuadorian; two identified only as "Hispanic" without mentioning a place of origin. Before the discussion, 51 percent of the participants supported declaring English the official language of the United States and 36 percent favored printing election ballots only in English. Among white participants only, 61 percent favored official-English and 46 percent favored English-only ballots. The reader can refer to appendix C for a more detailed explanation of the recruitment procedures and for descriptions of the participants, including a comparison between the demographics of the sample and the rest of New Jersey and the United States. The information in the appendix shows that the focus group sample is, on average, slightly more educated, affluent, and Democratic than the rest of the state and nation, slightly more middle-of-the-road (fewer conservatives *and* fewer liberals), and considerably more Hispanic. Among whites in particular, my sample underrepresents the views of people with lower incomes and lower levels of education. The reader should keep these differences in mind when reading the remainder of the book.

PROCEDURES

At the beginning of each discussion, participants were asked to tell the group how they and their families came to be Americans. Then the moderator read the text of HJ Res 37, aka "the English language amendment" (ELA)—a proposed amendment to the United States Constitution that would declare

---

[3] I did not distinguish among "white ethnics" (e.g., people of Irish, German, or Italian descent). A Hispanic colleague moderated the Hispanic groups, and I moderated the others.

[4] Sixteen of the 87 groups that I contacted—or 18 percent—were only for women, as opposed to eleven—or 13 percent—that were only for men. Three of the fourteen focus groups included in the study were only for women, whereas none of the groups were only for men. Two focus groups consisted only of women from mixed-sex organizations.

English the official language—and asked participants how they would want their representatives to vote if and when the resolution came to the floor of the House. HJ Res 37 was introduced in 1997 (105th Congress); the proposed amendment was first introduced in 1981 (97th Congress) and has been reintroduced in every Congress since. It states:

> The English language shall be the official language of the United States. As the official language, the English language shall be used for all public acts including every order, resolution, vote or election, and for all records and judicial proceedings of the Government of the United States and the governments of the several States.

The rest of the discussion was only loosely guided by the moderator, who tried to ensure that participants discussed other language issues, such as bilingual ballots and bilingual education, and their more general ideas about what it means to be an American (see appendix D for moderator question guide).

METHOD OF ANALYSIS

Each two-hour discussion was tape-recorded and transcribed. The unit of analysis is the "completed thought," which I define as (1) the dialogue of one speaker at one time or (2) the minimum amount of comments necessary to communicate the speaker's main point. Definition 1 was used when a speaker said little, and definition 2 was used when a speaker said a lot at once (see appendix C for examples).

In analyzing the transcripts, one of the first things I was looking for was whether the four conceptions provide an appropriate framework to use if the goal is to study both how Americans define American identity and how their definitions shape policy preferences. To do this, I first divided the dialogue from the transcripts into two parts. The first part contains general discussions about the nature of American identity (participants were asked, "What is it that makes us American?"); the second consists of opinions toward language policies and how people justify those opinions. The analysis in this chapter focuses on the first part, and the policy-related portions of the discussions are analyzed in the next two chapters.

The first step in the content analysis was to decide which of the broad conceptions of American identity were being discussed in any given thought. The categories included in the coding scheme are liberalism, civic republicanism, ethnoculturalism, incorporationism, and hybrids (a combination of any of those four). There were also four other coding options at this stage: concrete concerns about taxes or government spending,[5] conceptions of national identity that do not fit into any of the other categories (e.g., "When I think of America, I think of crime"), too vague to be classified (e.g., "Being American

---

[5] Public opinion research often pits symbolic concerns against more tangible or economic ones as predictors of policy preferences. The "taxes" category was included to account for this alternative hypothesis and is discussed in chapter 7.

means believing in certain ideals"), and statements that did not reference a conception of American identity (e.g., "I'm in favor of the ELA because the best way to learn the language is to do everything in English"). This last category was used only when participants discussed particular language policies. Next, the liberal, civic republican, ethnocultural, and incorporationist thoughts were subject to a second, more specific round of coding designed to capture the particular elements of the broader conception being discussed. These items were arrived at through a combination of a priori expectations and a cursory reading of three randomly selected transcripts.[6] Four transcripts were double-coded, with 82 percent overall agreement between coders.[7] Table 5.1 lists the specific items in this second, more detailed round of coding.[8]

American Identity, in Their Own Words

The focus group discussions provide a total of 3,748 completed substantive thoughts.[9] Fifty-six percent of these thoughts do not refer to any of the language policies under investigation but consist instead of general statements about American identity. These thoughts are the subject of analysis in the remainder of this chapter. Table 5.2 displays the number of thoughts that were coded as belonging to each broad category of American identity in the coding scheme. It shows that, including hybrids, roughly 78 percent of the nonpolicy discourse is accounted for by the model, with liberalism being the most common means for discussing American identity, followed closely by civic republicanism. Smith's framework does not tell the whole story, but it does provide a rather comprehensive guide for describing how people think about and discuss what being American means to them. I now turn to the patterns within each of the main categories to get a better understanding of how people interpret these complex conceptions of American identity and to see if the expectations described earlier are borne out.

---

[6] Three randomly selected transcripts were read to develop the coding scheme. Both the discourse of participants and hypotheses derived from theoretical expectations were used in its creation. Then, one transcript was coded to test its appropriateness. Revisions were made and another transcript was coded. Final revisions were made and then all transcripts were coded.

[7] The coders then discussed points of disagreement and made relevant changes. The revised codings are used in the final analysis. Coding materials are available upon request.

[8] Note that some of the categories listed in table 5.1 only make sense for those thoughts that directly refer to a particular language policy (e.g., opposition to the law because it is divisive or ethnocultural).

[9] Thoughts that were completely irrelevant to the topic at hand were removed from the analysis (e.g., "Are you taping yet?" "Is your hair naturally curly?"). All figures for the remainder of the book refer to substantive thoughts only. The mean number of substantive completed thoughts per group was 268, with a minimum of 167 and a maximum of 531 (531 is an outlier; the second highest number of substantive completed thoughts is 340). The number of completed thoughts does not vary systematically according to the ethnic or gender makeup of the group.

TABLE 5.1
Components of American Identity Included in the Content Analysis

Liberal Categories	Ethnocultural Categories
Civil/political rights	*(Acceptance of ethnoculturalism)*
Private/public distinction	Nostalgia/"good" vs. "bad" immigrants
English necessary for economic success	English as American
	Blames immigrants for their "station"
Obey laws	Ascriptiveness of American identity
Freedom	Anti-immigrant sentiments
Economic opportunity	Other ethnoculturalism or ethnocultural
Work ethic	hybrid
Majority rule	*(Rejection of ethnoculturalism)*
Individualism	Critical of ethnocultural tendencies in
Tolerance	America
U.S. as land of plenty	Need to fight ethnoculturalism
Rule of law	Not American because not white and blonde
Other liberalism or liberal hybrid	Language law is ethnocultural

Civic Republican Categories	Incorporationist Categories
Language law would be exclusionary	*(Multiculturalism)*
Isolation from the rest of the community	U.S. characterized by distinct cultures
	Important to maintain differences
Balkanization/too much diversity	Laments loss of culture
Local control over decision making	Critical of melting pot myth
Being able to communicate	Government to help maintain differences
Responsibilities/duties of citizens	*(Melting pot assimilationism)*
Ceremony/ritual/myth	U.S. characterized by cultural assimilation
Important to feel American	Melting as blending/"American" as dynamic
Voting	Vague references to the melting pot
Participation/volunteerism	Government to help with assimilation
Language law is divisive	Other incorp/incorp hybrid
Self-governance	
Other republicanism or republican hybrid	

Liberalism

Nineteen percent of the substantive thoughts were coded as being liberal in nature, making it the most popular conception of American identity in the study. This pattern accords with what many observers have written about the dominance that liberal principles have had over American political consciousness. Table 5.3 lists the different aspects of liberalism in the coding

TABLE 5.2
Completed Thoughts by Conception of American Identity

Conception of American Identity	N	%
Liberalism	401	19.19
Civic republicanism	390	18.66
Ethnoculturalism	324	15.5
Incorporationism	308	14.74
Hybrid	200	9.57
Tax/spend	11	0.53
Other	170	8.13
Unclassified	286	13.68
Total	2090	100

scheme and shows the number of thoughts that invoke each one when the nature of American identity was being discussed. The liberal principles of freedom, tolerance, and the rule of law were common means of expressing liberal sentiments, as was economic opportunity. Civil rights and individualism were not as common as conventional wisdom would lead one to expect, but they still appeared fairly frequently.

FREEDOM, RIGHTS, AND TOLERANCE

The most common liberal sentiments associated the United States with freedom. Tolerance and the provision of civil and political rights follow from

TABLE 5.3
Liberal Definitions of American Identity

Liberal Categories	N	%
Freedom	56	13.97
Civil/political rights	14	3.49
Tolerance	36	8.98
Economic opportunity	45	11.22
Work ethic	39	9.73
English necessary for economic success	20	4.99
Rule of law	26	6.48
Obey laws	16	3.99
Individualism	14	3.49
U.S. as land of plenty	12	2.99
Private/public distinction	11	2.74
Majority rule	9	2.24
Other liberalism or liberal hybrid	103	25.69
Total	401	100

this principle; although sentiments invoking rights and tolerance were coded separately, these categories will be discussed together. When combined, they account for over 26 percent of all liberal thoughts. One textbook example comes from June, a member of the public-speaking group.[10] When asked what makes us American, she said, "I'd have to say for me personally, it's freedom. It's our ability to do what we want, when we want, and how we want."

June was by no means the only participant to border on the cliché when discussing liberalism's privileged position in American identity. Another example of America being the land of rights and freedom comes from Patricia and Naomi, two members of a local historical association. In answering the same question posed to June, they responded with:

> PATRICIA: I think the old . . . the saying "I totally disagree with what you're saying but I will defend your right to say it," you know, "to the end," or something. . . . It epitomizes an American attitude if it's working because I think that's probably more bred in us than we realize. That you may hate what the person is saying, you hate what they're standing for, but you have enough respect, it's not like you're going to go out and shoot him because you disagree. You just say, "Well, he's a dope." And that he has a right to be. . . .
>
> NAOMI: And in some countries they would. I mean, I think that's what distinguishes us, in some countries they would.
>
> PATRICIA: . . . or be put in jail or exiled or . . .
>
> NAOMI: Right. Or ostracized.

A similar idea comes from Cindy, in one of the career-related groups, who discussed her involvement in a pro-choice march during the administration of a pro-life president. She said:

> When you march past the Bush White House and you're able to exercise your opinion that's contrary to that of the president, in front of the White House and not get arrested, it's just an absolutely profound moment. Some things I did down there [in Washington, D.C.] I take with me as just being uniquely American.

This widely endorsed cluster of ideals involving the freedom of the individual to do what she wants and her tolerance of other people's rights to do what they want, particularly with regard to speech, is not just considered "good," it is also seen as "American."

ECONOMIC OPPORTUNITY AND THE WORK ETHIC

Liberal statements associating the United States with economic opportunity or describing Americans as people who work hard to take advantage of those opportunities account for another 26 percent of the liberal thoughts that describe American identity. As with the statements about freedom and rights,

[10] Names of all participants have been changed.

economic imagery seemed to come naturally to the participants whose thoughts were often laden with phrases one might expect to see in a description of Horatio Alger's writings. One example comes from Roberta, a member of a hobby club. When asked what makes us American, she said, "If you work hard enough and you use your head, you can usually do pretty well. That's not like many other countries." A similar sentiment comes from Bob, in another hobby group:

> I don't think there's any reason for anybody to come to this country from another country except to make themselves or for them to have a better life. I don't think there's anyplace else in the rest of the world that anybody can think like that. Other countries I think they can think about it, here they can do it.

The unique economic opportunities that America has to offer, the fact that the streets are "paved with gold" or can become so if one tries hard enough, is seen as the primary reason why immigrants would choose to come here, a quality that makes America unlike anywhere else.

RULE OF LAW

Another common liberal sentiment people used to define the United States was the rule of law. Statements referring to our nonarbitrary observance of laws and our respect for the processes by which they are made account for 6.5 percent of the liberal discourse. One extended, but poignant, example comes from Tim, in one of the career-related groups:

> It was so profound when Richard Nixon resigned under the pressure he was under, and Ford took over. A television reporter commented that that evening after leaving the briefings at the White House and so forth, he walked out in front of the White House and there was a traffic policeman there who was directing traffic. And he realized that this was . . . probably 90 percent of the other countries in the world, when there was a change of government so dramatic as this, there would be tanks and armed troops in front of the main house. But it was just this cop. And he said this is the great thing about America. We have this rule of law and this structure.

Tim reminds his fellow discussants that respect for the rule of law in the United States provides a level of stability that should not be taken for granted. And as with the other examples quoted in this section, the subtext of Tim's speech is "only in America."

"OTHER LIBERALISM"

According to table 5.3, many thoughts were coded as "other liberalism." These thoughts typically combined more than one aspect of liberalism. People often talked about the "right" to "freedom" or the "freedom" to "prosper." Other thoughts included in this category involve vague references to the principles in the Constitution or other important documents. Still other thoughts were coded as "other liberal" if they referred to principles of liberalism that perhaps should have been included in the coding scheme but were not. These principles include the importance of being self-sufficient and a preference for minimal interactions between citizens and the state.

I thought certain aspects of the liberal tradition would be discussed more than they were. These include individualism and the principle of majority rule. When asked about the nature of American identity, for example, only a few people occasionally offered a vague observation about "valuing the individual." At no point did people explicitly pit individual rights against group rights or argue that the former should trump the latter. Equality is another important aspect of the liberal tradition that participants rarely discussed explicitly. As is well-known, tensions exist between liberty and equality. Yet that all people should be treated equally or that freedoms and rights should be enjoyed equally by all is a central component of the liberal philosophy. Americans have often expressed a preference for equality of opportunity over equality of results (Kingdon 1999), a tendency that minimizes the tensions between liberty and equality and that seems to be at work here. In many of the statements quoted earlier, and others like them, a reverence for equality of opportunity is implied, but conversations rarely focused on equality openly. Instead, the emphasis was consistently placed on freedom and on the market economy without explicitly using the language of equality.

In the end, however, the Hartzian thesis is validated and the American Dream comes out strong. It is clear that liberal principles influence the language participants use when called upon to describe what it means to be an American. Sometimes their reverence for the work ethic, for freedom of expression, or for the myth that anyone can "make it in America" comes across as textbook and suggestive of an almost brainwashed mentality. Although they may have been successfully indoctrinated, however, the participants in this study are by no means guided by a single philosophy when they define American identity. As the rest of this chapter will demonstrate, an understanding of the main tenets of liberalism is not, on its own, enough to provide an understanding of how they think about the American character.

Civic Republicanism

Participants rely on tenets of civic republicanism to define American identity in 18.6 percent of the substantive completed thoughts under investigation in this chapter, which suggests that the civic republican tradition is a worthy competitor to liberalism in the battle for the American psyche. Although aspects of these two traditions make them often compatible with one another, liberalism emphasizes the *rights* of *individuals* whereas civic republicanism em-

TABLE 5.4
Civic Republican Definitions of American Identity

Civic Republican Categories	N	%
Ceremony/ritual/myth	65	16.67
Participation/volunteerism	47	12.05
Voting	33	8.46
Responsibilities/duties of citizens	45	11.54
Important to feel American	27	6.92
Balkanization/too much diversity	26	6.67
Self-governance	17	4.36
Being able to communicate	16	4.1
Local control over decision making	11	2.82
Language law would be exclusionary	11	2.82
Isolation from the rest of the community	10	2.56
Other republicanism or republican hybrid	82	21.03
Total	390	100

phasizes *responsibilities* of *citizens* and the promotion of the common good. Table 5.4 displays the different aspects of civic republicanism in the coding scheme and shows the number of thoughts that invoke each one when the nature of American identity was being discussed. It shows that the most common aspects of civic republicanism that participants invoked deal with the ceremonies and rituals that promote emotional attachments to the national community (e.g., reciting the Pledge of Allegiance), the responsibilities of citizens (e.g., participating in community life and voting), and fears about the "balkanization of America."

CEREMONY/RITUAL/MYTH

The most common civic republican concern to emerge in response to questions about American identity involves the importance of rituals and ceremonies in bringing people together to forge a sense of common purpose. Rituals and ceremonies both foster and reflect patriotism. As Merriam writes (1966 [1931]), they serve to create and maintain loyalty to the society and promote positive attachments across both space and time. This aspect of civic republicanism accounts for just under 17 percent of the civic republican discourse and usually appeared in references to parades, the Pledge of Allegiance, or national holidays.

At the end of each group, participants were asked to say what they thought the most important topic their group discussed was. In a charity group, some women mentioned that the discussion awakened a sense of urgency about their pride in being American. They added that it is important to think about where that pride comes from and how it can be maintained. Then two of the women, Eileen and Ellen, said:

> EILEEN: Well, just thinking about that, the groups that come in—just whenever you see a group of new citizens as they're taking the pledge, isn't that exciting?
> ELLEN: Oh, isn't that exciting? It's enough to make you cry.
> EILEEN: It is!

Several participants described being overcome by emotions at public events and argued that such events and emotions are important in reminding us of who we are. Another version comes from Mary Ann, a member of a hobby club. When asked what makes us American, she said:

> OK, I think what makes us Americans, too, is we've learned our history. We've learned to respect our country, the flag. I don't think there's any of us that can go to a parade and not have one little tear. It's a patriotic thing, I guess.

And then there is Lisa, a member of a career-related group, who said, "Sometimes I feel kind of silly about [being proud to be American], that it's sort of a childish and naïve notion of . . . I think about Bruce Springsteen and 'Born in the USA' and boy, I love that song."

Having an emotional attachment to a nation may not be uniquely American, but having an attachment to *this* nation is, participants argue. And the rituals, songs, and ceremonies that sustain such an attachment are crucial in setting America and Americans apart from other countries and peoples. That 87 percent of the 1996 GSS respondents said that "feeling American" is either very or somewhat important in making someone truly American bolsters the evidence presented here that suggests that the focus group participants see feeling American and the means of creating that feeling as key features of American identity. In fact, an additional 7 percent of the civic republican thoughts explicitly mention that it is important for Americans to think of themselves primarily as American and to not have their main loyalties lie with some other locus of social organization.

PARTICIPATION AND VOTING

Another frequently cited aspect of the civic republican conception of national identity is that the United States is a place where people are involved in public life. Participation in all its forms, from volunteering in charity groups and joining the PTA to voting and making sure that government is truly "by the people," is seen as a more central feature of life in the United States than in other countries. And when participants acknowledge that voter turnout rates are low or that people seem to have become complacent or apathetic, they argue that the American people are not being true to themselves—they are being "bad" Americans. Statements that speak to the importance of participation in public life, through either volunteering or voting, account for 20.6 percent of the civic republican discourse.

When women in a career-related group were asked what makes us American, they responded with several descriptions, one of which focused on the American tendency to help one another:

> JUNE: I'm not coming up with the right word. I'm coming up with the word charity. But we are a nation that pulls together in whatever problems there are. In the Oklahoma City bombing . . .
> MODERATOR: You mean like volunteering?
> JUNE: Yeah, volunteering. And money. I mean if there's a story in the paper about some sad case, people send in money like crazy. Everybody's willing to help and pull together.
> MODERATOR: And you think that's unique to here?
> JUNE: I don't have experience in other countries.
> ALICIA: But it certainly seems that you find that pulling together in an emergency.
> SOMEONE ELSE:[11] The Red Cross goes out and helps in other countries whenever there's disasters, but I think we as Americans also reach out.

Often, conversations like this one then turned to lamentations of how Americans can and should be more involved than they are.

The following is an extended exchange from another career organization that focuses on the importance of voting in American society. When asked what the government can expect from its citizens, the following conversation occurred:

> CAMILLA: The most important thing is to go out and vote. People dying around the world for the right to vote. And we have elections, and I have to tell you . . . I understand a lot of people don't like to vote in the primary, but when I went to vote in the June election at 8 o'clock at night, from my party, I was number ten.
> LISA: But Camilla, it was uncontested. What's the point?
> CAMILLA: So what? Go out and express yourself. But even in the general election, it's . . .
> LISA: You see a ballot with one name on it, it's like, "OK, I could go do this, but what's the point?"
> CAMILLA: It's the principle and the idea behind it. I would never think of not going to vote.
> PAULA: What if there's nobody you want to vote for?
> LESLIE: So you write in a name.
> CAMILLA: You write in a name.
> PAULA: Who do you write in?
> LESLIE: Your name. Anyone's name.

[11] The speaker could not be identified on the recording.

CAMILLA: That is such a precious right, that ability to vote. It is taken so lightly now and people just don't go out and take the time to vote.

DENISE: My favorite line is that if you don't vote, then you can't bitch.

LESLIE: You've got to be in it to win it.

CAMILLA: Voting is so important for the kind of government that we have.

Much of the emphasis here is on the act itself and the rewards it brings, both in terms of individual satisfaction and for the larger good of the society. Even if your write-in candidate has no chance of winning, it is important to be out there and involved, they maintain. The ability to do that is seen as a privilege that sets the United States apart from many places in the world, and when we fail to take advantage of that privilege, it is seen as both a symbolic failing and a real threat to "the kind of government we have."

DUTIES OF CITIZENS

Civic republicanism is characterized by an emphasis on the responsibilities of citizenship. Beyond being informed and involved in public affairs, citizens also need to work together to overcome collective action problems of various kinds, and they need to be "other regarding" in a more general sense if the project of self-governance is to succeed. Participants in the study occasionally spoke of such duties. As with voting, they lamented that Americans often fail to live up to what is expected of them. Such thoughts were typically expressed by making general statements about citizens owing something to one another. One example comes from Amy, a woman in a hobby club. When asked about the most important topic her group discussed, she said, "I think what we've been talking about is more taking responsibility and being what my grandmother would have called a decent human being, which isn't always language connected, but it's the society that we all find ourselves in." She argues that we owe it to one another in our society to be virtuous, or "decent." What that entails, exactly, is left unclear, but Amy knows that it is an important part of what life in America is, or should be, about.

Another common way people expressed the idea that citizens have obligations was to discuss the importance of paying taxes. In some cases, people said that the *only* obligation citizens have is to pay taxes, and those thoughts were coded as liberal and as describing a limited government philosophy. In other cases, people talked about the responsibility of citizens to pay taxes in order to provide common goods and promote the well-being of the community. Such thoughts are more civic republican than liberal because they emphasize the collective over the individual.

"OTHER CIVIC REPUBLICANISM"

Finally, as with liberalism, there is a catch-all "other civic republicanism" category. These statements include multiple civic republican sentiments and concerns that should have been included in the coding but were not. One particular concern stands out as one that should have been a part of the coding procedure. Many participants voiced support for the idea that vibrant communities are a unique and essential component of American identity and expressed general thoughts about the importance of community life. I had initially expected community-related concerns to mainly involve fears about the "balkanization of America" or the disintegration of communities over time. I did not plan for the affirmation of community strength, but it turns out that people are more positive about the vitality of community life than I anticipated they would be or that scholars like Putnam might expect. An example comes from Betty, a woman in a career-related business organization. When asked what makes us American, she responded:

> I think a word that comes to my mind is community. I think if you go across the United States, and you stop maybe 1,500 miles from here, or 1,000 miles south or whatever, and there's a Little League game, those kids get ice cream if they win, or pizza or something like that. I've been in restaurants where these kids come in with these uniforms on and they do the same thing 1,500 miles west of us or 1,000 miles south that we do here in New Jersey. We're all alike. We're kind of like molded into a community of people. And we all have little governments and police departments and schools and churches and stores. And it's the same thing, no matter where you go, they all have churches and stores and it's community. And you become the United States by putting all these little communities together. So that's what it means to me.

No one listening to Betty at the time or reading her statement now has trouble creating a mental image of the scene she describes. The image of vibrant communities speckling the landscape of America, each with a white church in the town square, children playing happily in the streets, and neighbors waving to each other as they walk down Main Street may be overly romantic, but it is powerfully ingrained within each of us, and it comes to mind easily when people are asked to describe what being American means. This is not to say that people do not fear the breakup of close-knit communities; concerns about the "balkanization of America" account for almost 7 percent of the civic republican discourse. These worries are discussed in more detail in the next chapter where they play a prominent role in people's justifications for why English should be the official language.

SUMMARY

The civic republican tradition appears to form a central component of how people think about what it means to be American. Without emotional attachments to the community, without concerned and involved citizens who work together to solve common problems and achieve common goals, much of what makes America unique would be threatened. The *ability* to do all of those things is seen as something that sets the United States apart, and the *responsibility* to do them is an obligation that people think their fellow Americans should meet.

CIVIC REPUBLICAN BIAS?

In light of these findings, it is reasonable to consider whether sampling the focus groups from among existing community organizations gives an inflated picture of the level of civic republican sentiment in the American public. There is logic to this concern, but data for testing its validity are limited. Measures of attachments to the tenets of civic republicanism are absent from surveys, and studies of political participation do not examine whether a link exists between membership in *apolitical* associations and civic republican beliefs. The recent interest in social capital has generated a wealth of studies that show that people who belong to voluntary associations are, in some respects, likely to be better *civic republicans* (i.e., they are more likely to vote; e.g., Putnam 2000, 1995; Erickson and Nosanchuck 1990), but I have been unable to find a single study that can comment on whether people who belong to voluntary associations are more likely than others to endorse civic republican conceptions of American national identity. Putnam (2000) contends that membership in local organizations declined dramatically during the latter half of the twentieth century. If it did (not everyone is convinced by his evidence), and if, *and only if,* members of local organizations are more supportive of the tenets of civic republicanism, then my findings might indeed exaggerate the prevalence of civic republican beliefs. The link between the two—membership in associations and national identity—is key and is precisely where data are lacking.

According to GSS surveys from 1990 to 1994, 69 percent of Americans belong to at least one community club or organization.[12] Surely, what that membership entails varies greatly from person to person and organization to organization. Some people attend meetings regularly and devote significant amounts of time to their groups while others write checks and read newsletters. Some groups exist only locally while others are part of national organizations. But again, studies connecting these differences to conceptions of national identity, to my knowledge, do not exist. Finally, it would be absurd to suggest that members of a gardening club would argue that a preference for gardening is an important characteristic for Americans to have, or for people

---

[12] Participants were asked: "Now we would like to know something about the groups or organizations to which individuals belong. Here is a list of various organizations. Could you tell me whether or not you are a member of each type?" The list of groups in their battery is fraternal, service, veterans, political, labor union, sport, youth, school service, hobby, fraternity/sorority, nationality/ethnic, literary or art, professional society, church-affiliated, or some other type of group. When nationality groups, ethnic groups, political organizations, and unions are omitted from the list, 66 percent belong to at least one of the remaining groups (Davis, Smith, and Marsden 1998).

in a doll collecting club to insist that maintaining doll collections helps shape who we are as a political community. Presumably, one's membership in these organizations is driven by a commitment to the hobby itself more than by a desire to embody the civic republican ideal.

I did examine the prevalence of civic republican discourse among the different *types* of groups in my study and find no systematic differences. For example, the mean percentage of civic republican descriptions of national identity in the three community service focus groups was 18.2, whereas the mean percentage for the remaining groups (which are largely hobby-based) was 19.3. One community service group even told me that they were violating one of their main rules by participating in the study: "Never talk about weight or politics."[13] Additionally, the prevalence of civic republican statements is only slightly higher in the female-only groups, contrary to what some research might lead us to expect (e.g., Conover 1988); the mean percentage of civic republican descriptions of American identity in the female-only groups was 19.7, whereas the mean percentage in the mixed-sex groups was 18.7.

Hibbing and Theiss-Morse (2002), using focus groups drawn from a more random population, confirm that people are well aware of civic republican norms despite their failure to live up to them. They find that many people are quite conflicted about the role of the ordinary citizen in public life. They find that on the one hand, people do not necessarily trust their fellow Americans to make wise decisions should they become more involved, nor do they necessarily trust that citizens who are politically active are promoting the public interest rather than their own self-interest. On the other hand, they also find that people readily blame themselves for their unhappiness with the political system. They observe, "[People] know they should be involved in politics and they know they are doing damage by not being involved. They understand their lack of involvement has made possible the very dominance of special interests that they despise" (127). Among this more randomly selected sample then, the image of an informed, involved, and other-regarding citizenry was still seen to be part of the American ideal, an ideal that is only sometimes realized. So although it is possible that people in hobby clubs are more likely to endorse civic republicanism than people who belong to no clubs, it is also possible that most people value the ideal and that some simply do a better job of living up to it than others. Among those who do not live up to the ideal, lamentations abound, as do litanies of reasons for why they are not as civic-minded as they should be.

In short, although it is reasonable to consider whether members of local organizations will invoke more civic republican concerns than other citizens, no solid data currently exist to test it, most citizens belong to at least one organization in some form, and logical arguments can be made against this concern

---

[13] See Hibbing and Theiss-Morse (2002, 189) for more on members of voluntary associations and their aversion to divisive political issues.

as well. This issue is one where the union of focus groups and surveys could be especially useful. Focus groups highlight the vitality of the civic republican ideal, and appropriately designed survey questions would allow us to examine more specifically the impact that different kinds of group memberships have on attachments to that ideal.

Ethnoculturalism

Almost 16 percent of the focus group discourse was coded as being ethnocultural in nature; it was not as common as liberalism or civic republicanism. More important, unlike these other two, it turns out that ethnoculturalism is a highly *contested* notion of what it means to be American. In fact, over half of the statements coded as ethnocultural were openly critical of America's history of racist practices. In other words, no one claimed that the United States should not be the land of opportunity or that Americans should not be patriotic, but many argued that the United States should not continue to define its members based on ethnic or other ascriptive characteristics. The extent of this vocal criticism of the ethnocultural tradition in America was not something I anticipated. I expected most descriptions of the United States to be positive or neutral, not critical. While some criticism is to be expected, its extent was remarkable. For example, if one person in a group said that being American means being free, another person would often point out the hypocrisy that has usually accompanied the doctrine of all men being created equally. A common theme among Hispanic participants in particular was that even though they are American citizens, they do not consider themselves Americans because they do not fit into the ethnocultural ideal. A majority—62 percent—of the anti-ethnocultural discourse came from the three Hispanic groups, 26 percent came from five of the all-white groups, and 12 percent came from two of the three heterogeneous groups.[14] Ethnicity obviously affects whether ethnoculturalism stands out in a person's mind as an unfortunate yet persistent aspect of American identity. People excluded from the ethnocultural ideal are more likely to criticize it; they are routinely—and often overtly—at the receiving end of it. But it would be a mistake to assume that such criticism is confined to them.

That said, not all of the ethnocultural imagery in the discussions was critical. A fair amount of support was still shown for this limited vision of who is and is not American, as can be seen in table 5.5, which shows the number of thoughts that refer to each ethnocultural category in the content analysis. Sixty percent of the thoughts that openly or implicitly endorse ethnoculturalism came from the all-white groups, 31 percent came from the heterogeneous groups, and 9 percent came from the Hispanic groups.

[14] Three all-white groups and one heterogeneous group had no anti-ethnocultural statements.

TABLE 5.5
Ethnocultural Definitions of American Identity

Ethnocultural Categories	N	%
Acceptance of Ethnoculturalism		
Anti-immigrant sentiments	41	12.65
Minorities as not American	18	5.56
Nostalgia/"good" vs. "bad" immigrants	14	4.32
Ascriptiveness of American identity	14	4.32
English as American	7	2.16
Blames immigrants for their "station"	4	1.23
Other ethnoculturalism or ethnocultural hybrid	19	5.86
(Subtotal)	*(117)*	*(36)*
Rejection of Ethnoculturalism		
Critical of ethnocultural tendencies in America	173	53.4
Not American because not white and blonde	22	6.79
Need to fight ethnoculturalism	8	2.47
Language law is ethnocultural	4	1.23
(Subtotal)	*(207)*	*(64)*
Total	324	100

ANTI-IMMIGRANT SENTIMENTS

Some participants were quite hostile toward today's immigrants and were not shy about letting me know. Statements suggesting that immigrants are harmful to the country or that they are just bad people comprise almost 13 percent of the ethnocultural discourse. But is it appropriate to say that general anti-immigrant statements reveal an ethnocultural conception of American identity? After all, such thoughts do not actually involve a speaker saying that immigrants can never become American. I maintain that criticizing immigrants for not living up to some romanticized ideal or supporting a general policy of "keeping America for Americans" is indeed based on a narrow and exclusive vision of who can and cannot be a member of the club. To fault immigrants, as a group, for bringing America down is to engage in scapegoating, an activity that makes one more willing to deny rights and opportunities to those who do not fit the dominant cultural image, especially in an age when most immigrants are nonwhite. The result is a belief that certain ascriptive characteristics are important in distinguishing Americans from others. In some cases such beliefs were expressed openly, while other cases were more subtle.

An example of the former comes from Ed, a member of a hobby club, who expressed outrage at how immigrants have ruined his hometown of Trenton:

ED: Yeah, they live ten in a room, live like animals. Where have you been? Don't you know where you're at? You don't know where you're at. Go up to the Trenton Motel. They got ten in a room up there. They come over here from over there, they're here six months, don't pay a bit of taxes, run on home with the money. Next six months they're back again.

JOHN: Should we try to teach them English, Ed?

ED: Teach them English? Shoot them!

JOHN: I don't know, just a thought, right?

ED: You got them taking our tax money . . . they don't pay taxes when they're here.

RACHEL: You mean they get relief?

ED: Sure they do. I don't know where you guys are living at, but boy . . . you're not living in the same town I am. These are disgusting people.

Ed's degree of hostility was rare, but the points he was making were not. Several people echoed his complaints about immigrants coming to the United States only to make money and send it home. One of the career-related groups had the following exchange when discussing why they think minorities often seem reluctant to adapt to American society more fully:

PAULA: My point here is that if they're that stuck in their own ethnic background, if their own culture and origin of where they came from is so important, what the hell are they doing here?

LESLIE: Money!

PAULA: So it's money. But you can't pick and choose. This is the game, play by the rules. You don't want to play? Go home.

LESLIE: And most of them do go home after they get the money. They don't stay here.

SOMEONE ELSE: They take the money and go.

The game to which Paula refers is that of shedding one's ties to an ethnic identity. If one chooses not do to that, or if one cannot do that, then one does not belong here.

MINORITIES AS NOT AMERICAN

A more subtle yet related expression of the ethnocultural tradition in America involves participants revealing that they simply do not see ethnic minorities as Americans regardless of citizenship status. Observing the traditions of one's ancestors and maintaining cultural distinctiveness often trump citizenship in the quest to define American identity. An example of this type of thinking comes from Jackie, a member of a charity group:

I think all people, when they come from a different country, they want to be American, and they get their citizenship and everything. But as soon as that happens, maybe one or two months down the line, they go back to their old ways, some of them. They really should learn what's going on in the United States if they're going to stay in the United States. But a lot of them go back to the old ways and they don't want to be bothered.

Jackie does not go on to say what those "old ways" are, but she clearly indicates that a person cannot be considered an American as long as "the old ways" are still present, even after acquiring U.S. citizenship. As with Paula and Leslie's earlier statements, this tendency to see minorities as not American is indicative of the "melting-as-cleansing" philosophy, or rather, a corruption of the melting pot mythology. Rather than acknowledging the dynamic nature of the nation as a whole, the "melting-as-cleansing" perspective dictates that ethnic minorities adapt to dominant cultural norms before they can be considered Americans.[15]

REJECTION OF ETHNOCULTURALISM

The language of ethnoculturalism was used not only to endorse this conception of American identity but also to condemn it. This condemnation accounts for 64 percent of the discourse that was coded as being ethnocultural in nature. Although these statements do not reflect open agreement with the idea that white male Protestants are the only ones who can be American, it is still appropriate to call them "ethnocultural" because the existence of this conception of American identity provides the framework people are using when they interpret questions about American identity.

As I showed earlier, anti-ethnocultural dialogue was especially common among the Hispanic participants. They routinely criticized the dominant society for its stereotypes, for defining American identity narrowly, and for having irrational fears about ethnic change. One example comes from women in a community service organization that serves a local Hispanic community. Luz is telling the others that she used to work at a department store and that white customers would get visibly annoyed whenever she spoke to Hispanic customers in Spanish but not when other languages were spoken in the store:

> Luz: Why are we forced—Spanish people—to speak the language, when they don't force other languages? Why do they get mad when they hear the Spanish language?
>
> Anna: The fear. "You're speaking something that I don't understand, so you change it, because I am afraid of you. I'm afraid of you being different."
>
> Luz: But why aren't they afraid of Jamaicans, why aren't they afraid of Chinese people?

[15] The prevalence of ethnocultural sentiments does not vary systematically with the mean income level of each group (i.e., it is not the case that ethnocultural sentiments were more prevalent in the lower income groups). The groups with the lowest income were the three Hispanic groups. The remaining groups had very little income variation across groups.

LINDA: Because there's more of us.

LUZ: Why are they not afraid of Italians?

ANNA: Because there's more of us. Because they're afraid that we're going to take over. We are going to be the biggest minority by the year 2000. And we're going to take power away from them, and that's scary.

Later, in the same group, Maribel and Anna discuss how Americans have very different stereotypes of people from different parts of the world:

MARIBEL: If somebody speaks French, it's, "Oh, it's so pretty. I love their accents."

ANNA: "Mmm. Talk to me, baby."

MARIBEL: And if somebody talks in Chinese, their Chinese language, it's not discriminatory. The stereotype, the Chinese people are so good with computers and intelligent, so Chinese is intelligence, French is romantic . . .

ANNA: We are welfare.

MARIBEL: We are welfare, [switches to Spanish] people eating plantains, five thousand kids in the household . . .

The speakers in these examples are objecting to the stereotyping of minorities, but they are also concerned with the extent to which negative stereotypes, anti-minority sentiments, and irrational fears of ethnic change are directed at Hispanics in particular.

Hispanics in the study were by no means the only ones to complain about how Americans treat white citizens better than nonwhite ones. The following exchange is from members in a hobby club responding to the question of what makes us American:

JACOB: I don't think we've changed much from the time we overran the country and forced anything and everything in the way out.

CHRISTINE: Right. Keep the Indians out, keep everybody out.

MILTON: I think that what those comments show is that there's a rift between our perception of what it means to be American and. . . . Or maybe it's this other thing of what it means. I think our perception is. . . . What does it mean to be American? Everyone's perception is well, we love freedom, we're fair and open to every idea. Oh, but you know, don't let that black guy move into my neighborhood.

JACOB: Well, yes. That's what was going through my head when I heard that comment, but what about skin color?

And Bob, in the same group, shared this story:

This is [in] New York City and I was working there, living there. I'm walking down to the train station after work. And anybody who goes into New York City knows that the bicycle riders there pretty much rule the pedestrian ways. If you step out into the street, you don't have to worry about the cabs; you have to worry about the bikers. So I'm walking across the street, or at least getting to that point. It says "walk," and one of the bikers comes up and it's a tall black guy that's obviously delivering packages or whatever. And he stops and he pulls out into the walkway for the pedestrians a little bit. And a person that looks Indian or Pakistani or whatever is walking there. He stops and he kind of moves over and he says something to the black guy. And the conversation went something like this, I guess it was, "Watch what you're doing" or whatever. And the black guy says, "I'll knock your ass back to your country. I'll knock your ass back to your country." Now, this is really hilarious in New York City, because what happened is this guy basically said, "You're the foreigner here." Anybody who wants to come into New York City, it's filled with people like that. To me, it struck me as very comical, this guy deciding right there on the spot by physical evidence, "You're not an American citizen, so therefore I can say this to you."

Americans tell themselves that they accept all kinds, but as many pointed out, the fact remains that they often rely on superficial characteristics to remind others that they are not welcome. The United States may be seen as the land of the free, but it is also seen as the land of the irrational, the judgmental, and the racist.

NOT SEEING ONESELF AS AMERICAN

Finally, a common ethnocultural theme among the Hispanic participants only was that they often fail to see themselves as American, despite having American citizenship, because they do not fit into ethnoculturalism's ideal type. This first example is from Emily, a member of a Chicano culture organization. When asked what makes us American, she said:

If you ask me, "What do you consider yourself, American or Mexican?" I'd pretty much say that I really don't know, because the definition of an American is really so sketchy because it's so undefined. I say that I'm an American citizen, but in my head "American citizen" is very different from the definition of "American," because you think American and your stereotypical American. If you ask any person from any other country what do you think of as an American, it's just like this stereotype— blonde hair, blue eyes, the hamburgers, that kind of thing.

Not only are minorities not seen as American by whites like Jackie, quoted earlier, but they are also not seen as American by themselves. Hispanic members of a hobby group expressed similar feelings. When asked what characteristics make people American, this exchange followed:

PALOMA: Stereotypically, when you just said American, I automatically thought a white family living in a nice house, white picket fence, two kids, they've got the dog and the cat, a nice car and they both work for some really big company and they're both doing good.

JANET: The bad thing about that is we naturally exclude ourselves from that ideal.

PALOMA: Yeah, I don't think of myself as an American.

VELMA: And we were raised here, you know?

PALOMA: I don't find that I fit in this country really like an American. When they ask me, "What are you?" I don't say American. I say Dominican. I feel like . . . I was born here, but I don't feel that America includes me at all. I live here, but that's it.

These quotes show that people from a variety of backgrounds have internalized the ethnocultural conception of American identity. Those who accept it and those who reject it both respond to questions about what being American means with racial and ethnic concerns. And statements from people with either viewpoint are disturbingly similar. What is said by those who accept ethnoculturalism is parroted back by those who reject it: if your ethnicity shows, you are not American. This withdrawal from national identity among ethnic minorities has been called "reactive ethnicity," and it occurs when real and perceived discriminatory treatment prevents people from thinking of themselves as Americans and strengthens their ethnic identifications (e.g., Portes and Rumbaut 2001).

SUMMARY

All of these examples validate Smith's claim that ethnoculturalism is a full-blown conception of American identity in its own right. Whether people agree or disagree with it, they acknowledge that it has dictated and continues to dictate how "American-ness" is defined.

Incorporationism

Smith's trilogy of ideals may be a compelling way to think about and discuss American identity, but it is not complete. It cannot incorporate the image of America as "a land of immigrants," where the defining characteristic is not liberty or participation or ethnic purity but rather the presence of countless ethnicities and cultural traditions. This emphasis on the immigrant legacy in the United States is not just a subset of ethnoculturalism (i.e., using the language of ethnoculturalism to interpret American identity). It goes beyond simply rejecting an exclusive conception of who Americans are; it offers an alternative. This incorporationist perspective looms large in how the participants describe American identity, accounting for 15 percent of the thoughts analyzed in this chapter.[16]

Based on my summary reading of the transcripts when creating the coding procedures, I came to expect that participants would discuss this conception of American identity in two main forms. The first would celebrate the extent of cultural diversity in the United States (multiculturalism), and the second would describe American identity as an evolving concept that constantly

---

[16] If I were to code the anti-ethnocultural statements described in the previous section as incorporationist, then incorporationism's share of the discourse would jump to 24.6 percent (surpassing even liberalism) and ethnoculturalism's share would drop to only 5.5 percent.

TABLE 5.6
Incorporationist Definitions of American Identity

Incorporationist Categories	N	%
Multiculturalism		
U.S. characterized by distinct cultures	97	31.49
Important to maintain differences	59	19.16
Laments loss of culture	17	5.52
Critical of melting pot myth	13	4.22
Government to help maintain differences	1	0.32
(Subtotal)	*(187)*	*(60.71)*
Melting Pot Assimilationism		
U.S. characterized by cultural assimilation	58	18.83
Melting as blending/"American" as dynamic	29	9.42
Vague references to the melting pot	19	6.17
Government to help with assimilation	2	0.65
(Subtotal)	*(108)*	*(35.07)*
Other incorp/incorp hybrid	13	4.22
Total	308	100

changes as more and more ingredients are added to the mix (melting pot assimilationism). Table 5.6 lists the frequency of these two perspectives along with their more concrete manifestations. Both multiculturalism and melting pot assimilationism were present, with the former being more common than the latter. As table 5.6 shows, thoughts that invoke a multicultural conception of American identity account for 61 percent of the incorporationist thoughts, whereas those that describe an evolving sense of national identity account for 35 percent.

UNITED STATES CHARACTERIZED BY DISTINCT CULTURES

Participants in every group talked about the United States as a place of unparalleled cultural diversity and described how encountering this diversity on a day-to-day basis is a unique American experience. Such observations were either neutral or, more often, positive in tone, with participants describing how wonderful it is to be exposed to so much difference. These thoughts account for 31 percent of the incorporationist discourse. One example comes from Luanne, a member of a career-related organization, as she describes the ethnic composition of her community:

> We have two Spanish masses at my church every week. At Christmas and Easter they have Spanish/English bilingual masses. We love it. We think it's great. I sing the Spanish songs, you know? And I try to understand what the priest is saying when

he does the homily in Spanish. . . . I'm used to working with people from all kinds of backgrounds, with all kinds of accents, on the phone, face to face. So it's just something that you pretty much weave into your daily living.

And participants in several groups commented on how fortunate children in America are today because of the endless opportunities they have to learn about other cultures. Shelly, in a hobby club, exemplifies this pattern in saying, "[One] thing that I think is interesting, which is something that I never had the advantage of doing when I was growing up, is this diversity of cultures and things which children are exposed to today, which I think is wonderful." It is understood as given that one will be surrounded by different cultures in America, a simple fact of everyday life that is described as both praiseworthy and unique to this country.

IMPORTANT TO MAINTAIN DIFFERENCES

Although the presence of multiple cultures is taken for granted by some, others warn that the preservation of diversity requires active maintenance. Pressures to fit into the dominant culture are strong and can lead to subsequent generations being cut off from ethnic traditions. Not only should we celebrate diversity, they argue, but we also need to work against homogenization. Only rarely did such calls mention specific government action. More often, people referred to the role of the family in ensuring that traditions are maintained across generations. Nineteen percent of incorporationist discourse was of this nature. Several Hispanic participants demonstrated this concern by discussing how difficult it will be to make sure their children grow up knowing Spanish. In one group, members bonded over shared memories of being embarrassed as children when their parents spoke Spanish or listened to Mexican music, seeing such cultural displays as old-fashioned, out of touch, and "dorky," only to now feel immense gratitude because these displays facilitated enduring ethnic ties. They said that they too will make sure their cultural traditions survive, no matter how much embarrassment it causes for their own kids. Encouraging people to celebrate cultural differences, they argued, can work against the desire to shed the trappings of a non-European background, and it is seen as an endeavor requiring conscious and continuous effort.

LAMENTING THE LOSS OF CULTURE

In addition to those who fear that diversity is going to fade if they do not work at preservation, several participants acknowledged that a lot of diversity has already faded. Regretting lost traditions was routine, making up almost 6 percent of the incorporationist discourse. People often expressed this regret by describing a sense of loss that comes from being unable to use the language of one's ancestors. An example comes from Maribel, describing the challenge of remaining fluent in Spanish:

[*in Spanish*] The problem is also that we forget our Spanish, in such a way that then we can't communicate with our own people in our own countries, [*switches to English*] because my Spanish has [*switches to Spanish*] there has been such a big transformation since I left Puerto Rico. It is incredible. [*switches to English*] Because now I can't even communicate with people from Puerto Rico. I can't communicate with people who were born in the Bronx or around here because their Spanish is so different and their English is so different too. So we have this mixture of stuff because we're trying to preserve something that we don't even know what it is sometimes.

Her difficulty completing the thought in either Spanish or English demonstrates her point as much as its actual substance. Similarly, another woman said she feels "cheated" in knowing only English.

As with anti-ethnoculturalism, regrets like these were not confined to the Hispanic focus groups. People of all backgrounds recalled fond memories of hearing Italian, German, or Polish in the house when all of the older relatives came around and mentioned how unfortunate it is that they or their children have not been able to learn that ancestral tongue. They argued that the diverse cultures that come together to make America what it is should be maintained. They feel that we are worse off, both as individuals and as a community, when cultural distinctiveness fades. Nowhere in the discussions, however, did participants argue that their identity as Americans should be second to their identity as members of a particular ethnic group or that the purpose of the American political system is to affirm group identities. There was no evidence that this type of "hard" multiculturalism carries any weight in how people understand the nature of American identity.

UNITED STATES CHARACTERIZED BY CULTURAL ASSIMILATION/"MELTING-AS-BLENDING"

In contrast to the celebration of distinct cultures that characterizes the multicultural component of incorporationism is the assimilationist idea that "American" is not a fixed concept. This theme grows out of the myth of the melting pot and acknowledges that Americans, as a people, change as the matrix of ethnicities making up American society changes. Rather than singling out a few key features as definitive of American-ness, melting pot assimilationism highlights the fluidity of American identity. The most prevalent means of voicing this conception of American identity was to refer to cultural assimilation or the idea that American identity is constantly in flux; such thoughts make up 28 percent of the incorporationist comments.

A concise example of how people talked about the evolutionary nature of American identity comes from Robert, a member of a hobby club. When asked what makes us American, he replied, "Managing to develop a culture that's uniquely different than sum of the parts, I guess." Another example comes from one of the career organizations. Here, the group is discussing how words and foods from various cultures eventually come to be thought of as "American":

> ALICIA: And also what makes the American society so rich is the fact that it's changing and all these cultures are being added to it. All these flows of immigration are really adding new elements to the culture.
>
> SALLY: Enriching it.
>
> ALICIA: Tacos are now an American food.
>
> REBECCA: And Thai is so popular.
>
> ANITA: I think other cultures teach us, too.
>
> SALLY: Pasta is American. Sushi is American.
>
> LUANNE: Thai food is getting to be pretty commonplace too.
>
> ALICIA: And even the English language is adopting words.
>
> SALLY: So that's why you want [English] to be the official language. We'll put "amigo" in the American dictionary. I'm sure it's there already.[17]

These examples describe the United States as a true melting pot—not one where all cultures "melt" away and everyone becomes homogenized, but one where different ingredients are added and the stew in the pot changes with each new component to form an identity that is, as Robert says, more than just the sum of its parts.

THE MELTING POT

The term "melting pot" itself appeared with regularity, by some as an accurate description of the American people and by others as a dangerous myth that erodes cultural distinctiveness. Both perspectives offer an incorporationist conception of American identity; the first emphasizes the dynamism of the whole, while the second emphasizes the "ingredients." The first approach often involved people like Mary, in one of the career groups, simply saying things like, "I think the melting pot is one thing that is typically American," whereas the critical stance involved speakers advocating alternative images such as a salad bowl or a mosaic. Linda, from the Hispanic community service group, offers the latter alternative when she says, "We're salad people. All different types of things all mixed in. We're not a melting pot. We are a salad."

These differing interpretations of a long-standing American civic myth invoke strong emotions on both sides. Some people praised the country's ability to adapt and evolve, arguing that we do not acknowledge and appreciate that ability often enough, while others bristled, "What if I don't want to go into that pot?" That people attribute such divergent implications to the melting pot symbol provides a concrete example of the complex role described in chapter 2 that political symbols can play in the opinion formation process.

[17] It is.

Many people associate the symbol of the melting pot with American identity, but their assessments of that association and their emotional reactions to it vary widely.

SUMMARY

The quotes and figures in this section demonstrate the existence of a set of images and concerns grounded in the immigrant legacy of the nation that people use to define what it means to be American, which means we need to develop other constructs if we are to be better equipped to understand how regular Americans think about American identity. We need better ways to measure the ideal people value that balances manyness and oneness, because, like other traditions, the immigrant tradition in America is something that people learn about from an early age and are taught to cherish. It comes to mind easily when people are asked to articulate what they think being American means. Whether the metaphor is a salad bowl or a melting pot, the tradition of cultural diversity is seen to be, as they say, as American as apple pie.

Hybrids

Although participants clearly discuss American identity in liberal, civic republican, ethnocultural, and incorporationist terms, they do not always distinguish among these traditions when they describe what it means to be American. As table 5.2 shows, hybrid statements—thoughts that combine elements of more than one tradition—account for nearly 10 percent of the discourse under investigation in this chapter. It should be made clear at the outset that the coding of hybrid thoughts is not simply a way to count thoughts for which the coders could not decide on an appropriate classification. Rather, hybrids are thoughts that clearly invoke tenets of more than one conception of American national identity.

Table 5.7 lists the different possible combinations included in the coding procedure and the number of thoughts that were coded as belonging to each one. The reader should remember that hybrid totals are a lower bound, only catching when the conceptual combinations are present within a single thought. An individual-level analysis would most likely show that people endorse multiple conceptions of national identity throughout the two-hour discussion at a higher rate than table 5.7 shows.

LIBERALISM AND CIVIC REPUBLICANISM

That civic republican and liberal sentiments are frequently expressed simultaneously should come as no surprise. As Smith himself points out, liberal principles, such as freedom, rule of law, and tolerance, can often work in concert with civic republican principles, such as self-governance and political involvement. Both traditions have the consent of the individual as a crucial starting point, and the boundaries between these clusters of ideals are often

TABLE 5.7
Hybrid Thoughts and American Identity

Type of Hybrid	N	%
Liberalism and civic republicanism	56	28
Liberalism and ethnoculturalism	42	21
Civic republicanism and ethnoculturalism	22	11
Liberalism and incorporationism	13	6.5
Civic republicanism and incorporationism	20	10
Ethnoculturalism and incorporationism	31	15.5
Other hybrid	16	8
Total	200	100

quite permeable. This combination accounts for 28 percent of the hybrid comments in the focus group discussions.

An example of how liberalism and civic republicanism can be seen as jointly descriptive of American identity comes from June (quoted earlier). When asked if citizens should expect anything from the government or vice versa, she answered:

> It's more that we should expect the government to have the ability to pass laws that are timely and are of the time, of particular issues that are going on . . . but that they go through fair and due process with coming up with the laws, that there are people within the country as citizens that are allowed to vote within it.

June rambles a bit as she goes on, but the values that can be gleaned from this statement are fairness, majority rule, and self-governance. Government is supposed to operate within a fair and legalistic framework, but it is ultimately up to us, the citizens, to make sure that things turn out the way we want them to.

LIBERALISM AND ETHNOCULTURALISM

The combination of liberal and civic republican principles may have been the most common type of hybrid, but it is also, arguably, the least engaging. From a theoretical standpoint, I was more interested in the combination of liberalism and ethnoculturalism because the simultaneous expression of liberal and ethnocultural beliefs constitutes "symbolic racism," a controversial concept in public opinion research. Symbolic racism is a modern phenomenon that involves the combination of anti-minority sentiments and beliefs in liberal principles such as the work ethic, individualism, and limited government. It manifests itself in claims that minorities violate these cherished liberal American values and leads people to oppose policies designed to counter the effects of racial discrimination, such as affirmative action.[18] Several scholars

[18] See appendix A in Kinder and Sanders (1996) for a review of the controversies surrounding the concept of symbolic racism.

have documented that many white Americans do indeed see minorities as violating these liberal American values (e.g., Kinder and Sanders 1996; Kinder and Sears 1981; and McConahay 1982). Although much of this work emphasizes attitudes toward African-Americans, I expected to see some of the same denigration aimed at immigrants and other nonblack minorities. In the end, the combination of liberal and ethnocultural beliefs did not appear as often as the symbolic racism literature might lead us to expect, but it does account for 21 percent of the hybrid thoughts.

A common means of expressing symbolic racism was to complain that immigrants take unfair advantage of social services. An example comes from Ellen, a member of a charity group. Her peers were talking about how difficult it can be to keep the country unified in the face of rampant diversity and she said:

> I think a lot of the philosophy has changed too. I think years ago when the first immigrants came, there was the philosophy of adding to the country, not taking from. They came and they worked. They were not coming to this country for a handout, to get on welfare. They worked hard.

According to Ellen, part of what made America a coherent whole despite the influx of many ethnic groups was that everyone, native or immigrant, shared a common desire to work hard and be self-sufficient. Immigrants today, says Ellen, do not share that desire.

A similar complaint comes from Amy, a member of a hobby club. When asked what the government has a right to expect from its citizens, she said:

> A lot of that problem is that people don't. . . . The older ones, when they came, came to better themselves. If not themselves, then their children. And it was, "You'll own one of those someday." They'd take the children down to the most beautiful houses in town. "Some day, we'll have one of those." The attitude today is, "I'm going to tear that down because it's not mine," or, "If no one's going to give me one, I'm going to destroy it."

Amy is specifically talking about "people coming over" and how they've changed from the earlier times. Amy and Ellen clearly combine support for the work ethic, self-sufficiency, and negative images of immigrants, and several other participants shared their concerns. They never mention that their complaints are directed at Hispanics or Asians in particular, but given that Hispanics and Asians make up over 70 percent of today's immigrants, they do not have to. As symbolic racism theorists would expect, several white participants in my study articulate a conception of Americans as people who work hard to better themselves and of today's immigrants as people who just don't cut it.

CIVIC REPUBLICANISM AND ETHNOCULTURALISM

Smith (1988) has acknowledged that the principles of civic republicanism have often "been used to shield deplorable local abuses" (232) and create a slippery slope that allows for the exclusion of others in the name of the public good. A well-functioning society, it has been argued, requires a certain amount of homogeneity, a need that has often allowed for the exclusion of others and the denial of rights based on ascriptive characteristics (for other discussions on this theme, see Hibbing and Theiss-Morse 2002; and Putnam 2000). Such combinations of civic republican and ethnocultural claims were not especially common in the focus groups. Thoughts that combine concerns from these two conceptions of American identity account for 10 percent of the hybrid statements.

INCORPORATIONIST HYBRIDS

Given the divergent interpretations of immigrant-based conceptions of American identity described earlier and the extent to which people celebrate the interpretation that is most pleasing to them, it is rather straightforward to envision how incorporationism may be expressed in concert with other civic myths. Regarding liberalism, it is easy to imagine beliefs about tolerance and freedom being blended with a celebration of cultural diversity. In this hybrid, liberal principles provide the private space and individual autonomy that allow people to either sustain or ignore their ethnic traditions. Regarding civic republicanism, people may emphasize the virtues of melting pot assimilation-ism in increasing our abilities to work together to achieve common goals. Fi-nally, ethnoculturalism and incorporationism, though often at odds with one another, may be blended by those who disparage immigrants for refusing to "melt" or by those who acknowledge the ethnocultural tradition in America while simultaneously promoting the cultural pluralist alternative.

It turns out that hybrid statements involving liberalism and incorpora-tionism were the least common. When such hybrids were expressed, they did not emphasize Americans' freedom to preserve their cultures or argue against group rights, but rather marveled that liberal principles can not only survive but also thrive in such a diverse setting as the United States. An ex-ample comes from Paula (quoted earlier). When asked about the most im-portant thing her group discussed, she answered with, "I think it's really pretty special that we are able to do this—talk freely in a group about how we'd like to change the government, make it different. How many places can you do that, freely, with so much different background and so much different input?"

Hybrid thoughts involving both incorporationism and civic republicanism were more common and indeed involved participants describing how the dy-namic nature of American identity allows us to continue to strive for the civic republican ideal. An example comes from Melanie, a member of a hobby club. Using her grandfather as an example, she describes how assimilation leads to the development of personal attachments to the nation, which in turn lead to the fulfillment of the responsibilities of citizenship:

> MELANIE: I know my grandfather was Irish, born in Ireland. And he came over I guess when he was a teenager. But he fought in World War I. And yet . . . I guess they questioned him, and he was not Irish. He was American. And that was very important to him. He was an American. He had fought for his country and his country was the United States.
>
> MODERATOR: And he had been born in Ireland?
>
> MELANIE: Yeah. I mean, he came over as a teenager so he didn't. . . . But I guess his life . . . I guess his good fortune, he felt, he owed it to the United States.

Melanie clearly articulates a conception of American identity that allows for one to become more American, a hallmark of melting pot assimilationism, and becoming more American makes immigrants more likely to do their part, she says. Ten percent of all hybrid thoughts were of this nature.

Finally, incorporationist thoughts were most commonly expressed jointly with ethnoculturalism. This type of hybrid accounts for almost 16 percent of the hybrid thoughts analyzed in this chapter. Several of these thoughts were indeed critical of immigrants for not assimilating enough. But almost half of the ethnocultural/incorporationist hybrids actually criticized the ethnocultural ideal. Hispanic participants in particular disparaged other Hispanics who try to shed their ethnicity so as to not stand out. Some even described their own efforts at trying to blend in, only to discover that their culture is not so easy to shed. Here is Linda, who was born in Puerto Rico, describing how she tried to "melt" so that the dominant society would accept her:

> With that melting pot thing, when you say that people try to assimilate, it has a lot to do with fear, and I try to fit in because I remember when I came here, I really tried so hard to look like everybody else. My God, I must have done everything I could to this hair, to make this hair straight. And I tried. I tried to look a certain way and act a certain way. But the reality is that no matter how hard I tried to fit in and how hard I tried to make these white people like me, it didn't happen. My hair is kinky and when I open my mouth all that comes out is my big accent.

Linda felt that to become American meant, among other things, to have straight hair and to not have an accent. Becoming more American and becoming more like whites were not processes that were easy to separate. Clearly, the ethnocultural and incorporationist conceptions of American identity are not easily reconciled. Because they are both prevalent in the American psyche, the focus group format allows for participants to struggle with this reconciliation and to share with each other the actions they have taken to do so. The tensions between these traditions have been with America since the founding, and the focus group participants show that they are still with us. Given the increasing ethnic diversity of the American population, such tensions should not come as a surprise.

SUMMARY

Conceptual hybridization is not a sign of flawed theory or of simple-mindedness. Rather, it is normal and understandable for a variety of reasons. First, each tradition has qualities that can be compatible with qualities from another. Second, citizens are rarely called upon to articulate their beliefs about national identity. Even though they carry notions of American identity around with them every day, it can be difficult to discuss what those notions are. It is reasonable that the competing concerns that have been absorbed and reinforced over years and years of experiences will be called forth and expressed. Third, as Smith shows, laws and judicial decisions throughout the nation's history have combined elements of these traditions, and the regular Americans participating in my study may simply be following their lead.

SUMMARY AND CONCLUSIONS

This chapter has covered a lot of ground and spanned a wide range of complex arguments in the course of studying the concerns people raise when asked to describe what being American means. The findings presented here complement the findings of the previous chapter, which relied on data from the 1996 GSS to examine attitudes about American identity and immigration policy. In both cases, people are virtually unanimous in their agreement that certain "adoptable" characteristics are important in setting Americans apart from people in other countries. For example, the GSS respondents and the focus group participants agree that Americans should have a strong emotional attachment to the national community. And in both cases, ascriptive definitions of American identity receive a fair amount of support while also receiving condemnation. Many GSS respondents say that only Christians or people who were born in the United States can be truly American, and several focus group participants indicate that they see people who deviate from dominant cultural norms as not being American. At the same time, many respondents reject the GSS items that tap into an ethnocultural conception of American identity, and many focus group participants criticize the United States for its history of using race and ethnicity to determine who can and who cannot belong. These similarities across the two methodologies should alleviate some concerns about the generalizability of focus group findings.

Yet these two chapters also have important differences, though I argue that these differences serve to highlight the strengths, not the weaknesses, of using focus groups. The GSS section on American identity is limited in the amount of information it can provide about which constructs resonate with regular Americans when they are asked to explain their national identity. The focus group method allows me to account for several sets of concerns that were overlooked in the GSS. Important philosophical influences on American political culture that have been the subject of scholarly works on American identity and that shape how issues and events are interpreted are absent from the GSS, yet play a major role in shaping the course of the focus group interviews. For instance, the extent to which the GSS can be said to capture civic republican concerns is weak at best, but the focus groups allow civic republicanism to be a major aspect of descriptions of American identity.

This chapter represents my attempt to join the many scholars who have tried to come to grips with the Holy Ghost of American identity. Rather than look at elite behavior, such as legislative activity or judicial decisions, my efforts have concentrated on providing a systematic analysis of how regular Americans respond when asked to come to grips with this mysterious yet alluring entity themselves. And unlike others who have written on the subject, I do so primarily for instrumental purposes. My ultimate aim is to examine how conceptions of national identity influence policy preferences. In order to do that, I first need to know which conceptions of identity to use in the analysis. Finding survey data, on its own, ill suited for the task, I turned to focus groups to provide information about how people think about being American. Doing so has yielded information that both confirms conventional wisdom and provides new insights. We already knew that liberalism is an important influence over American political consciousness, and showing that it shapes attitudes is not particularly noteworthy. But looking *only* at liberal ideas of tolerance and freedom or at ethnocultural ideas that use ethnicity to delineate American identity will repeat past errors of overlooking important considerations that shape what people think it means to be American, an error that will only be compounded when the analysis turns to policy preferences. Demonstrating that my more nuanced approach to the study of American identity contributes to our understanding of how identity shapes policy preferences is the focus of the next two chapters.

Discussing Language Policy

MUCH OF THIS BOOK has been concerned with establishing that there are multiple conceptions of American national identity and that these conceptions have the power to shape how people feel about political issues. The purpose of the next two chapters is to examine how these several notions of American identity are related to policy preferences on official-English and English-only ballots.[1] By drawing on Smith's tripartite description of American national identity—consisting of liberalism, civic republicanism, and ethnoculturalism—I improve upon public opinion research that has sought to understand the relationship between identity and opinions. Smith's treatment of American identity encompasses a broader range of concerns than is typically included in surveys that aim to measure how Americans define their national identity. In developing each component as a distinct tradition with its own intellectual and legal history, Smith avoids placing these three traditions along a single dimension with liberal norms at one end and ethnocultural beliefs at the other. Adding incorporationism to the model improves the analysis even further, for it reflects yet another widely accepted conception of what being American means. As the goal of the study is to investigate how citizens use national identity to make sense of the language debate, analyses that include a variety of conceptions should prove to be more insightful than those that use a more narrow range of possibilities.

I find that although discourse that invokes these conceptions of national identity appears frequently in discussions about language and ethnicity, mere adherence to these traditions is not always enough to determine whether someone will support or oppose restrictive language policies. Abstract notions of American identity have multiple manifestations. The direction in which they influence opinions depends on which of those manifestations are most salient during the discussion and on the specific implications participants draw from their own interpretations of these civic myths. The only conception of national identity with a straightforward relationship to language policy preferences is ethnoculturalism, which conforms to the story line prior empirical research attributes to conceptions of national identity more broadly: ad-

[1] My initial intent was to have bilingual education be an equal partner in this analysis, but discussions on that topic were quite different from the discussions on the other two policies; they were largely driven by concerns about effectiveness, not identity. Therefore, I address bilingual education separately in chapter 7.

herence is associated with support for restrictive policies while rejection is associated with opposition.

The Relationship between Identity and Preferences

Imagine two people who believe that Americans should be active in public life. One might argue that without an official language, citizens are less able to get along and work together in civic affairs to achieve common goals, while the other might argue that an official language would make it too difficult for people to participate. These two people value the same norm—being involved in one's community—yet arrive at different policy preferences. Unfortunately, we do not know whether and how these concerns influence official-English attitudes because they have not been studied yet. The default has been to (mis)characterize all official-English supporters as ethnocultural. While some official-English supporters indeed harbor anti-immigrant sentiments, it is easy to imagine that others have more legitimate concerns about the well-being of the community.

This scenario informs the assumptions that underlie my expectations regarding all of the notions of American identity under investigation here. The first assumption is that national identity should not be thought of as a single dimension. People are not simply liberal or ethnocultural, and these two components of American identity are not polar opposites. As I have argued, people can adhere to either one, or to both, and other important conceptions of American identity are overlooked when a dichotomous measure is used.

Second, it is not necessarily the case that each notion of American identity consistently leads to a particular policy preference. For instance, it is not the case that liberal ideals always lead one to oppose restrictive policies. Framing, context, and interpretation all play a part in whether and how different components of national identity influence opinion formation. If the debate is not framed in liberal terms, then liberalism might not be influential in this issue area despite its centrality to definitions of "American-ness." Further, symbols that are widely cherished can be interpreted differently by different people. The direction in which liberalism, civic republicanism, ethnoculturalism, and incorporationism shape preferences will depend on whether they are associated with the policy in question and the particular aspects of each one that are emphasized by the individual.

In this sense, the ways in which conceptions of national identity are used among ordinary Americans might appear to differ from the ways in which they are used by policy makers, especially if one examines my claims in the context of Smith's analysis. In his work each civic tradition tends to point in one, and only one, direction regarding citizenship laws. For example, if a person believes in the rule of law and individual rights and freedoms, then the liberal tradition says he is eligible for citizenship. Likewise, if a person is a white

Christian, then he can belong, according to the ethnocultural tradition. That clarity breaks down, however, once we turn to other policy areas. What exactly is the liberal prescription when it comes to deciding whether the government should print documents in multiple languages? As we saw in chapter 3, partisans on either side of the issue can come up with an answer to that question that supports their view. This difference has more to do with the nature of the policy in question rather than with an inherent difference in how elites and masses rely on civic traditions when devising a preferred policy. When it comes to determining eligibility for citizenship, each civic tradition functions in more or less the same way: if people embrace or otherwise meet the prescriptions of the tradition, they can belong. But when it comes to language policy, the guidance provided by competing conceptions of national identity is much less straightforward. It is still the case that with each tradition, as long as the policy in question promotes (or does not threaten) its prescriptions, then the policy is acceptable. The difference is that it is much less clear whether a particular policy promotes (or threatens) those prescriptions. That activists and lawmakers on both sides of language conflicts invoke similar traditions supports the case that differences in policy type rather than differences between elites and masses drive the seemingly disparate nature of how American identity is implicated in citizenship law and language policy.

It is not necessarily the case, however, that both sides will invoke the same particular norm. Instead, people might appeal to different aspects of the same overarching civic tradition to endorse opposing views. As we saw in chapter 3, activist supporters of official-English note that intrusions into public life will not occur if English is made the official language, whereas opponents contend that official-English infringes upon freedom of speech. Both sides are looking to the liberal tradition when they are making these claims, but they are appealing to different aspects of that tradition.[2] Yet it might also be the case that both sides do indeed look to the same particular norm but interpret its relevance in terms of language policy in contradictory ways. The example described earlier of two people's desire for an informed and involved citizenry leading to opposite preferences is a case in point. The extent to which either of these possibilities actually plays out in practice among ordinary Americans remains to be seen. But before moving on to the empirical analysis, I offer brief descriptions of how we might expect each tradition to feature in the focus groups in light of the phenomena discussed thus far.

LIBERALISM

The "problem" with liberalism with regard to immigration and ethnic change is that it is more or less silent on issues relating to the manner in which new

---

[2] Smith himself notes the internal tensions within the civic traditions (1997, 20, 30). His main goal, however, is to establish ethnoculturalism as an alternative civic tradition to liberalism and civic republicanism, not to explore these internal tensions.

members should be incorporated into the limited contractual government. This is not to say that liberalism does not address interactions among citizens and governments. Rather, it emphasizes the individual and limits the demands that the state can make on its people. As such, people might not find liberal prescriptions all that useful when considering mandating a single public language. Perhaps language issues will not prime the sorts of concerns we associate with liberalism, such as individual autonomy, economic freedom, and rule of law. Liberalism teaches people to value being free to do what they want and being tolerant of other people's right to do what *they* want; it does not place much stock in forging common ties with fellow citizens.

However, I showed in chapter 3 that activists on both sides of language conflicts invoke liberal norms when making their case. Politicians and activists who oppose official-English criticize such laws as discriminatory and as violations of free speech. For example, Rep. Sheila Jackson-Lee (D-TX), arguing against the English Language Empowerment Act of 1996, says, "The Founders of this country recognized the danger of restricting its citizens' freedom of expression. Language, like religion, is an intensely personal form of self-expression which must not be subject to governmental regulation."[3] On the other side of the issue, U.S. English proclaims it supports making English the official language because, along with other reasons, doing so will allow immigrants to pursue the American Dream and achieve economic success. One of their print ads depicts a man with dark hair and a moustache sweeping the floor of a room with folding chairs scattered about. The accompanying text states: "Immigrants who don't learn English can really clean up America." U.S. English also goes to some lengths to point out that official-English laws will affect only public, not private, enterprises.[4] If these ways of framing the issue reach the mass public, then symbols associated with liberalism can fuel both support for and opposition to official-English laws. Therefore, it is reasonable to expect that overall, liberalism will not play a large role in discussions of language policies. But when it does, people against official-English will argue that it violates freedom of speech or other rights and liberties, and people in favor of it will argue that making English the official language will sustain the American Dream and will not intrude on private interactions.

CIVIC REPUBLICANISM

The civic republican tradition speaks to the concerns raised by debates about language policy more clearly than does the liberal tradition. Civic republicanism is fundamentally concerned with the interactions among citizens and how such interactions can best promote the public good. The ability of citizens to govern themselves and act in ways that promote this public good are largely dependent upon whether the design of public policies enhances or

[3] See *Congressional Record*, 142, no. 116, part 2 (August 1, 1996): H9749.
[4] See U.S. English website at www.usenglish.org.

hinders those activities. Whether public life is conducted in one or multiple languages profoundly shapes the alternatives available for achieving such ends. Civic republican themes should therefore feature prominently in discussions about restrictive language policies. Yet interpretations of how these symbols lead to a well-functioning community of informed and involved citizens can vary, such that some people may be led to favor English-only policies and others to oppose them. When people fear that Americans do not have enough in common (a frequent claim of official-English activists), they should be more likely to favor regulating language use. Alternatively, when people emphasize the importance of having an informed and involved citizenry, they should be more likely to oppose official-English laws. Analyses of activist rhetoric do not have much to say about this last concern, but given its centrality to the civic republican tradition, and given the civic republican tradition's centrality to conceptions of American identity, I expect it to surface in the focus group discussions, particularly when participants debate English-only ballots.

ETHNOCULTURALISM

Unlike liberalism and civic republicanism, it is rare to see ethnoculturalism explicitly endorsed, at least as far as mainstream political discourse is concerned. Despite this lack of public endorsement, subtle nods to the idea that certain ascriptive characteristics define who is and who is not an American are still common. Debates about whether to make English the official language or to provide voting materials only in English directly relate to these types of beliefs. Language issues would not arise if everyone spoke English and so these debates, by their very nature, suggest that the stereotypical image of an American as a white, English-speaking person of Anglo-Saxon descent is being challenged. Since this image is so clearly implicated in the existence of language debates, ethnocultural themes should emerge in discussions about language policy proposals.

When ethnocultural beliefs are expressed, they should lead to support for restrictive language policies. Proponents of official-English laws who invoke ethnocultural sentiments will express discomfort with ethnic change and show contempt for immigrants who do not conform to the dominant modes of interaction in American society. In light of the findings presented in chapter 5, however, which show that explicit critiques of ethnoculturalism are common, this expectation needs modification. Many people are openly critical of America's legacy of treating its nonwhite or non-English-speaking residents worse than their white and English-speaking counterparts, and those who offer such critiques are likely to view official-English laws as contributing to that legacy. Thus, ethnocultural discourse should consist of two forms: endorsement and rejection. Endorsements should be associated with support for official-English, whereas rejection should be associated with opposition.

INCORPORATIONISM

I argued in earlier chapters that Smith's typology overlooks an important conception of American identity, namely the idea of the United States as a nation of immigrants and the profound impact it has had over the development of political culture in American society. Within the category of incorporationism I found two main strands, multiculturalism and melting pot assimilationism. Recall that multiculturalism is characterized by a celebration of cultural diversity in the United States and melting pot assimilationism emphasizes the evolving nature of what being American means; as more and more ingredients are added to the mix, the very idea of American identity changes. Both interpretations appeared often in discussions about American identity and should therefore play a role in the opinion formation process regarding language policy. By definition, multiculturalism should be associated with opposition to restrictive policies. No matter how well-intentioned such proposals may be, a multicultural interpretation of the incorporationist civic myth should lead people to resist policies designed to homogenize. At the same time, there is no reason to expect people to endorse "hard" multiculturalism; the preponderance of evidence suggests it is unlikely that people will advocate group-based rights or ethnic separatism. There is no similarly logical relationship as far as melting pot assimilationism is concerned. People might think that a common language is part and parcel of the evolutionary experience and therefore support official-English, or they might think that this evolutionary process would take place on its own, as it has in the past, and not need governmental regulation.

Measuring Policy Preferences

The previous chapter concentrated on whether the four-part typology provides an appropriate framework for studying the relationship between conceptions of American identity and policy preferences. To do that, I divided the focus group discourse into two sections. The first is the subject of chapter 5 and consists of those statements that deal with general feelings about being American. The second contains all statements that refer to a particular language policy and provides the set of thoughts analyzed here. I use the same coding procedure from the analysis in chapter 5 but with two additional steps. First, each statement was marked according to which policy, if any, it referred (official-English, English-only ballots, bilingual education). Next, if the statement pertained to a particular policy, it was marked to indicate whether it expressed support, opposition, ambivalence, or no opinion.[5]

I also created a code for comments that did not explicitly mention support

[5] See appendix E for examples of ambivalent and opinionless policy-related thoughts.

Table 6.1
Opinion Direction of Completed Thoughts by Policy Type

Policy	N	%	Direction	N	%
English as official language	938	56.5	Support	226	24.1
			Oppose	213	22.7
			Ambivalent	141	15.0
			No opinion	358	38.2
					100
English-only ballots	101	6.1	Support	34	33.7
			Oppose	30	29.7
			Ambivalent	17	16.8
			No opinion	20	19.8
					100
Bilingual education	231	13.9	Support	12	5.2
			Oppose	52	22.5
			Ambivalent	34	14.7
			No opinion	133	57.6
					100
Americans should speak English	389	23.4	n.a.	389	100
Total	1659	100		1659	

for declaring English the official language per se, but rather argued that everyone in America should speak English. I suspected that people who made such comments would also support making English official. Indeed, many participants did not distinguish between the formal pronouncement and the desired condition and thought that the former would promote the latter. Despite the overlap between expressed and implicit support for official-English, I coded implicit thoughts as a separate category because the relationship between support for official-English and for the value of speaking English is not one-to-one. In the end, 60 percent of the participants who expressed the general belief that Americans should speak English also supported making English official. The remaining 40 percent were largely opposed to making English official but argued that people should still speak English. By using a separate category for these views, I avoid mischaracterizing those participants who draw distinctions between making English official and the value of speaking English.[6]

Table 6.1 shows how many statements were made in support for or opposition to each policy and how many express ambivalence or no opinion. The policy-related portion of the focus groups was dominated by official-English,

[6] Eighty-one of the 108 participants mentioned the importance of knowing English. This does not mean, however, that the remaining 27 participants think it is acceptable for citizens not to learn English.

due in part to the design of the interview protocol, which began with a reading of a proposed amendment to the Constitution to designate English as the official language.[7] As the emphasis of this chapter is on how symbolic notions of national identity shape when people support or oppose restrictive policies, the analysis that follows concentrates on thoughts that express a clear preference or argue that everyone should speak English.

FINDINGS

The same 1,659 completed thoughts presented in table 6.1 are categorized in the left half of table 6.2 according to the conception of American identity invoked. More than half of the policy-related discourse is accounted for by the model, with civic republicanism being the most common tradition, although liberalism and ethnoculturalism are not far behind. Note that the row labeled "No identity" (thoughts that do not invoke a particular conception of American identity) contains the highest number of thoughts. This result is due to the inclusion of thoughts on bilingual education in the table and is discussed in more detail in chapter 7. The right half of table 6.2 excludes thoughts on bilingual education. It also excludes thoughts that are ambivalent or do not state an opinion on the policies in question. It categorizes only those thoughts that explicitly argue for or against official-English or bilingual ballots, or argue that everyone should speak English. It is these thoughts that are analyzed in this chapter. In other words, the remainder of this chapter deals with those thoughts in the upper right quadrant of table 6.2 (cells in bold).

Liberalism

About 12 percent of all substantive policy-related thoughts are coded as liberal. Most refer to declaring English the official language. It turns out that liberal discourse is a prominent player in discussions about the language(s) in which official government business should be conducted and is associated with support for official-English more often than with opposition. The symbols associated with liberalism were not invoked when the focus group participants discussed whether election ballots should be printed only in English. Table 6.3 lists the different aspects of liberalism in the coding scheme and shows the number of thoughts that invoke each one for each policy position. Within the broad concept of liberalism, there are two main strands. The first promotes rights, freedom, and tolerance and is what many people bring to

---

[7] To remind the reader, the text of the ELA is: "The English language shall be the official language of the United States. As the official language, the English language shall be used for all public acts, including every order, resolution, vote or election, and for all records and judicial proceedings of the government of the United States and the governments of the several states."

TABLE 6.2
Policy-related Thoughts by Conception of American Identity

Conception of American Identity	All Policy-related Thoughts		Without Bilingual Education, Ambivalent or Opinionless Thoughts	
	N	%	N	%
Liberalism	191	11.51	112	12.6
Civic republicanism	280	16.88	221	24.8
Ethnoculturalism	184	11.09	144	16.1
Incorporationism	62	3.74	36	4.0
Hybrid	139	8.38	110	12.3
Tax/spend	41	2.47	22	2.5
Other	6	0.36	1	0.1
Unclassified	297	17.9	147	16.5
No identity	459	27.67	99	11.1
Total	1659	100	892	100

mind when they think of the dominant political philosophy in the United States. The second emphasizes economic opportunity, the market economy, and the freedom to follow private individual pursuits. In chapter 5, I showed that both strands are powerful symbols of American identity among the participants. The data here show that participants still invoke these principles when discussing language policy and that they tend to use the rights-based strand to explain opposition to language restrictions, whereas they rely on the economy-based strand to explain support. They also show that concerns about economic success overwhelmingly constitute liberal statements saying that people in the United States should speak English.[8] Although I had not anticipated the frequency with which liberal concerns would be associated with support for official-English, it is more accurate to say that these concerns are offered as reasons to *not oppose* official-English rather than as reasons to support it. I elaborate on this point later.

CIVIL/POLITICAL RIGHTS AND FREEDOMS

As table 6.3 shows, most liberal thoughts against the ELA objected on the grounds that it would discriminate against ethnic minorities, violate civil rights, or restrict basic freedoms. For example, Joan, a woman in a hobby club,

[8] χ^2 significance tests of independence are not included because of the high number of cells with fewer than five observations. Fisher's exact tests for tables 6.3 to 6.5 all yield $p < 0.001$ for official English and $p < 0.01$ for English-only ballots.

TABLE 6.3
Liberalism and Language Policy Preferences

Liberal Categories	Official-English		English-only Ballots		All Should Know English
	For	Against	For	Against	
Freedom	0	5	0	0	0
Civil/political rights	0	9	1	0	1
English necessary for economic success	6	2	0	0	39
Public/private distinction	25	0	0	0	4
Obey laws	0	0	0	0	0
Economic opportunity	0	0	0	0	0
Work ethic	1	0	0	0	1
Majority rule	0	0	0	0	1
Individualism	1	0	0	0	0
Tolerance	0	0	0	0	1
U.S. as land of plenty	0	0	0	0	0
Rule of law	0	0	0	0	1
Other liberalism or liberal hybrid	4	7	0	0	3
Total	37	23	1	0	51

explains that she opposes the ELA because it is reminiscent of overt discrimination from previous eras. She says, "I think that that particular piece of legislation, the way it's stated now, sounds kind of discriminatory. It reminds me of the 'No Irish Need Apply,' that kind of thing that you saw." A more emphatic example comes from Yasmine in a community service organization:

> I'm against it because it's illegal. The First Amendment says you have a right to freedom of speech. And therefore if that goes through and that becomes a law, it's directly in violation to the First Amendment of the United States Constitution. . . . It's illegal and directly against not only the U.S. Constitution's First Amendment, but civil rights laws. So, no. No. It's illegal and it's not fair. That's what I think.

Similarly, Andrew, in a career-related group, says, "I think there's a danger there, when zealots get a hold of something like this and start to restrict and restrict. . . . I'm against anything that restricts freedom of speech or expression, in any language, really." Most participants envision the United States as a place where people are more or less free to say what they want without being censored or discriminated against, and some fear that the ELA would violate this sacred image by placing restrictions on the languages in which people communicate. Sixty-one percent of the liberal opposition to official-English was of this flavor.

ENGLISH NECESSARY FOR ECONOMIC SUCCESS

An aspect of liberalism frequently mentioned in support of making English the official language is the desire to structure social relations in a way that would promote opportunities for economic success. Some participants argued that without a command of the English language, people are not able to take advantage of the economic opportunities that America has to offer. This argument could speak to a more civic republican–based vision of citizenship, particularly if people said that language minorities threaten the stability of the community or fail to meet an obligation of self-sufficiency when they do not achieve economic success (Kymlicka 1994; Mead 1986). But participants who invoke economic success as a reason to support the ELA or assert that everyone in America should know English do so in a purely instrumental fashion, focusing on the individual. They see Americans not as people who have an obligation to be successful but as people who value industry and initiative because of the personal benefits such attributes confer. But the ability to get ahead, they maintain, can only be realized by those who know English.

The argument that knowing English is essential if people living in the United States are to succeed economically accounts for six of the thirty-seven liberal thoughts in favor of the ELA. The extent to which this sentiment was used to argue that people living in America should know English is striking, constituting 76 percent of all liberal thoughts that make this claim.[9] People who made this argument often stated their case by describing acquaintances whose poor English skills brought hardships or by sharing the success stories of a neighbor or distant relative who was able to "make it in America" thanks to his or her determination to learn English. Merle, for example, a member of a hobby club, was eager to explain his support for the ELA and shared the story of a hair stylist he knew who was held back because she only spoke Spanish:

> And there you had a woman who had so much talent, but the amount of money that she could make was very limited. But we helped her and encouraged her to take classes to learn the English language. This woman now quadrupled her pay. . . . So I think not learning the English language could really curtail you from being successful.

Later in the same group, John describes a memorable message his grandfather gave him about the importance of learning English:

> I remember in my house, my grandfather knew German, and I took German in high school. And I come back and he says, "Well, what are you taking German for? Where you gonna go with that?" I said, "Well you speak German I thought, you

[9] More than half of the people who used this justification for everyone knowing English indicated elsewhere that they favor declaring English the official language.

know you learned it from your parents. I thought I could have a conversation with you in German." He says, "German never got me anywhere. I speak English and you gotta speak English."

Merle's hair stylist and John's grandfather were two of many characters to appear in the stories participants told to convey a simple message: without English, you'll never "get anywhere."

For some, the strong link between knowing English and economic security was a reason for thinking everyone should learn English but *not* for favoring the ELA. Indeed, among those who oppose official-English laws but say it is important for people in the United States to know English, economic success was the most common reason offered. Again, people made this case by telling stories of people and places they know. Antonio, who opposes the ELA, describes how economic class and English acquisition go together in the border town where he grew up:

> [My city is] about 70 percent Hispanic or Mexican-American. . . . And you have Hispanics of all different levels of the economic spectrum. And I think as you go down, like in income, Hispanics with high income, I think they know less Spanish. And as you keep going down, getting to new immigrants and the ones that earn less, they're the ones who speak Spanish. . . . As you're there longer and the more you succeed, and the English language becomes part of you, you see that that's what's important to survive economically.

Antonio sees that learning English is beneficial for economic independence but does not think it requires getting the Constitution involved. In short, while most people who noted the link between English and economic success were supporters of the ELA, opponents did so as well, and they discussed this link in terms of the personal benefits at stake, not societal obligations.

PUBLIC/PRIVATE DISTINCTION

The most common liberal justification for supporting, or rather for not opposing, the ELA is that the proposal would affect only public, not private, interactions. Statements of this nature account for 68 percent of all liberal comments in favor of making English official. That the United States is a place where the private sector is protected from too much government intrusion came up from time to time in the general discussions about what being American means but not often when compared with other liberal principles like freedom and tolerance. But when discussing specific policy alternatives, the need to maintain the distinction between public and private spheres of life became more important. Many participants agreed that the language(s) in which private individual concerns are pursued should not be infringed upon by the state and indicated they would oppose the proposal if they thought it would interfere with private relations. An example comes from Mary Jane, a member of a charity group:

> I think that if people want to speak their native language in the privacy of their home or in a social gathering or what have you, that would be fine. But as far as anything public, yeah, I think it should be unified in English and English only.

Other times, the public/private distinction was raised to dismiss the fears of people who oppose the law. In dismissing those fears, some participants accused opponents of official-English of being too sensitive and of misinterpreting the intent and scope of the proposed legislation. Such comments suggested that the line between public and private would be respected and that people who fear that this law would prohibit them from speaking other languages are overreacting.[10]

Note that the belief that government should not regulate private interactions was not actually used to say we should *support* making English the official language, but was invoked to explain why should *not oppose* it. People do not make the nonsensical case that "we need to make English the official language because in this country we do not allow government to interfere in our private affairs." Rather, they say, "I support the ELA because it applies to public affairs only," implying they would have a different preference if they thought the amendment would cross the sacred line between public and private. So, although this value does not *cause* support for the ELA, *it makes support possible* by providing a universally accepted framework through which people interpret the debate.

SUMMARY

The focus groups show that certain aspects of the liberal tradition in America attract people to official-English legislation while other aspects serve as a repellent. Participants value that Americans have the freedom to express themselves, and people who fear that the ELA would encroach upon this cherished norm are against it. Most people accept the liberal notion that, by and large, they should be left alone to pursue individual goals. In making that case, however, they do not go so far as to argue explicitly against the concept of group rights (although they might have if they had been asked about it outright). One manifestation of this belief, the image of Americans as people who work hard to fulfill their potential and strive for economic success, leads some to support the ELA because they feel that this ideal cannot be realized without a command of English. A second manifestation, that government should

---

[10] The problem with this reasoning is that it mischaracterizes the views of people on both sides of the debate. No supporters in the focus groups, in Congress, or at pro-official-English organizations say they want to regulate speech in the home, and opponents never say that they think such intrusion will happen. Opponents do appeal to free speech, as seen in the quotes from Yasmine and Rep. Jackson-Lee, but they do so within the context of rights and freedom, not while debating the line between public and private affairs.

not regulate private interactions, promotes support by making it acceptable for them to advocate language restrictions.

Civic Republicanism

The image of the active citizen paying attention to political affairs and working to promote the general welfare is a prominent symbol in American political consciousness. Yet, by and large, public opinion scholars have not explored how this deeply held attachment relates to policy preferences. In the focus groups, civic republican concerns account for more policy-related thoughts than liberalism, ethnoculturalism, or incorporationism (see table 6.2). Civic republican concerns are invoked in 41 of the 101 statements that refer to printing election ballots only in English and account for 28 percent of the statements saying that everyone in the United States should know English (compared with 13 percent for liberalism, 18 percent for ethnoculturalism, and 5 percent for incorporationism). These numbers suggest that the power of the civic republican ideal to affect policy attitudes has indeed been neglected. Table 6.4 lists the aspects of civic republicanism in the coding scheme and shows the number of thoughts that appeal to each one for each policy view. As with liberalism, multiple aspects of this tradition are relevant to debates about language policy. Some emphasize unity and the ability of people to communicate with one another, concerns generally raised in support of the ELA and everyone knowing English. Others focus on participation in political and community affairs and are not uniformly associated with a particular policy view. When people express the desire to maximize both the quantity and quality of participation, they tend to oppose restrictive policies; when they only talk about maximizing quality, they voice support.[11] Another aspect of civic republicanism that shapes attitudes on language issues is a preference for local decision-making control.

BEING ABLE TO COMMUNICATE/TOO MUCH DIVERSITY

The data show that people frequently refer to concerns about the community when discussing language and ethnic change. Some argue that a certain degree of homogeneity is required to maintain healthy and well-functioning communities. Others add that the diversity we celebrate in America has gone too far and has resulted in the breakup of social ties. They note that ethnic and linguistic diversity make it harder to get along and communicate, and without successful communication, there can be no community. The word "balkanized" is used frequently. For example, Tim, a member of a career-related group, in sorting out the potential benefits and drawbacks of making English official, says:

[11] The maximization of "quantity" means increasing the sheer number and diversity of people who participate in the political process; the maximization of "quality" means ensuring that people who are involved are politically knowledgeable.

TABLE 6.4
Civic Republicanism and Language Policy Preferences

Civic Republican Categories	Official-English		English-only Ballots		All Should Know English
	For	Against	For	Against	
Balkanization/too much diversity	17	0	0	0	18
Being able to communicate	3	0	1	1	42
Language law is divisive	0	4	0	0	0
Language law would be exclusionary	0	19	0	9	1
Importance of voting	0	0	2	7	3
Participation/volunteerism	0	0	4	1	2
Local control over decision making	5	14	1	1	0
Isolation from the rest of the community	1	1	1	1	13
Responsibilities/duties of citizens	0	0	1	0	7
Ceremony/ritual	0	5	1	0	0
Important to feel American	0	0	0	0	0
Self-governance	0	1	0	0	0
Other republicanism or republican hybrid	8	4	0	0	22
Total	34	48	11	20	108

I think that culturally we're facing, and I think the world is facing, a certain balkanization where people tend to want to stay in their own groups and communicate in their own languages as well, which is, I think, detrimental to . . . certainly our country, ultimately. So if the intention of [the ELA] is to try to break that down, perhaps that's a worthy goal.

The following comments from Harriet and June, supporters of the ELA and members of a public-speaking group, also demonstrate the frustration people can feel regarding the lack of a common sense of identity in the United States. When asked what the most important topic their group covered was, they replied:

HARRIET: The textbooks will tell you we're an individualistic society as opposed to a communitarian society. But I don't think anybody's completely thrilled with the lack of community here. And if we let go of the language . . . that's not healthy. It really isn't.

JUNE: I guess the most important thing we talked about tonight, in my opinion, was probably, again, the language issue and whether or not it's going to unify us or divide us or keep us from being connected to. . . . Are we going to be connected with everyone in our society? That's probably the most important issue.

Another common civic republican concern is simply the need to communicate with one another. At its most basic, this concern is practical: a society cannot function with a multiplicity of languages. A common manifestation of this view is to complain about driving exams being offered in several languages. For instance, Kate, a member of a business organization, asks, "How about the driver's license? How can someone go for a driver's test in a different language, yet all of our signs are in English? How about when you've got street names or stop signs that say stop?" Others similarly discussed the dangers of having drivers who are not able to know where they are or understand the rules of the road. It's a matter of safety and of order; a single public language can provide both and thus enhance the well-being of the community.

A loftier version of this theme is that people get along better when they speak the same language, and when people get along better, community life improves. Ernie, for example, a member of the public-speaking group, says:

I'm speaking as an American. Here in America, most everybody speaks English. For everybody to get along and communicate, everyone should learn English at least. And I feel that there's nothing wrong with having a second language, whatever it is. But for all of us to understand each other, English should be understood by everybody who is a citizen or who lives in America.

The idea that communication is necessary for a sense of unity and harmony is more commonly used to express the belief that everyone should speak English rather than in explicit support for declaring English the official language. But 78 percent of those who use communication as a reason for everyone knowing English also explicitly support the ELA elsewhere during the discussion.

Occasionally, wanting to promote unity and minimize social divisions actually led people to oppose the ELA, but this was relatively rare (see "Language law is divisive," table 6.4). One instance comes from Milton, a member of a hobby group, who says, "The biggest problem I have with the English-Firsters, or the ones who want to make it official, is that it's so divisive. [It's] a divisive issue, and that's why my personal vote is that we have to be as little divisive as possible." By and large, however, people who lamented divisiveness in America supported making English the official language.

PARTICIPATION/VOTING/LANGUAGE LAW IS EXCLUSIONARY

Political participation is essential to the success of self-government according to the tenets of civic republicanism. As such, I expected people to think that policies should be designed so as to make participation possible and meaningful. But what this means exactly in terms of support for official-English is not straightforward. I thought that people who emphasize participation would oppose official-English policies because of their potential for excluding some members of the polity from community life. I expected people to argue that because many Americans do not speak English well, we should provide services and ballots in several languages to ensure that all citizens can fulfill their civic duty by participating meaningfully. It turns out in some cases, wanting to be sure everyone can take part in the political process does indeed lead to opposition to restrictive policies. But in other instances, an emphasis on being informed and involved leads to support.

Table 6.4 shows that civic republican–based opposition to the ELA is fueled mainly by fears that minorities will be excluded from the political process. An example comes from Gloria, a woman in a community service organization. She argues:

> I'm nay for that proposal. And just for the reason that how are people that speak different languages going to understand anything that's being said as far as the politics or anything else? That's why I'm against it. Because at some point they need to know what's going on. And if it's in English and they don't understand, they're basically being sanctioned for it because they don't know the language.

Similarly, Rena, in a career-related group, says, "I feel that an amendment would marginalize an already marginalized population and would make them even more on the fringe," and, "I don't think it would really have any kind of impact, except just alienating people who are already feeling alienated." Gloria and Rena know that people cannot be informed about and involved in their political and social surroundings if they do not speak the language in which the majority of public discourse occurs, yet they feel that declaring English the official language will make it harder, not easier, for language minorities to be a part of "what's going on." This fear of excluding minorities from participating accounts for 40 percent of all civic republican discourse against the ELA.

So far, concerns about political participation seem to be associated with opposition to restrictive language policies. Looking at views on whether election ballots should be printed only in English, however, reveals a more complex scenario. Many statements against this proposal did follow the anticipated course: fears of excluding ethnic minorities from the political process and general claims about the importance of voting were by far the most common reasons given for opposing English-only ballots. Yet statements of *support* for this policy were also driven by concerns about general participation in the community and having an informed citizenry. This divergent pattern stems from the alleged long-standing incompatibility in the ideal of a self-governing society between wanting to maximize both the quantity and the quality of participation.

The following excerpt from a discussion among members of a community service organization illustrates the type of reasoning I expected to find:

> DAVE: If you think in terms of the computer age that we're in, it's not too far-fetched to imagine that you go up to the polling booth and they ask you which language you would like your ballot to be in, you press the button, and, boom, it can come out in more than forty. So technologically it is becoming possible to [do] something more than just pay attention to the large ethnic subgroups that might be Spanish or might be French or Japanese or Vietnamese.
>
> GARRETT: When you install your computer Windows in Word, if you will, in Microsoft, you have your choice of a half-dozen languages there that you can press the button and put it into.
>
> DAVE: But the point is, it would be more important to have every citizen able to make an informed choice and to participate in the voting process. And if you have to do it in multi-language to do that, to make it happen, then I'd be for it.
>
> ALICE: Yes. Yes.
>
> MODERATOR: Other people?
>
> TOM: Say that again, Dave?
>
> DAVE: I'd say it's better to have citizens make an informed choice and to partici-pate in the voting process. And if the price we have to pay to do that is to provide the ballots in multiple languages, then I would say we should.

Dave's emphasis is on the quantity of participation, but he does not see quan-tity and quality as necessarily in tension. Rather, the quality of participation is improved by making information more accessible and encouraging greater involvement.

Cindy, in a career-related group, shows how the symbol of participatory public life in America can lead to the opposite policy view. She argues that being informed is crucial for meaningful and effective participation and that people cannot be adequately informed without a command of English:

> MODERATOR: Cindy, you mentioned earlier when you were trying to parse out what the different effects of [declaring English the official language] might be, you said you aren't really comfortable messing with the Constitution, but the idea of having all ballots in English, that is fine with you. Could you say a little more about that?
>
> CINDY: I agree with that. I really do believe that potential for a lot of very hor-rific things in this country comes from uninformed decisions in the voting booth. And if you can't understand the English language and you can't comprehend what's going on in the news because you don't understand English and you can't read an English newspaper, I do not comprehend how you'll be able to make an in-formed decision at a voting booth.

According to this reasoning, people must know English to participate because that is the language in which political debate occurs. When people who are not able to follow mainstream political discourse have a say at the ballot box, the sanctity of voting is tarnished and decisions that are made could be harmful.

This next exchange between Doug, Bob, and Milton, members of a hobby group, further illustrates the tension between quantity and quality that underlies the participatory aspect of civic republicanism:

> Doug: I guess my opposition [to having bilingual ballots], at the risk of seeming inconsistent [with my earlier opposition to the ELA], I don't think that any of the ballots ought to be in anything but English. And the reason is that you have to participate in a dialogue, and to understand what's going on, I think you ought to be able to speak English.
>
> Bob: And if you want to talk in more detail about issues and stuff like that, there are plenty of different language newspapers out there so they could talk about that in that particular language. But when it comes to a legal standpoint, it should be English.
>
> Milton: Is anyone concerned that we only have 40 percent or fewer people in the United States vote regularly in elections? Does anyone worry that some of that is attributable to the fact that they might not understand what the ballot proposals are or what the elections are about? And if that's the case, would more accessibility and their understanding of the language on the ballot help that? I think we have a problem in so few people vote.

Doug suggests that people who do not know English will not know "what's going on" and should therefore not take part in the project of self-governance. Milton cynically counters that Doug need not worry because the lack of accessible information is effective at keeping language minorities away from the polls. Like Dave, from the community service club, Milton suggests that providing information in other languages could both increase the number of voters and provide them with the tools necessary to prevent the results of their involvement from being "horrific."[12]

Both sets of viewpoints espouse the civic republican call for citizens who are both informed and involved. For some people, increasing involvement means allowing uninformed people to take part, a possibility that offends their notion of a participatory system of government. Imagine a New England town meeting packed with people who obstruct meaningful debate by offering their views on subjects about which they know little. Add multiple languages to this scenario and the situation becomes even more frustrating and ineffective. Cindy and Doug fear that bilingual voting materials will get more people involved but not necessarily more informed, a combination worse than having

[12] On the pre-discussion survey, Milton said he favors having ballots printed in other languages in addition to English. Although he sounds ambivalent in the quote provided here, his answer to his own question would most likely be yes, bilingual ballots would help in terms of accessibility and understanding and would therefore result in more participation.

language-minority citizens who are both uninformed and uninvolved. Others, like Dave and Milton, agree that providing voting materials in multiple languages will increase involvement, but it will do so mainly because it would increase awareness. For them, the civic republican call for a participatory society requires us to promote quantity along with quality, and increased quantity would be a natural by-product of actions taken to improve quality.

LOCAL CONTROL

A third civic republican concern that featured prominently in the focus group discussions is the notion that certain issues should be left to communities to settle on their own. This argument was a common justification for opposing the ELA even though it hasn't been a factor in activist rhetoric in concrete policy battles. For activists, advocating local control would mean accepting that some places could opt for the "wrong", policy, but for ordinary citizens, the enduring civic republican image of citizens playing a role in deciding their local policies shapes how they interpret the debate. People argued that no single policy is right for every locality. This sentiment appeals to the notion of active citizens deliberating and debating over which policies will foster the public good in their community. Given that communities vary greatly in their ethnic composition, people argue, official-English is perhaps an issue that is best decided by towns and cities themselves. Those who felt this way argued that one national language policy cannot provide an appropriate way for all places to conduct interactions between their citizens and government. This concern accounts for 29 percent of civic republican thoughts against the ELA.

Francine, Marge, and Ron, members of a historical society, had an exchange that illustrates this sentiment:

> FRANCINE: Working at it from the educational side would accomplish the goal [of having people learn English] in a much more gentle and effective way than foisting from above on all the states how to deal with . . . another thing that states usually know better how to . . .
> MARGE: This is what our society has done. If it sees an ill, it decides to pass a law instead of letting the community deal with it in its own way.
> FRANCINE: That's bad.
> RON: Yeah.
> MARGE: Another federal mandate coming down from Trenton, or coming down from Washington.

Another example comes from Alicia, a woman in a career-related group. Her peers say that although providing government services in other languages sounds like a good idea in principle, there are so many language minorities in the United States that it could easily get out of hand. When asked, "Where do you draw the line?" Alicia responds, "Let each region, state, county, whatever, decide where to draw the line. Obviously, in Florida, Spanish has become the predominant language in many areas. Probably Piscataway [in New Jersey] has a high Hispanic population. . . . So let each locality determine what needs to happen." Note that none of these statements indicate that the speakers see anything wrong with some communities deciding to provide materials and services in English only. Rather, they say the best approach is to let individual communities decide for themselves the language(s) in which government business will be conducted.[13]

SUMMARY

The previous examples demonstrate that the notion of an active and informed citizenry resonates with many of the participants in the study. They have an image of Americans attending political rallies, pulling levers in voting booths, and being a part of the governing process. Yet the widespread attachment to this ideal vision does not result in consensus on public policies designed to address the incorporation of language minorities into the political process. For some, this image cannot be sustained if public discourse is not conducted with one common language. For others, the image falls apart if the outlets for participation, by design, restrict involvement.[14] This complex relationship between civic republicanism and policy preferences substantiates my claim that the civic republican tradition of American identity deserves more attention in public opinion research.[15]

Ethnoculturalism

While few people will agree with overtly racist or ethnocultural statements, many still do not see ethnic minorities as Americans. They possess static definitions of American identity that do not adapt to the changing reality of the country's demographic makeup. Along these lines, many members of minority groups do not think of themselves as being American because they do not fit

[13] On August 4, 1999, the city of El Cenizo, Texas, a city where more than 60 percent of the residents speak little or no English, declared Spanish the official language for public city business. Advocates say that the ordinance is intended to connect residents with the local government and "snap the population out of its political lethargy" (McLemore 1999). It would have been interesting to hear what the supporters of local control over the decision making in this policy area would say about this development.

[14] There were also twenty-two thoughts expressing the value of knowing English that were coded as "other republican." No dominant pattern emerged from these thoughts. Some mentioned that learning English is a show of hospitality; others felt that allowing other languages in public discourse would make political corruption more likely; still others involved the simultaneous expression of multiple republican images.

[15] As in chapter 5, I checked for civic republican bias in the community service groups. For the community service groups, the mean percentage of civic republican thoughts in the policy portion of the discussion was 24, whereas the mean percentage for the other groups was 26. The mean in the female-only groups was 23, whereas the mean in the mixed-sex groups was 27.

that static image. As I showed in chapter 5, attitudes relating to this tradition were expressed regularly when the participants discussed what they think makes them American, and it turns out that they appeared frequently in the policy-related portions of the interviews as well. Some participants justify their support for the ELA by appealing to this unfortunate American tradition, and others explain their opposition by condemning it.

Ethnocultural discourse accounts for 16 percent of the policy-related thoughts analyzed here. Seventy-two percent of these thoughts accept the ethnocultural tradition and 28 percent reject it. Most anti-ethnocultural sentiments—53 percent—came from the three Hispanic groups, 25 percent came from the all-white groups, and the rest came from the heterogeneous groups. On the flip side, most endorsements—72 percent—came from the all-white groups and 25 percent came from the heterogeneous groups. Again, it is not surprising to find that ethnicity affects whether people see the ELA as a tool to promote ethnic exclusions. Yet, as before, the critiques of ethnoculturalism are not confined to Hispanics.

Table 6.5 lists aspects of ethnoculturalism included in the coding scheme along with the number of thoughts that invoke each one for each policy view. It shows that when people think there is something special about the English language or when they see ethnic minorities as not being real Americans, they tend to favor making English the official language. When, on the other hand, they disapprove of the ethnocultural tendencies of their fellow Americans and fear that this proposal will encourage those tendencies, they oppose the ELA. It also shows that ethnocultural imagery was not invoked when participants debated the merits and drawbacks of English-only ballots. The concerns that this policy raises fall squarely within the realm of civic republicanism.

ENGLISH IS AMERICAN

The most common ethnocultural idea invoked to express support for making English the official language was that the English language is an integral part of American identity. More than asserting the virtues of having a common language, these statements reflected an attachment to English in particular and account for 62 percent of all ethnocultural comments made in support of official-English and 38 percent of all ethnocultural thoughts claiming that people living in the United States should speak English.[16] A common example comes from Jacob, a member of a hobby group, who said, "If they're going to live here, they should speak our language, the language." Another comes from Denise, in a career-related organization, who argues, "It's time for the government to simply say this is a country that speaks English and that's what we're going to use as our official language." Josie, in the public-speaking

---

[16] Of the participants who used the centrality of English to American identity to argue that everyone in America should know English, 90 percent also supported the ELA elsewhere.

TABLE 6.5
Ethnoculturalism and Language Policy Preferences

Ethnocultural Categories	Official-English		English-only Ballots		All Should Know English
	For	Against	For	Against	
Acceptance of Ethnoculturalism					
English as American	23	0	0	0	26
Nostalgia/"good" vs. "bad" immigrants	5	0	0	0	18
Minorities as not American	0	0	0	0	10
Anti-immigrant sentiments	4	0	0	0	4
Blames immigrants for their "station"	0	0	0	0	1
Ascriptiveness of American identity	1	0	0	0	5
Other ethnoculturalism/ ethnocultural hybrid	4	0	2	0	1
(Subtotal)	*(37)*	*(0)*	*(2)*	*(0)*	*(65)*
Rejection of Ethnoculturalism					
Language law is ethnocultural	0	23	0	0	0
Critical of ethnocultural tendencies in America	0	11	0	0	2
Need to fight ethnoculturalism	0	2	0	0	2
Not American because not white and blonde	0	0	0	0	0
(Subtotal)	*(0)*	*(36)*	*(0)*	*(0)*	*(4)*
Total	37	36	2	0	69

group, also thinks that we should make English official because it would reaffirm her image of who Americans are. She says, "When in Rome, you do as the Romans do. You join a country. You participate in its culture. We cannot deny that we are a culture of English-speaking people."

NOSTALGIA/GOOD VS. BAD IMMIGRANTS

Another way people expressed support for the ELA and for everyone knowing English was to compare what they consider to be good immigrants with bad immigrants, or rather, those who know English with those who do not. People recalled the good old days when their relatives came through Ellis Island and worked hard at becoming American. They regret that those days are gone and that today's immigrants are of a different breed. These comparisons make up 14 percent of ethnocultural thoughts in favor of the ELA and 26 percent of ethnocultural thoughts arguing for everyone to know English.[17] Merle (quoted earlier) is critical of immigrant groups whose members do not know English, and he compares them to what he says immigrants used to be like:

> My grandmother spoke mostly Italian but your children, you told 'em, "It's so important to learn the English language," [and] I don't see that today. . . . With some groups it's like, "Well, why should I *have to* do it?"

Bill, in the same group, adds:

> One of the big differences that I see is the attitude of the people today. You know, we've had a couple of people [here] say that their parents spoke a particular language [and] they encouraged the children to learn English. In a lot of cases today, the parents do not encourage the children.

By criticizing language minorities for not living up to romanticized notions of "the good immigrant," these statements reveal exclusivist beliefs about what it takes to be an American. Statements in the next section are even more explicit in this regard.

MINORITIES AS NOT AMERICAN/ANTI-IMMIGRANT SENTIMENTS

Another way people voiced support for the ELA was to describe ethnic minorities, as a group, as being foreigners or not American. Similarly, ethnocultural support for English as the official language sometimes emerged in blatantly anti-immigrant statements. This combination of images—minorities as not American and immigrants as unwanted—reveals a belief that some people are just not able to be as American as others. Seventeen percent of all ethnocultural thoughts invoke these notions, either to support making English the official language or to say that people living in America should know English.[18] Shelly, a member of a hobby club, illustrates this entrenched ethnocultural tendency to assume that language minorities are not American when she complains about hearing other languages around town:

> There are a lot of people that don't speak good English, or understandable English, in the trades here. And as a native American, it's difficult sometimes when you go into a place and you don't understand what the person is saying, in your own country. . . . I don't understand it. And, I mean, this is my country, and English is my language, and yet I have to deal with people who do not speak it so that I can understand what they're saying.

She feels that people who do not speak English or who have accents that make their English difficult to understand are not respecting that they are guests in

---

[17] All participants who said everyone in America should know English because that's what their ancestors did and what other good immigrants do also supported the ELA elsewhere.

[18] Again, all participants who used these ethnocultural images to argue that everyone in America should know English also supported the ELA elsewhere in the discussions or on the pre-survey.

her home. It does not enter her consciousness to distinguish between ethnic minorities who are and are not citizens.

A more incisive attack comes from Leslie, a member of one of the career-related organizations, who not only disparages minorities for not knowing English but also suggests that many of them are faking it:

> Twenty years ago I never thought in a million years I'd be talking like this. If half the people who claim they don't know how to speak English were put in the situation where they had to speak English to save their lives, watch how quickly the English would come pouring out. Forgive me, God. I never thought I'd become one of these people.

When probed as to why people would not use English when they really know it, she replied, "They don't want to. They're learning that if they continue not to want to speak English, we will accommodate them," implying that language minorities have us duped and lawmakers are being taken for a ride to subsidize this un-American lifestyle.

REJECTION OF ETHNOCULTURALISM

Not all people who incorporate the language of ethnoculturalism into their vocabulary do so as a show of endorsement. As I showed in chapter 5, many people are critical of America's ethnocultural legacy. Here, objections to this tradition are common reasons for being against the ELA. Not surprisingly, anti-ethnocultural statements account for all of the ethnocultural discourse that opposed official-English legislation. This type of opposition was not confined to Hispanic participants; half of the people who relied on anti-ethnocultural sentiments to voice their opposition to the ELA were non-Hispanic whites. That said, there does seem to be a relationship between ethnicity and using anti-ethnocultural rhetoric to express opposition; 41 percent of Hispanic participants versus 10 percent of white participants used condemnation of this tradition to convey their opinions.

Anna, a Hispanic member of a community service organization, lashed out against the potential for this law to reinforce a particular caricature of Americans:

> I think [this law] sends the message to the country that we are all one people, that we are all English speaking, and by that I think there is a hidden message that we are all white, that we are all one culture. . . . I think it just sends the message that we are one people, disregarding everybody else, that we're one big, white, conservative America. That's what we say when we say we're only going to speak English.

Cheryl, a member of the historical society, offers a tamer angle on the same theme:

> I feel that there's something about this legislation that implies a threat and not only a threat but an implied message that America is for Americans. And I think that we

less and less want other people in this country, even though new immigrants are certainly contributing to the country. I think there is an underlying anti-not-born-in-this-country implication in that legislation and that I really disagree with.

Here the language issue is framed through ethnocultural imagery, and opposition is situated within that frame by refusing to accept its narrow definition of who does and does not belong.

Some people interpreted the proposed amendment as a backlash against the growing number of Hispanics in the United States. Most participants who voiced this concern were of Hispanic descent. Participants in one of the Hispanic groups in the study touched upon the anti-Hispanic tone they sensed in the ELA. The following is an excerpt of their responses when asked what they would say about the language issue to their local representative in Congress if they had his ear for five minutes. They said they would ask the politician to address their fears that the ELA is meant to remind Hispanics that they are not true Americans:

MARIA JOSE: I think I would need to know more as far as exactly what their intentions are in that bill before I could really say whether I'd be against it or not. I really want to know what are they trying to limit or are they trying to limit anything? What are the issues behind it and what the effects will be, truly.

VELMA: But they would not really say, "We are targeting Hispanics."

MARIA JOSE: That's what I'm saying. I would want to make sure, I would want to know like are there going to be . . .

JANET: There's no way you could make sure of that. You can't make sure. I would tell these people, "no." We don't have a law right now. Everything is in English anyway. . . .

MANOLO: You give them a little bit and they'll take a lot.

ANTONIO: It's a dangerous document. . . . Because of what we've been talking about, that it could be interpreted in different ways. . . .

MANOLO: It's like maybe an indirect way of white America trying to tell Hispanics to stay in their place.

SUMMARY

It would be misleading to say that certain aspects of the ethnocultural tradition are associated with support for official-English legislation while other aspects are associated with opposition. The defining element of ethnoculturalism—an ascriptive basis for national identity—is central to both policy preferences. The main difference between those who use ethnoculturalism for support and those who use it for opposition is whether they endorse or reject it. By referring to people with poor English skills as guests in the native English speakers' land or by castigating newcomers for not being more like an idealized image of "the good immigrant," people reveal that they simply do not see language minorities as Americans.

People in the focus groups are less guarded than pro-official-English activists tend to be. One won't find statements like Shelly's or Leslie's on the website for U.S. English, for example. There are indeed official-English activists who do make ethnocultural statements, but they tend to be fringe elements. Ordinary citizens, on the other hand, are not in the public eye, which permits their ethnocultural attachments to emerge. Conversely, people who use ethnoculturalism to voice opposition to the ELA object to the stereotypical American and harbor fears that making English official would only serve to burn that image into the American psyche even more than it already is.[19] They do not accept that to be an American, one needs to be a white English-speaking Protestant of Anglo-Saxon descent, but the existence of this conception of American identity provides a framework through which they interpret the merits and dangers of the ELA.

Incorporationism

In rejecting the ethnocultural conception of American identity, some participants offer an explicit alternative, one that is derived from our immigrant legacy. To understand the nature of American identity and to contemplate how the nation should address language issues, this immigrant tradition needs to be taken into account. But to confuse matters, people who reject ethnoculturalism are not the only ones to draw upon incorporationism for inspiration; that the United States is a nation of immigrants is acknowledged and respected by nearly all participants in the study. As I showed in chapter 5, one understanding of the immigrant legacy emphasizes ethnic distinctions, while another focuses on the assimilative powers of American society. Given the prominent role that incorporationism played in discussions about American identity, it makes sense to look for such discourse in debates about language policy.

It turns out, however, that the occurrence of incorporationism pales in comparison to the occurrence of liberalism, civic republicanism, and ethnoculturalism. It accounts for just 4 percent of the completed thoughts in the policy-related discussions. Only 36 thoughts both invoke incorporationism and explicitly express either support for or opposition to restrictive language policies. This number may be small, yet as table 6.6 indicates, a pattern still emerges. Table 6.6 lists the manifestations of incorporationism in the coding scheme and shows the number of thoughts that invoke each one for each policy position. The data show that the multicultural version of incorporationism

[19] Although concerns that are more appropriately labeled as liberal (such as fears of discrimination or violating rights) are behind anti-ethnocultural sentiments in some cases, the thoughts described here were couched in the language of ethnoculturalism. To be faithful to the dialogue, unless the speaker specifically mentioned phrases like "discrimination" and "rights," these thoughts were coded as being anti-ethnocultural rather than pro-liberal.

TABLE 6.6
Incorporationism and Language Policy Preferences

Incorporationist Categories	Official-English		English-only Ballots		All Should Know English
	For	Against	For	Against	
Multiculturalism					
U.S. characterized by distinct cultures	2	5	0	0	2
Important to maintain differences	0	1	0	0	5
Laments loss of culture	0	1	0	0	1
Critical of melting pot myth	0	0	0	0	0
Government to help maintain differences	0	0	0	0	0
(Subtotal)	(2)	(7)	(0)	(0)	(8)
Melting Pot Assimilationism					
U.S. characterized by cultural assimilation	0	0	0	0	7
Melting as blending/ "American" as dynamic	0	1	0	0	3
Vague references to the melting pot	1	0	0	0	2
Government to help with assimilation	3	0	0	0	1
(Subtotal)	(4)	(1)	(0)	(0)	(13)
Other incorporationism/ incorporationism hybrid	0	1	0	0	0
Total	6	9	0	0	21

is associated with opposition to language restrictions, whereas melting pot assimilationism is associated with support.[20] It also shows that this conception of national identity is not called forth to discuss the issue of bilingual voting ballots. Civic republicanism is clearly the main conception of American identity that this policy invokes.

MULTICULTURALISM

Of the nine incorporationist thoughts that emphasize cultural distinctiveness and voice an opinion about making English official, seven express opposition. An example of using multicultural sentiments to oppose the ELA comes from Maribel:

[20] Fisher's exact test yields $p < 0.148$.

If you look back into the history of the United States, many, many, many states, before they even became states, had other languages as . . . written everywhere. German was spoken in many places. Even signs, the stores, a lot of the legal documents were written in the language of many different communities that created the United States as we know it today. So we've been in contact with many different languages in this country, and laws and different other government official-use documents have been written in other languages in the past, so I don't know why now . . . [doesn't finish the sentence]

According to Maribel, there has never been a time when the American public was not characterized by a multiplicity of cultures and languages, and the country has managed to get along just fine thus far. Other thoughts that used multicultural interpretations of the incorporationist tradition to express opposition to official-English made similar arguments.

Table 6.6 shows that twenty-one thoughts invoke incorporationism to argue that people living in the United States should speak English. Eight were coded as being multicultural in nature. No single argument characterizes these thoughts. Some people said that knowing English is necessary to be truly able to celebrate and appreciate each other's cultures and backgrounds. One person said it is better to do everything in English if one can, but that accommodations should be made for the many people who cannot do everything in English. And there were still others, like Merle, who talked about the importance of knowing English to get by but also acknowledged the value of preserving one's own cultural heritage:

Well, what I'm trying to say is, I think it's so important to learn the English language. Now . . . I think people realize that it's important to keep their heritage too. I would want, if I ever have children, I would want my children to learn the Italian language, you know, and also be proficient in the English language.

Merle wants his descendants to be connected to where they came from and to be able to take pride in their Italian background. He is not talking about an evolving national character or praising the melting pot. Rather, he is aware of the need to learn English but also wants the Italian part of his heritage to remain a distinct part of the family's identity. Only about half of the participants who used multicultural discourse to say everyone should speak English indicated elsewhere that they support the ELA.[21]

MELTING POT ASSIMILATIONISM

A technique I use throughout my analysis is to examine thoughts that say everyone should speak English and to look for whether the people who invoke a given value to make that argument also indicate support for governmental regulation. If there is a perfect or near-perfect overlap, as there is in the case of people who say everyone should know English because that is what the good

---

[21] None of the multicultural statements advocated "hard" multiculturalism.

immigrants from earlier generations did, I can conclude that the value in question most likely leads to support for language restrictions on a consistent basis. If there is little or no overlap, I can conclude that the value in question points to a respect for the virtues that having a common language can bring but does not necessarily imply the next step of favoring governmental regulation. The case of melting pot assimilationism illustrates why this approach is useful. My assertion that the assimilationist version of incorporationism leads to support for language restrictions rests primarily on the fact that all people who referred to America's assimilative powers in arguing that everyone should know English also indicated elsewhere that they support the ELA.

First, notice that four of the six incorporationist statements in favor of making English the official language invoke an assimilationist stance, which suggests that this image might lead to support for official-English. But if the thirteen assimilationist thoughts in favor of everyone knowing English are spoken by people who are against the ELA, then the data would become more difficult to interpret. It turns out that all speakers who used assimilationist rhetoric to say that everyone should know English say elsewhere that they support the ELA, a pattern that is in stark contrast to the multicultural version of incorporationism. Here, people talked about how what it means to be American evolves over time, and they argued that a common language has helped the multiplicity of cultures come together to form this new thing called American identity. Learning English is seen as a part of the process of becoming American. As we have seen in many instances before, a participant's desire for people to know English slides easily into support for an official-English proposal. It is not always the case that these two sentiments go together (as we saw in the liberal case of economic opportunity), but they do in the case of melting pot assimilationism.

SUMMARY

The relationship between incorporationism and language policy preferences is difficult to untangle. The immigrant legacy does not seem to provide much help to the participants in my study as they try to make sense of complex debates about language. Instead, they primarily discuss language debates in terms of rights, economic opportunity, political participation, and America's ethnocultural past. Yet many participants describe the United States as a nation of immigrants and use incorporationism to describe what they think being American means. And the few incorporationist thoughts that do appear display rather clear patterns.

One could reasonably argue that the anti-ethnocultural statements described in the previous section are implicit endorsements of multiculturalist incorporationism. I chose to include them under the umbrella of ethnoculturalism because they do not explicitly advocate an alternative, but if those statements are counted as incorporationist, then incorporationism's share of the policy-related discourse doubles to 8 percent, with the lion's share of that portion arguing against the ELA (and ethnoculturalism's share drops from 16 to 12 percent).[22] Even so, this 8 percent still lags behind the other three. Although the image of the United States as a nation of immigrants is a powerful one, it was not spontaneously brought to bear as frequently in this policy area as liberalism, civic republicanism, and ethnoculturalism. Given the apparent affinity between the myth of the melting pot and concrete policy debates about issues that arise from ethnic change, the comparatively small number of incorporationist comments among the focus group participants when they debated the ELA is curious and suggests that further investigation into the role that this conception of national identity plays in the American mind is needed.

DELIBERATION AMID CONFLICT AND CONSENSUS

Throughout the analysis in these past two chapters, I have noted where differences in group composition (e.g., gender, ethnicity, nature of the organization) did or did not yield systematic patterns of discourse. Because one benefit of focus group methodology is the ability to examine the social nature of opinion formation, it is worth ending this chapter with another observation in this regard, particularly in light of the growing interest in deliberative democracy and debates about its relationship to conflict and consensus. In particular, deliberative democracy scholars have been interested in whether discussion leads to more or less conflict when people start out disagreeing—and when people already agree, whether discussion makes them even more extreme in their views (e.g., Mendelberg and Oleske 2000; Sanders 1997). My focus groups by no means provide definitive answers to these questions, but they do exhibit the potential for increased dogmatism when group members are in accord and for increased understanding when group members disagree.

I categorized groups as "conflict" or "consensus" on the basis of my impression of the overall discussion and on how participants responded to language policy questions on the pre-discussion survey. Six groups (three female-only, two ethnically heterogeneous) exhibited consensus in favor of official-English; two groups (both Hispanic) exhibited consensus against; and six (one female-only, one Hispanic, and one heterogeneous) exhibited conflict. I examined the impact of conflict and consensus in an exploratory fashion, by simply looking at how participants responded to a question at the end of the focus group that asked, "What is the most important topic that your group discussed?" All groups, whether characterized by conflict or consensus, said that discussing the nature of American identity was very important and that people should spend

[22] With anti-ethnocultural thoughts counted as incorporationist, Fisher's exact test yields $p < 0.001$.

more time doing it. Most groups also said they had not previously recognized the importance of language issues.

Consensus groups, whether in agreement for or against the ELA, reiterated the importance of their position. They expressed hope that other Americans would think about language policy and said that if they did, they would come to feel as the group felt. Although this is hardly strong evidence of increased dogmatism (aka group polarization), consensus groups did convey that they wanted other Americans to "see the light." Without contrasting interpretations being offered, members in consensus groups behave as Elder and Cobb (1983) would expect. Recall Elder and Cobb's assertion that people often fail to recognize that prominent symbols in the political sphere can have divergent interpretations and meanings "because all [people] are reacting to the same objective stimuli and tend to assume that the meaning they find there is intrinsic to the symbols involved and thus common to all" (10). In consensus groups, participants indeed share common interpretations of enduring symbols and assume that other Americans would share them too, if only they stopped to think about it.

Conflict groups, on the other hand, said the most important thing was to recognize not only the salience of the issue but also its complexity. The more one discusses language conflict, they argued, the less sure one becomes of his or her views. For example, Marge, in the historical society (a conflict group), said the most important part of the discussion was realizing

> that there are so many different shades of gray it's not funny. And no one head can come up with answers on any issue. And the more discussion that we can have on issues, you don't see the layers until the discussion comes out and somebody brings their point into it and it makes you think.

Conflict groups, in other words, operated as proponents of deliberative democracy would hope. People listened to and respected each other, were open to new ideas, and emerged with a more nuanced perspective. No conflict group ended with consensus for or against official-English, but they did agree that language policy is one tough and important topic.[23]

Conclusions

The four conceptions of American national identity under investigation here provide cognitive tools for Americans to interpret the issues that arise from ethnic change. The ideas associated with these conceptions featured prominently when participants explained their attitudes toward restrictive language

---

[23] Disagreement in the focus groups remained quite civil. Settings where discussants are strangers or where the policy implications are more immediate would likely exhibit more aggressive conflict, which could alter the patterns seen here (Mendelberg and Oleske 2000).

policies. People who support making English the official language and printing election ballots only in English justify these policies as ways to promote either economic self-sufficiency (liberalism), a greater sense of national and local unity, or a common basis for communication (civic republicanism). Others justify support for restrictive policies by arguing that the United States is too "balkanized," that uninformed people threaten the integrity of the voting process (civic republicanism), that the English language is an integral part of American identity, that today's immigrants are a "letdown" (ethnocultural-ism), or that language laws will help to stir the melting pot (incorpora-tionism). That the proposed legislation is not seen as crossing the sacred line between public and private (liberalism) also provides a way for people to ex-press their support. Alternatively, people are more likely to oppose restrictive policies if they fear that these laws will violate civil rights (liberalism), exclude minorities from the political process (civic republicanism), or promote the idea that Americans should all look and sound alike (ethnoculturalism). Oth-ers oppose the ELA when they think that it would be an affront to America's immigrant legacy (incorporationism). Finally, people also oppose the ELA when they feel that language issues should be dealt with on a community-by-community basis (civic republicanism).

This analysis demonstrates that enduring conceptions of what it means to be an American affect how people interpret public policies that address issues of language and immigration, but that the relationship between identity and opinion is not as straightforward as previous research would suggest. The lib-eral, civic republican, and incorporationist conceptions of American identity are internally conflictual, and ethnoculturalism is contested. These tensions have been overlooked by more traditional survey-based analyses. It turns out that the only straightforward relationship between identity and language pol-icy preferences is that when ethnoculturalism is endorsed, it leads to support for restrictive language policies and when it is rejected, it leads to opposition. Endorsements of liberal, civic republican, or incorporationist norms could go either way, depending on the particular aspect of each one that comes to mind, and the ethnocultural tradition provides a target for some of the most vehement opposition to making English the official language.

So why is it that people sometimes employ civic traditions in seemingly contradictory ways? What factors determine whether a person will zero in on freedom of speech while another will concentrate on English as a means of achieving economic success? Why does a concern for an informed citizenry lead to support for official-English for some people but to opposition for others? While there are many potential explanations, it is very likely that individual-level social and demographic factors play a key role in determining these trajectories. Ethnicity, for example, seems to be a potent determinant of preferences and of the justifications for those preferences among the Hispanic participants, although it was less straightforward as a determinant for whites.

The kinds of independent variables used in the statistical models in chapter 4 are all worthy contenders in explaining whether there is any systematic component to the findings described here. As Chavez (2001) writes:

> Key symbols may be universally recognized within a society but the meanings attached to a symbol may be subject to contestation, reformulation, or refraction by the reader . . . because readers bring with them different histories and power positions within society. Issues of gender, race, class, age, language, immigrant history, and citizenship status all frame the give and take that forms the process by which meaning is communicated. (36)

Focus groups, however, are limited in the extent to which they can isolate the independent role each of these factors plays for individuals in shaping how national symbols are interpreted and employed. They are best at revealing the patterns discussed in this chapter, but are less useful for examining these individual-level relationships. The challenge now is to combine the insights from the focus groups with the strengths of survey analysis to pursue the questions raised by my findings. Yet as I have argued as various points, existing surveys are not up to the task. Thus, an important next step in this research agenda will be to design surveys that are capable of carrying out such tests and of exploring how endorsements of particular conceptions of American identity interact with individual-level characteristics.

The matrix of influences regarding how symbols are interpreted and how they factor into the opinion formation process includes individual-level demographic and attitudinal factors, the prevailing norms of the day, and the framing of particular policy debates by elites and activists. The analysis in this book has so far taken several steps in putting these pieces together in the realm of language policy. I have focused on establishing the prevailing norms regarding national identity, examining how those norms are invoked by elites to advance their preferred policies, and showing how ordinary Americans rely on them when sorting out their views on this complex and contentious issue area. The individual-level determinants need further study, a task that depends on future survey analysis with appropriate question design. The focus groups do not allow for neat conclusions about the causal story underlying individual-level patterns. But they do allow relationships between broad conceptions of American identity, their particular manifestations, and policy preferences to be studied in a way that surveys do not.

The analysis in this chapter points to some other conclusions that are also worthy of future investigation. One in particular is that the factors that drive support for one policy may differ from the factors that drive support for another. Two seemingly similar policies can have different levels and *causes* of support among the public. As tables 6.3 through 6.6 show, the issue of bilingual ballots does not elicit liberalism, ethnoculturalism, or incorporationism. The cognitive link between ballots and participation appears to be strictly civic republican in nature. The ideals embodied in the civic republican tradition provide a more useful framework than the ideals embodied in the other traditions for thinking about the merits and drawbacks of printing election materials in more than one language. This phenomenon is even more pronounced in the discussions regarding bilingual education, which were largely driven by concerns about effectiveness rather than identity, as I demonstrate in chapter 7. In short, the considerations that inform preferences will vary even though the policies being examined are derived from a common political issue. I elaborate on the differences across policy domains and on other factors that are at work in the processes discussed thus far in the next chapter.

CHAPTER SEVEN

Mixed Messages

HYBRIDS, TAXES, AND THE CASE OF BILINGUAL EDUCATION

I DEMONSTRATED in the previous chapter that a model of American identity consisting of liberalism, civic republicanism, ethnoculturalism, and incorporationism provides a compelling and fruitful model for analyzing attitudes about language policy. The content analysis of focus group transcripts revealed that each conception is invoked regularly to justify policy preferences and that each one has a complex and contested relationship to how people feel about the unity or multiplicity of languages in the public sphere. Yet it also revealed that a sizable proportion of the thoughts are not accounted for by a model that only looks at pure expressions of these sentiments. The remaining portions of the discourse can be grouped into three separate and intriguing clusters, and these clusters are the focus of this chapter.

First, elements from liberalism, civic republicanism, ethnoculturalism, and incorporationism are often blended in practice, both among elites and among ordinary Americans when they discuss what being American means and how they feel about restrictive language policies. One goal of this chapter, then, is to analyze the extent to which hybrid expressions are used to explain views on language policy and the direction in which they do so. This analysis provides a more complete understanding of the relationship between identity and opinions than has been established previously and allows me to investigate the role of symbolic racism, or racial resentment, in debates about language and ethnic change. In addition, the possible existence of "symbolic nativism," a construct analogous to symbolic racism, is explored.

Second, public opinion scholars often test whether symbolic predispositions are more powerful than tangible or economic concerns in influencing how people feel about immigration, ethnic change, and minorities more generally. Conventional wisdom holds that short-term, self-regarding, material interests dictate human behavior. Much effort has been devoted to testing the validity of this view of human nature. In light of this effort, I examine whether the participants in my study invoke tangible economic issues when they discuss making English the official language. Such concerns did not arise much during the focus groups and were always associated with a preference for language restrictions when they did. The relative weakness of self-interest as a factor shaping opinions is in line with much public opinion research. I maintain, as others do, that group interest is a more powerful force linking interests and attitudes than self-interest.

Third, I address the extraordinary extent to which the issue of bilingual education does not fit within the general argument that conceptions of American identity should dominate discussions about language policy. Conversations about bilingual education primarily emphasized concerns about effectiveness, not identity. A detailed description of this finding and speculation about its cause constitute the final section of the chapter.

Privileged, Responsible, White, Immigrant Citizens and Language

The coding procedure guiding the analysis here is the same one used in earlier chapters. Each completed thought was marked to indicate whether it combined more than one conception of American identity and to indicate which conceptions were being combined. Then, each thought was marked to indicate to which policy it referred, if any, and whether it expressed support for or opposition to that policy. And again, there is a fourth policy option for thoughts that express support for the idea that everyone in the United States should speak English but do not explicitly endorse a particular policy. I want to reiterate that the hybrid categories are not simply to catch thoughts where coders could not decide which conception of American identity was being invoked. Unclear thoughts were coded as being just that. Rather, hybrid categories are for thoughts that clearly mix elements of more than one conception of American national identity.

There is no reason to expect citizens to talk about complex political issues in a way that fits neatly into theoretically delineated categories. I showed in chapter 5 that hybrid thoughts constitute just under 10 percent of all substantive discourse in the portion of the focus groups that deal with what participants think American identity means. I therefore expected hybrid thoughts to feature at least as prominently in the policy-related discussions. But would these hybrids lead to support for or opposition to restrictive language policies? I showed in chapter 6 that liberalism, civic republicanism, and incorporationism can all be used to justify either support for or opposition to making English the official language, and thus I am unable to make a blanket prediction about what combinations of these ideals will do. Whenever ethnoculturalism is expressed jointly with another tradition, I expect it to trump its companion(s). In other words, a person who combines an endorsement of an ethnocultural conception of American identity with, say, an emotional attachment to political participation should favor the English Language Amendment (ELA) and English-only ballots. Likewise, a rejection of the ethnocultural conception of American identity should trump whatever else may be included in that statement. Why do I grant such power to ethnoculturalism? The analysis in chapter 6 showed ethnoculturalism to have the clearest and most consistent influence on language policy preferences: endorsement leads to support and rejection leads to opposition. I expect this relationship to hold and that liberal, civic republican, or incorporationist ideals will be used to bolster the policy preference being advocated.

In the end, hybrid thoughts make up just over 8 percent ($n = 139$) of the policy-related discourse (and 12 percent of the policy-related discourse expressing an explicit opinion for or against official-English or English-only ballots. Continuing the trend from chapter 5, liberalism and civic republicanism appear together most often, making up 31 percent of the hybrid discourse. The proportions of the remaining possible permutations range from 5 percent (ethnoculturalism and incorporationism) to 22 percent (civic republicanism and ethnoculturalism). Table 7.1 lists the different hybrid categories in the coding scheme and shows the number of thoughts that invoke each one for each policy position.[1] It is difficult to discern a clear pattern from the numbers alone, except to say that the combination of civic republican and ethnocultural concerns seems to promote support for language restrictions, as do any hybrid thoughts involving incorporationism. In the following sections, I look at these thoughts in more detail in order to get a better sense of the underlying phenomena that these numbers signify.

LIBERALISM AND CIVIC REPUBLICANISM

Thoughts that combine elements of liberalism and civic republicanism are the most common form of policy-related hybrid, although they refer only to the ELA, not to English-only ballots. On balance, this combination leads respondents to oppose the ELA, but it also leads them to say that everyone in the United States should know English. Recall that I created this fourth "policy" option to capture cases where a person uses a symbolic predisposition to justify why he believes that everyone in the United States should speak English but also thinks that governmental regulation should be avoided. At first glance, it seems that the joint expression of liberal and civic republican sentiments may constitute such a case. But looking at the particular thoughts involved reveals a more complex pattern.

First, it turns out that twelve of the thirteen people who combine liberal and civic republican language to say that everyone should know English indicate elsewhere that they *support* making English the official language. This overlap perhaps suggests that two different types of liberal-civic republican arguments are being employed—one to support restrictions and one to oppose them. However, I find that people who use this hybrid to support official-English and people who use it to oppose restrictions both rely on the same type

[1] As in chapter 6, I only look at the ELA and English-only ballots here. Bilingual education is addressed separately later in this chapter. Fisher's exact test yields $p < 0.01$ for official-English, $p > 0.1$ for English-only ballots.

TABLE 7.1
Hybrid Thoughts and Language Policy Preferences

Type of Hybrid	Official-English		English-only Ballots		All Should Know English
	For	Against	For	Against	
Liberalism and civic republicanism	3	13	0	0	16
Liberalism and ethnoculturalism	3	2	3	0	7
Civic republicanism and ethnoculturalism	8	1	2	1	13
Liberalism and incorporationism	2	0	0	0	5
Civic republicanism and incorporationism	2	0	0	0	10
Ethnoculturalism and incorporationism	1	0	0	0	5
Other hybrid	3	1	1	0	8
Total	22	17	6	1	64

of argument. Whether they oppose the ELA or say that everyone should speak English, these thoughts all unite statements about the need for English for economic success with concerns about language minorities being excluded from the political process and from the community. For example, Robert, a member of a hobby club, uses both liberal ideas about personal success and civic republican ideas about being part of the political process to argue against the ELA. He says:

Well, I think it's beneficial to have a record of doings with government in English. But I think the thing that concerns me the most is people that don't speak English as a first language, giving them access to government and allowing them to transact some level of business in their own native language. It shouldn't be a hindrance to those people getting ahead, to force people to transact business with the government in English.

He is concerned about the ability both to access government and to get ahead, and he worries that both will be hindered if English is declared the official language. Yet as Katherine, a woman in a charity group, demonstrates, those same concerns can lead a person to say that everyone should know English. In response to people in her group telling the stories of relatives who worked hard to learn English when they came to the United States from Europe, she says:

That's what you need to do. You need to learn the language and learn what is here. And if you want to get ahead and you want to get along in this country, just as if we went to another country and we were going to live there, then we would have to learn that language to be able to live there.

Both getting ahead and being a part of what is going on in the community at large are considered to be quite important. For some, this means that language minorities would be denied those opportunities if English were to be made official. For others, the onus is on the immigrants to keep up with the dominant society.

The pattern revealed here—the use of both liberal ideas about economic freedom and opportunity and civic republican ideas about community involvement to express divergent preferences—provides a concrete and salient example of the phenomenon that Edelman (1985 [1964]) and Elder and Cobb (1983) describe. Ideas about economic opportunity and about the ability of all Americans to take part in the political process are everywhere in American society. Most Americans are not only aware of these myths, but also believe that such opportunities and abilities are unique and positive components of what makes the United States stand apart from other countries. The universal worship of a civic myth, however, does not guarantee the uniform assessment of its implications. As Elder and Cobb write:

> The meaning of the message is heavily colored by the significance to the receiver of the symbols involved and his or her own interpretation of their meaning. The same symbol may communicate different things to different people. . . . This heterogeneity of interpretation is likely to go unrecognized, however, because all are reacting to the same objective stimuli and tend to assume that the meaning they find there is intrinsic to the symbols involved and thus common to all. (10)

In this case, participants agree on what the symbolic myths mean but not on what those meanings suggest they do about citizens and residents who do not know English. A complex relationship between individual-level factors, prevailing societal norms, and elite framing, combined with the universal acceptance of the myth (which then obscures multiple interpretations), leads to patterns such as these.

LIBERALISM AND ETHNOCULTURALISM

Antiblack sentiments combined with an adherence to traditional liberal norms like individualism and the work ethic constitute what has been termed "symbolic racism" in the public opinion literature. It is argued that symbolic racism has become a dominant influence over white Americans' attitudes toward racial politics over the past few decades (e.g., Kinder and Sears 1981; Kinder and Sanders 1996). Given the consistency of such findings across studies, we might expect symbolic racism to play a role in attitudes about policies that address the needs of nonblack minorities. If it does, it would be represented by the simultaneous expression of liberal and ethnocultural beliefs. In other words, it would involve participants harboring anti-immigrant sentiments, adhering to ascriptive notions of who Americans are, and believing that new immigrants violate cherished liberal norms. Symbolic racism, when expressed, should be associated with support for language restrictions.

Table 7.1 shows that symbolic racism, as described earlier, did not appear often, although it does seem to be associated with support for restrictive policies and the idea that everyone in the United States should speak English. That said, two of the liberal and ethnocultural statements in favor of everyone knowing English were critical of America's ethnocultural legacy. These thoughts involved speakers saying that it is important to know English because minorities are destined to be mistreated in this ethnocultural society or that knowing English is a weapon for keeping discrimination at bay. For example, Luz, a member of a community service organization, says, "When we have kids we have a tendency of raising our kids in English because we have fears that they may be treated different and we want them to be as equal because they were born here." Luz's children—though of Hispanic descent—are Americans, born and raised in the United States, and thus deserve equal treatment, the same as any other American. But Luz knows better—she knows that reality differs from the ideal and feels that knowing English could mitigate disparities in treatment.

Anne, a woman in a charity group, provides one of the few instances of classic symbolic racism being used to justify support for making English the official language. She says, "[Mexicans in California] complain they need more tax dollars for this or that because they're not equal. Well, they make themselves separate [by not learning English]. So it is personal responsibility." But this type of argument did not come up as often as I thought it might or as often as empirical symbolic racism research would suggest. To think about why, I turned to another study involving focus group research in the suspicion that the answer might lie in type of results that different methodologies can provide. Roberta Sigel used both focus groups and a telephone survey to study how women view gender relations (1996). In most instances, the findings from each methodology complement the other nicely, bolstering the other's strengths and making up for each other's weaknesses. Sigel finds, however, that nearly all of the women in the focus groups said that they personally have been victims of gender discrimination and are quite resentful of it, while few of the telephone respondents claimed to be victims or displayed any anger. She attributes this finding to the more personal and nondirective (i.e., loosely guided and open-ended) nature of the focus group, which facilitates an emphasis on personal experience and creates a comfortable environment in which to express anger—something women are socialized to avoid, especially when talking on the phone to a stranger.

In the present study, it might be that participants simply use more overtly exclusionary rhetoric than they would when on the phone with an anonymous interviewer, thus eliminating the need to express resentment in terms that invoke traditional liberal norms. Though many participants do not think that Hispanics are simply unable to become Americans (at least at the level of awareness), their language is often ethnocultural in nature with no hint of liberalism in sight. This tendency is evident in the extent to which participants refused to distinguish between recent immigrants and minorities who are also U.S. citizens, a tendency that survey research has not sought to document. The inability of participants to consider this important distinction could explain why we see less symbolic racism and more pure ethnoculturalism. It could be that symbolic racism and the type of ethnocultural discourse I find are actually quite similar. Both illustrate that people no longer explicitly refer to ascriptive characteristics when talking about natural ability or the granting of rights and liberties, but an examination of a more subtle kind shows that such ascriptive beliefs are still common. The different methodologies—surveys and focus groups—result in different manifestations of this subtlety.

Another possibility is that the transfer of theories developed to study how white Americans feel about policies aimed at reducing inequalities between blacks and whites, such as affirmative action, is not entirely appropriate. The social and historical factors that have characterized the relationship between blacks and whites in America and that made the emergence of symbolic racism possible (see Mendelberg 2001) may be unique to that particular facet of American society. In other words, the modern ways in which whites disparage African-Americans or view race relations more generally might not apply directly to how the dominant American culture views the increasing Latino and Asian populations. The phenomenon of holding anti-minority views and believing that immigrants violate cherished American values may still have a role to play in debates about language policy, but rather than being liberal in nature, the cherished values in question might instead be civic republican or incorporationist.

CIVIC REPUBLICANISM AND ETHNOCULTURALISM

I wrote earlier about the affinity between an ascriptive vision of American society and a preference for well-functioning self-governing communities—and about how such an affinity can lead to exclusions in the name of the public good. This affinity did not appear much in the general discussions of what being American means, yet it plays a larger role in discussions about regulating language use. Table 7.1 indicates that civic republican–ethnocultural hybrids are quite common and, in general, lead respondents to favor language restrictions. This type of hybrid accounts for 36 percent of all hybrid thoughts in favor of the ELA and 20 percent of all hybrid thoughts indicating that everyone in the United States should know English. All participants who used this hybrid to say everyone should know English indicated elsewhere that they support the ELA. Thus, unlike the liberal-republican or liberal-ethnocultural cases, the civic republican–ethnocultural mix appears to be uniformly associated with a preference for language restrictions.

This pattern suggests that a different type of symbolic interaction than the more familiar one involving liberalism and ethnoculturalism may be a factor here. Symbolic politics research points to liberalism and ethnoculturalism as providing the vocabulary that makes modern expressions of racism possible, but perhaps the joint expression of civic republicanism and ethnoculturalism forms a more compelling attitudinal construct in this context. The lack of additional data prevents my analysis of this construct from being more than speculative at this point. More directed research designs are needed to investigate whether the simultaneous expression of civic republican and ethnocultural beliefs constitutes "symbolic nativism," a feeling that immigrants threaten cherished civic republican norms and the public good, and if it represents a modern way to express anti-immigrant views, just as symbolic racism is a modern way to express antiblack views.

Many of the thoughts in this category combined the need for a common language in order to have a well-functioning society with the belief that English in particular is a necessary part of being American. Other thoughts involved explicit comparisons between immigrants from the turn of the century and immigrants today, with speakers arguing that immigrants today do not work as hard at pursuing the good of the larger community as earlier, "better" immigrants did. These thoughts do not demonstrate in any conclusive way the validity of my symbolic nativism proposition, but the prevalence of civic republican–ethnocultural hybrids suggests it is an idea worth investigating further in future analyses. And as I discuss later, adding the civic myth of incorporationism to ethnoculturalism takes this line of reasoning even further.

INCORPORATIONISM HYBRIDS

Twenty-five thoughts involve speakers simultaneously invoking incorporationism and at least one other conception of American identity. I discuss all twenty-five together because, as table 7.1 illustrates, they all express support either for the ELA or for everyone knowing English. Without exploring these thoughts in more detail, the numbers alone suggest that they most likely emphasize melting pot assimilationism rather than multiculturalism, since the analysis in chapter 6 showed that the former tends to be associated with support for language restrictions, while the latter tends to be associated with opposition. It turns out, however, that many of these hybrids stress cultural diversity and the challenge of maintaining the diversity that makes the United States unique while simultaneously promoting other traditional American values. This pattern is particularly true of the civic republican–incorporationist hybrids, which stress the importance of fostering the common bonds that allow for the maintenance of a coherent self-governing society in such a diverse setting.

A typical example comes from Mary Jane, a member of the charity group, who says, "We are just a really rich nation in differences in people, but there's got to be some kind of unification." This sentiment invokes the fear of the "balkanization" of America described in the previous chapter, but it does so while explicitly referencing, and even celebrating, the nation's plethora of cultural backgrounds. And in some cases, speakers introduced their reverence for cultural assimilation while simultaneously praising diversity *and* expressing fears of diminishing community cohesion. Such hybrids reveal the complex ways in which the political culture can pull citizens in different directions as they try to interpret the social and political changes they see around them. It has been well established that the routine demands of daily life alone can prevent citizens from holding constrained political views. In the absence of detailed knowledge and ideological sophistication, people rely heavily on long-standing predispositions to help them arrive at policy preferences. But those long-standing predispositions are often in tension with one another, and the focus group participants illustrate the frustration that can result from such conflict. How are people to reconcile the competing calls for diversity and cohesion—two enduring civic myths that they endorse? Among the speakers who invoked this particular combination of ideals, the English language seems to provide what they need in order to reach a compromise. If people can at least talk to each other in the same language, then perhaps the dangers of diversity can be kept at bay.

Ethnoculturalism was sometimes added to this mix of concerns, with speakers criticizing today's immigrants for expressly avoiding assimilation. They compared today's immigrants with immigrants of old, or today's Latino immigrants with other immigrant groups, and blamed them for not allowing the melting pot to do its work. The following extended exchange from one of the career-related groups provides an example. It begins with Paula, who has two adopted children from India, explaining why regulating language has become more imperative now than it was in previous generations:

> PAULA: My grandparents were forced to speak English and that's how they learned. They were forced to speak English, they made their children speak English. So they learned. The attitude [today] is different. And the cultural isolation is very different. There isn't that feeling of incorporation. I'm really not quite sure why that has happened, but it has happened. Yet at the same time there are other nationalities and people of ethnic backgrounds that are still coming over that are assimilating like that. Look at the Indian population. Not just my children, but the Indian population has come over speaking a very different language. Even when they learned to speak English, because of the way they speak their native language, their accents are very difficult. And yet they strive to speak English. And they've assimilated into the culture and the economy so much faster by participating in . . .

LESLIE: That's because they have the desire to assimilate. The cultural desire. Just like the Europeans did.

PAULA: That's right. They want to participate as Americans and they have an appreciation for what they are getting here and they don't want to use it, they want to participate in it. And they're assimilating so much more easily than the people that . . . I don't know why they want to stay like that, but it seems like that particular comparison is a pretty obvious example that if you want to fit in and you speak the language, people are willing to accept you. As different as the Indian people are . . . they speak English and they have heavy accents and they still wear their beautiful Indian garb, and nobody holds it against them because in many ways they participate and they speak the language. I think it's holding the Hispanic populations back.

LESLIE: That's right. It is.

The entire exchange contains a variety of symbolic civic myths, including civic republicanism (participation) and liberalism (economic opportunity). Yet Paula and Leslie explicitly target Hispanics as not doing their part, as actively resisting the melting pot process that they see as being a central component of becoming American. Hispanics, as a group, are seen as not knowing English and as consciously working against learning it. Paula and Leslie see this as a fundamental difference between Hispanic immigrants today and European immigrants of earlier generations. These types of complaints were not especially common, but again, whether this type of preference justification might in fact be more widespread and constitute an immigration analogue to symbolic racism is something that needs to be explored further than the data at hand will allow.

SUMMARY

It is important to remember that the number of thoughts coded as hybrids represents a lower bound of sorts. My coding procedure does not take into account that a person may invoke one tradition to explain her view at one point in the conversation and then invoke a different tradition at a later point. It only captures those thoughts that combine elements of more than one tradition at one moment of the discussion. Participants are not displaying ideological innocence when they incorporate more than one tradition into their decision-making calculus. On the contrary, they are showing that they follow their leaders quite well, leaders who tell them that liberalism, civic republicanism, ethnoculturalism, and incorporationism all shape what being American means. Each tradition provides distinct predictions and prescriptions, yet policy makers and citizens often do not observe the boundaries imposed by theorists. To date, this phenomenon has not been modeled in survey-based analyses; to do so would require separate measures for each tradition and allowing for interactions among them.

Tax and Spend: The Role of Interests

A rival hypothesis to theories of symbolic politics contends that policy preferences will be shaped not by the myths and values associated with conceptions of American identity but rather by concerns about tangible interests. This hypothesis is often tested using measures of both individual-level and aggregate-level economic concerns.[2] It has also been tested with noneconomic measures of self-interest in specific policy domains, such as whether gun owners are more opposed to gun control measures than non–gun owners and whether smokers are more opposed to cigarette taxes than nonsmokers (Wolpert and Gimpel 1998; Green and Gerken 1989). It has been generally understood in these analyses that self-interest should be defined narrowly in order for it to be a meaningful concept. Its operationalization is usually restricted to the desire to protect or promote the short-term material interests of oneself and one's family. If the definition is expanded such that any action that is taken to satisfy any individual need, including psychic needs, is said to be evidence of self-interested behavior, then the concept ceases to provide any leverage as an analytical tool.

Since human nature is widely viewed as consisting almost entirely of the pursuit of self-interest (narrowly defined), public opinion scholars have logically tested whether self-interest is indeed a causal factor driving attitudes and behaviors. For the most part, the self-interest hypothesis fails to perform well, despite its intuitive appeal. Sears and Funk (1990) explain that short-term tangible concerns are more likely to shape preferences when the costs and benefits associated with a policy are both clear and substantial and when political leaders expressly politicize self-interest (e.g., Reagan asking, "Are you better off now than you were four years ago?"). But costs and benefits are rarely clear or substantial, and Americans in general are not inclined to blame the government for their personal economic (mis)fortunes (Sniderman and Brody 1977; Feldman 1982; Mutz 1998), a combination of factors that works against the ability of tangible cost-benefit calculations to influence policy preferences.

It is unclear whether an official-English policy is likely to invoke tangible concerns. It is entirely possible that any given individual will expect the tax burden resulting from the provision of multilingual materials to be severe and that politicians and interest groups will politicize the economic aspects of the issue. For instance, the cost of providing government services in other languages is among the many reasons the interest group U.S. English cites as its motivation for supporting official-English policies. Basing its calculations on an estimate that Canada spends three cents per citizen per day to provide government services in French and English, the U.S. English website notes that

[2] See Sears and Funk (1990) for an excellent overview of "symbols versus self-interest" research.

the American equivalent, if the United States were to adopt language policies similar to those in Canada, would total over $3 billion per year. The site then lists all of the other things that this large sum of money could buy, including 354,986,558 American flags (3 × 5 nylon), 64,102,709 prescriptions, 119,931 new teachers, and 106,673,759 copies of the latest *Harry Potter* book.[3] Likewise, the English First website lists three primary goals, one of which is to "eliminate costly and ineffective multilingual policies." This kind of framing could indeed lead people to think about language policy in terms of economic costs.

But in reality, the individual-level economic impact of providing services in other languages is unnoticeable, and the comparison with Canada is overblown. Moreover, most of the existing state-level official-English policies have had little, if any, noticeable impact other than increasing ethnic tensions (Tatalovich 1995). Therefore, it is also reasonable to expect that short-term tangible interests will play an insignificant role in focus group discussions about official-English policies. Thus, I did not expect these concerns to appear often, but when they did, simple logic suggests that they would be used to justify support for language restrictions, with participants arguing that financing bilingual programs costs them and the government too much money. To evaluate the validity of these expectations, I included a code for thoughts that invoked the financial and economic burden of multilingualism.

Relative to the symbolic predispositions that have been the focus of the analysis thus far, economic concerns emerged only infrequently during the policy-related portion of the focus groups. They account for only 2.5 percent of the thoughts that refer to one of the three policies or to the idea that everyone should speak English (see table 6.2). Most, twenty-four thoughts, refer to the ELA, four to English-only ballots, five to bilingual education, and eight to everyone knowing English. Of the twenty-four economics-based thoughts that refer to the ELA, only ten explicitly offer an opinion and, not surprisingly, all ten voice support. Likewise, all thoughts that refer to English-only ballots support the idea. Finally, all participants who brought up economic concerns to say that everyone in the United States should speak English indicated explicit support for the ELA elsewhere. Recall that the discussions began with the moderator reading the proposed ELA and asking participants how they felt about it. Participants were not prompted to respond with concerns about American identity; if they wanted to talk about how much bilingual programs cost, they were not discouraged from doing so.

An example of an economic justification rather than an identity-based justification for one's views comes from June, a member of the public-speaking group. At the end of each focus group, participants were asked what they would say to their representative or senator about language issues if they had

---

[3] Figures as listed on the U.S. English website (www.usenglish.org) on August 16, 2003.

his or her ear for five minutes. June said she would advise Senator Toricelli (D-NJ) to bear in mind the costs associated with not requiring government to conduct its business only in English. She said:

> I'm just going to go with the economics again. It's an economically based . . . We're spending far too much money . . . in my opinion, we're spending far too much money on multiple amounts of languages and those particular things. I'm not saying cut out all the funding, but just be more careful with what you spend the money on.

Another example comes from Denise, a woman in a career-related organization, who had the following exchange with the moderator:

> DENISE: I don't know what the source of this proposal was, but I think. . . . This is my perception; it's not fact. But I hear stories about [how] everything now has to be printed in different languages, which is foolish and expensive. So I just think it's gotten out of hand.
> MODERATOR: And why is it foolish?
> DENISE: It's foolish because these are generally programs run by the government that we pay for.

For these women, a simple cost-benefit analysis in the truest sense of the phrase leads them to think multilingual materials are a waste of money that could be better spent elsewhere. What they think being American means is irrelevant. The programs are simply seen as an inefficient or misguided allocation of resources.

Although such reasoning was not nearly as common as identity-based arguments overall, it turns out that concerns about government spending were the only real rival to civic republicanism, though a distant one, whenever the topic of English-only ballots was discussed, accounting for 6 percent of the ballot-related comments in which an opinion was offered. An example comes from Brian, one of June's colleagues in the public-speaking group, who said, "Today we spend hundreds and hundreds of millions of dollars on separate balloting of votes in separate languages. Some places, over two hundred different languages—I'm [thinking of] California. It is insane." Unfortunately, the Voting Rights Act does not require covered jurisdictions to keep track of costs associated with providing bilingual voting assistance. Still, in 1997, the General Accounting Office (GAO) issued a report detailing the information it was able to compile. Although the report's estimate of the cost of providing such assistance in the 1996 election is imprecise, it does suggest that "hundreds and hundreds of millions of dollars" is an implausibly high assessment. The report also indicated that California's twenty-one covered jurisdictions provided assistance in only six (not two hundred) languages other than English: Chinese, Vietnamese, Japanese, Spanish, Filipino, and Wintun, a Native American language spoken in Colusa County (U.S. General Accounting Office 1997). Would Brian and others who used this type of argument still oppose bilingual ballots if they knew how much was actually spent on them and how few language groups receive assistance? This is a question I cannot answer here, but I can say with a fair degree of confidence that the people who said we spend too much on bilingual materials have no idea how much we really spend. Perhaps they would readjust their accepted level of spending to have a lower threshold, or they may say that any amount is too much, or they might even change their policy preference in light of new and accurate information, but this is an empirical question for another day (e.g., Hochschild 2001; Theiss-Morse 2003a). What can be said at this point is that the nature of the policy in question seems to affect the extent to which cost-benefit calculations will be invoked, even within a single issue domain. Bilingual ballots is an issue where the tangible costs are perhaps more obvious, or at least easier to imagine, than official-English. And as Sears and Funk would lead us to expect, participants were proportionally more likely to invoke economic concerns in their discussions of the former than the latter.

Another valid question is whether invoking economic concerns is simply a cover for less admirable motivations, such as racism or anti-immigrant sentiments, especially in light of some people's willingness to rely on grossly inaccurate information about the costs of programs and the number of language groups to which assistance is provided. While there is no way for me to know for sure, I can say that only ten out of eighteen people who raised tax concerns used the language of ethnoculturalism elsewhere (in any form, including hybrids) to support official-English or English-only ballots. This imperfect relationship suggests either that the remaining eight participants are flawless in their self-monitoring abilities or that it would be premature to conclude that tangible concerns about government spending are simply a façade masking exclusionary beliefs.

SELF-INTEREST OR GROUP INTEREST?

In the case of language policy, as in the case of so many other policies, it is more accurate to view interests working on a symbolic group level rather than on a material individual level. Opinions are said to be shaped by group interest when people's concerns about the well-being of the group or about the relative standing of their group in society determine support for a particular policy. Kinder and Sanders (1996) and Bobo (2000), for example, note that Anglo opinion about affirmative action is shaped, in part, by concerns about whether it will hurt whites' chances for getting promotions or for getting admitted to universities. Other research has shown that demographic context, such as the changes that result when immigration patterns lead to more contact between people of different ethnic backgrounds, can also promote the salience of group interest. The classic example of this kind of context-related group interest, sometimes called "realistic group conflict," is Key's (1949) description of the southern Black Belt—areas in southern states that had both the highest proportion of blacks and the most severe racial conflict. Greater contact, it is argued, leads to greater competition between groups over scarce resources, such as jobs or status. More recent studies confirm that contact with members of different ethnic groups can promote group-interested beliefs and behavior and, consequently, group conflict (e.g., Forbes 1997; Glaser 1994; Hero 1998).[4]

Most of the research on group interest and group conflict has focused on the conflict that arises between different ethnic groups. The group identity under investigation here, however, is an ethnic one only for those who define the United States ethnoculturally. When the content of the national identity is defined in such a way, then the findings of group conflict studies should apply. That is, invoking ethnoculturalism to justify one's support for making English the official language can be interpreted as a response to perceived threats to the in-group's place in the social hierarchy by an out-group, which in this case consists of nonwhite, non-English-speaking immigrants.

But what about when national identity is defined in nonethnic terms? Do perceived threats to one's group, when that group is defined in terms of a liberal or civic republican ideology, promote policy preferences aimed at protecting that identity? In these cases, the out-group can be difficult to identify. For instance, for people who oppose the ELA because they feel it would undermine America's liberal character, the threat is not prompted by extra-national groups but rather by internal interest groups or politicians promoting their own efforts to protect their own cherished view of American national identity. Yet as my arguments throughout the book should make clear, the impulse to protect one's group is quite universal and persists even when the group's identity is defined ideologically. This manifestation of group interest does not always conform to the more traditional ethnically based in-group–out-group conflicts that so much of public opinion scholarship investigates, but the desire to protect a cherished identity when it is threatened is still at work. Regardless of the particular identity content being protected or the particular entity that is seen to be a threat, the perception of threat promotes defense.

I do not, however, see group interest as being at odds with symbolic politics because, as I discussed in chapter 2, whether the perceived threats are real or not is largely irrelevant to their effects. Mere contact does not constitute an actual threat, but it can generate a widespread *perception* of threat, and that is what really matters. For example, Kinder and Sanders (1996) found that whites who were resentful of blacks were more likely to perceive threats (at both the individual level and the group level) than others, and that the perception was then a significant predictor of anti–affirmative action attitudes more so than objective measures of social standing. The authors conclude, "Threat is not so much a clear-eyed perception as it is an emotion-laden atti-

[4] See Forbes (1997) for a comprehensive evaluation of the competing hypotheses that increased contact between different groups will lead to more (or less) conflict between them.

tude" (90). Likewise, Huddy and Sears (1995) found that whites with anti-Latino views were more likely to perceive economic and educational threats from Latinos than were whites without anti-Latino views, controlling for a variety of demographic factors, including income and having children in heavily Latino schools. They write, "Perceived educational conflict had a strong impact on opposition to bilingual education programs but did not arise directly from any personal threats posed by them" (142). Oliver and Mendelberg (2000) also argue that the impact of context works "less through realistic conflict over resources than through psychological states that produce out-group animosity" (589). In other words, it is people's reactions to contact with different groups that matter, not necessarily whether contact actually generates threats to either tangible or abstract goods. These findings recall Edelman's (1985) observation that "whatever seems real to a group of people is real in its consequences regardless of how absurd, hallucinatory, or shocking it may look to others in different situations or at other times" (199). What matters is that the threat seems real to the perceiver because that is what leads to real consequences in terms of subsequent beliefs, orientations, behaviors, and, ultimately, public policies. The perception of threat is an essential component of symbolic politics theories. It does not, however, need to stem from an objectively realistic understanding of actual threats.

In sum, the familiar story of group interest being more powerful than tangible short-term self-interest describes the situation here just as it does in so many other policy domains. Often what is being protected is symbolic. Here, the perceived threat is to an abstract conception of group identity rather than to a material good. For some, the defense of that identity leads to support for language restrictions, while for others it leads to opposition. Arguments about group interest and symbolic politics are not incompatible because the veracity of the threat is largely irrelevant to the perception of the threat and its impact over policy preferences. In fact, it could even be argued that one cannot understand the dynamics of threat without understanding the power of symbolic predispositions.

By Any Means Necessary? The Case of Bilingual Education

Finally, there is another important set of thoughts from the focus groups that is largely devoid of identity-related myths and symbols—thoughts about bilingual education. My original intent was to have bilingual education feature as prominently in the analysis as official-English and English-only ballots. But this intention was thwarted by a rather formidable obstacle: discussions about bilingual education consistently had little, if anything, to do with conceptions of American identity. In the remaining pages of this chapter, I show that most participants who discussed bilingual education seemed to agree that schools should do whatever they can to ensure that limited English proficient (LEP) students learn English. Where they differed was on the means they thought to be the most effective way of achieving that end; some participants favored English immersion, or English as a second language programs (ESL), and others favored transitional bilingual education programs (TBE) in which students receive some instruction in their native language. Participants offered little to no support for programs designed to maintain immigrants' native cultures. Sometimes when elaborating on why it is important for language-minority students to learn English, participants brought up familiar concerns about economic success or political participation, but more often, the discourse simply focused on effectiveness. I argue that the lack of identity-based opinions is due primarily to the nature of the policy itself.

BILINGUAL EDUCATION AND POLLS

But before discussing the focus group data, it is useful to go over the tangled state of public opinion about bilingual education as it is depicted in surveys and in concrete educational battles. Looking first at polls, one quickly finds that it is very difficult to figure out what it is that people even want, let alone why they want it. One factor that makes deciphering public opinion on bilingual education difficult is that people have very different understandings of what the term *bilingual education* actually means or what bilingual education programs actually entail. Some survey questions provide definitions, but even there, definitions often vary from survey to survey. And that gets me to a second factor that makes deciphering public opinion difficult, which is that practically every survey asks about bilingual education in a different way. This variety of question wording makes time trends hard to discern and results in a confused picture of what people want public schools to do.

For instance, the 2000 GSS found that 75 percent of the respondents *disagree* that "bilingual education programs should be eliminated in American public schools."[5] This question wording is new and is most likely in response to Ron Unz's efforts to get states to pass ballot initiatives ending bilingual education. To date, he has been successful in California (Proposition 227), Arizona, and Massachusetts, and unsuccessful in Colorado. This GSS finding suggests that getting his initiatives passed will continue to be a challenge. However, a similar question asked by the Pew Research Center for People and the Press in 1999 found only 49 percent saying they disapprove of "doing away with bilingual education and requiring that all public school students are taught in English only" and 49 percent saying they approve.[6] And a 1998 poll from the Roper Center found that only 33 percent favor bilingual education over English immersion.[7] In the GSS question, no definition of bilingual education is offered; the Roper question defines bilingual education as providing

---

[5] Data and wording were retrieved from LexisNexis.

[6] Data and wording were retrieved from Polling the Nations.

[7] Data and wording were retrieved from Polling the Nations.

gradual instruction in English while other subjects are taught in the native language and defines immersion as providing intensive training in English, and the Pew question clearly offers English-only instruction as the replacement for bilingual education, although it leaves bilingual education undefined. Providing definitions in survey questions is important, especially when there is a lot of confusion about what particular policies entail. When questions offer definitions, we get a better sense of the kinds of instruction people are saying they'd prefer.

But the Roper and Pew questions only offered two alternatives. Another question wording that is sometimes used, and that some people would argue is a more accurate characterization of the actual options out there, offers three alternatives: immersion, teaching students in their native language only until they know enough English to succeed in mainstream classes (TBE), or teaching students in their native language and in English throughout their education (cultural maintenance). Yankelovich surveys in the mid-1990s found people to be about evenly split between the first two alternatives, with slightly more favoring immersion over TBE in a 1995 poll and slightly more favoring TBE in a 1993 poll. The cultural maintenance option got very little support (Lapinski, Peltola, Shaw, and Yang 1997).

But it's not just the opinions from national random samples that are difficult to decipher. The picture does not get much clearer when we look at surveys targeted at immigrants or Hispanics. The 1995 Yankelovich poll just mentioned, for example, found Hispanics to be evenly split between all three alternatives. The 1991 Latino National Political Survey (LNPS) asked respondents whether they support or oppose bilingual education, without offering a definition, and found about 80 percent of Latinos supporting it. The survey then asked people what they thought the main objective of bilingual education is. Most people said the objective is to learn two languages, some said it is to learn English, and only a few said the goal is cultural maintenance (de la Garza et al. 1992). Yet according to an exit poll from the *Los Angeles Times*, nearly 40 percent of voting Latinos in California supported Proposition 227 in 1998 (Schmid 2001). Crawford (2001) notes that preelection polls in California "found that the idea of intensive English instruction was popular in immigrant communities" (45) and that "attacking bilingual education did not result in the polarization that many had expected" (44). And a 2002 national survey of Hispanics by the Latino Coalition found that 68 percent of respondents said that the main purpose of bilingual education programs should be "to make sure that students learn English well" rather than "to teach immigrant children in their native language so that they don't fall behind in other matters."[8] To the extent that the results of these disparate questions can be com-

[8] The Latino Coalition is a nonprofit, nonpartisan organization that conducts research on how public policies affect Latinos in the United States. It also lobbies legislators to advocate policies that they deem beneficial to Latinos in the United States. The entire survey can be found at www.thelatinocoalition.com.

pared, it seems that there is no clear consensus among Latinos, but that support for learning English quickly has grown somewhat over time.

In a 2002 national survey of immigrants from a variety of ethnic backgrounds, Public Agenda gave respondents two options, asking, "Do you think all public school classes should be taught in English, or do you think children of immigrants should be able to take some courses in their native language" (Public Agenda 2003, 52)? Sixty-three percent said that all classes should be taught in English. There was some variation by national origin, but even the group with the lowest support for the immersion option, Mexicans, was still at 51 percent. The survey then asked, "When it comes to students who are new immigrants, is it more important for the public schools to teach them English as quickly as possible, even if this means they fall behind in other subjects or to teach them other subjects in their native language even if this means it takes them longer to learn English" (Public Agenda 2003, 53)? Seventy-three percent chose the former.[9]

Regardless of ethnicity, it seems that when people are given only two alternatives—immersion or some form of bilingual education—people favor immersion. When TBE is framed as an alternative *in between* immersion and cultural maintenance, no clear winner emerges. Sometimes it's immersion and sometimes it's TBE, but it's never cultural maintenance. Among Hispanics and immigrants, the data point to an increased preference over time for learning English quickly through immersion instead of through more transitional approaches. Thus, the complex picture we are left with from existing survey data is that among Hispanics and immigrants, there is growing support for immersion, while at the same time national majority-white samples are not overwhelmingly embracing the Unz approach of eliminating bilingual education outright.

My goal, however, is not just to examine what kind of program people prefer, but to learn more about *why* they favor one alternative over another. For example, are Hispanics today increasingly likely to favor immersion because they consider it to be the most effective way of learning English, or do more abstract norms and values drive their preferences? Likewise, is support for TBE driven by pedagogical or symbolic motivations? Existing surveys do not provide much clarification here either. First, surveys do not ask people to explain their policy preference. Questions that ask people what they think the goal of bilingual education should be are a step in the right direction. Data from those questions suggest that learning English quickly is clearly a priority. When framed as a choice between learning English while falling behind in other sub-

---

[9] There is a vibrant debate over whether TBE programs actually delay the learning of English. In their survey of research on the effectiveness of alternative approaches, Hochschild and Scovronick (2003) conclude that any type of program can be effective at teaching English as long as the program is implemented well and given appropriate resources: "In other words, good programs work and bad programs do not" (154; also see Crawford 2001).

jects, or learning other subjects while taking longer to learn English, immigrants overwhelmingly choose learning English. But what about nonimmigrants? What about the voters passing the Unz initiatives? Individual-level regression analysis would be a good way to get at this question. As I argued in chapters 2 and 4, however, the few national surveys inquiring about bilingual education rarely ask an appropriate range of background questions that enable tests of whether conceptions of American identity shape preferences.

Citrin and colleagues (1990) examine what factors determine whether Californians would or would not pay more taxes for bilingual education. It turns out that their "Americanism" scale, while a significant predictor of attitudes on bilingual ballots, is not significant (in their final model) when it comes to bilingual education.[10] In fact, few traditional political cleavages turn out to be significant, except for resentment toward Latinos and Asians, and one's level of education. This finding suggests that concerns about effectiveness might indeed be an omitted variable that determines one's preferred programmatic alternative.

Huddy and Sears (1995) also examine the determinants of whether people oppose bilingual education, using a composite scale as the dependent variable. They attribute opposition to a combination of prejudice and the perception that bilingual education threatens the interests of whites. Their composite scale includes some items about potential effects of bilingual education, but the distinct analytical value of these items gets obscured when combined with measures of racial threat and general opposition to bilingual education. And no items ask respondents to evaluate the extent to which the different types of programs are effective at meeting desired ends. Thus, the alternative hypothesis that opinions on bilingual education are determined by concerns about effectiveness more so than by perceptions of American identity or other abstract beliefs is still untested.

BILINGUAL EDUCATION AND ACTIVISTS

Perhaps returning to analyses of activist rhetoric will help. Do partisans in bilingual education battles cast their positions in terms of any of the four conceptions of national identity, or do they claim that their policies would simply be the best method of reaching the shared end of teaching English to LEP students? Surveying analyses of activist rhetoric, it becomes immediately clear that both sides generally do portray their approach as the best way to get the job done. The question is whether they claim that their approach will advance particular American civic traditions as well.

Schmidt (2000) provides one of the most thorough examinations of contemporary bilingual education rhetoric. Looking first at supporters (the group he calls "pluralists"), he notes that American norms and values—particularly

[10] The authors note that Americanism is significant when measures of resentment toward Latinos and Asians are removed from the model.

liberal ones—are often invoked to advocate TBE programs, but the case is made that TBE enables us to realize these norms *because* it is more effective at educating students than immersion. This was the prevailing rationale for implementing bilingual education programs in the first place. He writes, "From the outset, then, bilingual education was justified as a means of promoting greater educational success, which in turn, would lead to greater social equality for language minority children and their communities" (131). Transitional bilingual education, in other words, would render the American Dream an attainable reality.

Over the years, he notes, a similar justification has been used by activists to promote cultural maintenance programs instead of TBE. The argument here is that programs that promote the culture of the immigrant provide recognition, which boosts self-esteem, which in turn leads to greater educational success. Yet even in this more radical strain, self-esteem is an instrumental goal, a means to academic achievement. Thus, the debate, as Schmidt sees it, is primarily over which method is most likely to create conditions that enable educational success. The liberal image of all Americans having equal opportunities for social mobility is invoked by proponents of TBE and cultural maintenance, both of whom argue that their preferred alternative is a better way *pedagogically* for realizing that American Dream.

The organized campaign against Proposition 227 in California, the most prominent bilingual education battle in recent memory, did not take this approach, however. In fact, it had trouble arriving at a coherent message of any kind (Crawford 2001). Opponents of 227 tried to follow the advice of their consultants, who advised them to avoid debating the merits of bilingual education and to campaign instead against specific aspects of the proposition. But their strategy backfired, as they were never able to capture the emotions or the imagination of the electorate and never offered a compelling alternative message. According to Crawford's postmortem, the anti-227 efforts addressed neither the effectiveness of bilingual education nor more abstract American values such as the American Dream. They "began with the premise that voters' minds were closed to considering the merits of bilingual programs. So, rather than engage them in discussion on the issue, the campaign sought to distract them with diversionary gimmicks" (49). If they had debated the effectiveness of bilingual education at teaching English and/or at being an essential stepping stone to economic success, Crawford believes, supporters of bilingual education in California might have given Unz more of a run for his money.

In describing opponents of bilingual education, Schmidt writes that they ("assimilationists") believe that "assisting language minorities toward greater equality through social mobility can only be attained through emphasis on efficient mastery of English" (140). Again, the liberal conception of American identity is advanced, and again, it is argued that the particular educational method in question—in this case immersion—is simply the best way to get there. Part of its effectiveness derives from changes in the students' self-concept as they immerse themselves in the language and customs of their new home. Schmidt elaborates the opponents' claims:

> Only when one internalizes an American identity—in which the adoption of English as one's true language plays a central part—will genuine equality of membership take place in one's own heart and mind. In this sense, the linguistic adoption of an American identity is instrumental to the attainment of social equality. (142)

Additionally, opponents fear that students who maintain cultural distinctiveness "risk the danger of permanent marginalization in U.S. society" (140), and they warn of the resulting social divisiveness such marginalization will cause. In this formulation, opponents also see themselves as protecting the civic republican ideal and as warding off the "balkanization" of America.

Unz himself invoked a hodgepodge of rationales for his initiative, some practical and some abstract. Civic republican concerns about the "balkanization" of America, for instance, immediately confront visitors to his website merely by typing its address: www.onenation.org. And although he has tried to downplay the association between his efforts and ethnoculturalist beliefs, Unz himself disparaged today's immigrants in a campaign letter for not being like his immigrant grandparents, who he said came to the United States to work hard, not to "sit back and be a burden on those who were already here" (quoted in Schmid 2001, 162). The liberal image of American identity also appeared in Unz's rhetoric when he promoted Proposition 227 as the immigrant's "ticket to the American Dream" (Crawford 2001, 43). Finally, the Unz campaign also highlighted the effectiveness issue. The charge that current bilingual education programs do not work at teaching English or at leading to academic achievement featured prominently in his campaign rhetoric. His website, for example, calls bilingual education a "dismal practical failure" with children "trapped in Spanish-almost-only classes for years." The official name of the campaign, "English for the Children," promotes this concern for concrete attainment of English mastery. Thus, we see three of the four conceptions of American identity invoked in support of English immersion along with concerns about which method is most effective at teaching English. In no accounts of the 227 debate is incorporationist notion of national identity described as playing much of a role.

Among activists, then, it seems that "effectiveness" is an important rationale for advocating their policies. But effectiveness at what, exactly? At teaching English, certainly, but that doesn't seem to be the main goal. Rather, teaching English is largely framed as an instrumental goal, necessary for achieving the shared end of making the American Dream a reality and, consequently, reducing social inequality. As Schmidt puts it, both sides "are in profound disagreement" (144) about how to do that. Civic republicanism appears to play a secondary role in anti–bilingual education rhetoric, but not much of a role at all among proponents. Proponents charge Unz and his supporters with nativist and ethnocultural motivations, but the Unz activists go to great lengths to dispel that image. If nativism is a driving force, they know it must be muted if they hope to achieve legislative success. Finally, there is not much evidence that cultural maintenance is promoted for its own sake. More often, cultural maintenance is promoted as a means for achieving liberal ends. To be sure, there are some "hard multiculturalists" out there too, just as we saw in chapter 3. But again, calls for maintaining cultural distinctiveness for its own sake do not seem to get much mainstream support or much attention in coverage of bilingual education battles. Rather, calls for group recognition and cultural maintenance are advanced as a means to gain self-esteem, which in turn leads to educational success, which in turn enables social mobility.

So what does all of this suggest for public opinion? Recall that the aim here is to examine why people prefer one alternative to another and to investigate the extent to which competing conceptions of American national identity play a role in determining preferences. I've already noted that effectiveness at teaching English seemed to dominate the focus group discussions on this topic. My review of survey data and activist rhetoric suggests that we shouldn't be surprised to see concerns for teaching English well play a major role. The question is whether teaching English was seen as the ultimate end or whether it was cast in instrumental terms, as a means for advancing or protecting particular notions of American identity.

BILINGUAL EDUCATION AND FOCUS GROUPS

In all, there were 231 thoughts about bilingual education in the focus group discussions. Of those 231 thoughts, 65 percent were coded as "no identity," meaning the speaker did not invoke any of the main conceptions of American identity under investigation in this book and did not raise concerns about government spending. How does this rate of identity-free thoughts compare with the other policy areas? Table 7.2 shows the percentage of thoughts for each policy area that were coded as belonging to each category in the first step of the coding procedure (including ambivalent and opinionless thoughts). It shows that only 26 percent of the official-English thoughts and 26 percent of the English-only ballots thoughts were identity-free, compared with the 65 percent for bilingual education—a rather striking difference.

Another unique aspect of bilingual education is that most thoughts on the subject did not express a particular opinion direction. This issue was characterized by more opinionless statements than the other two policies. Table 7.3 shows that nearly 58 percent of the statements about bilingual education were opinionless, while the equivalent figures for official-English and English-only ballots are 38 percent and 20 percent, respectively.[11] As with official-English

---

[11] See appendix E for a more detailed description of opinionless statements.

TABLE 7.2
Percentage of Thoughts for Each Policy by Identity Type

	Policy			
Identity	Official-English	English-only Ballots	Bilingual Education	Total
Liberalism	14.07	0.99	3.03	11.02
Civic republicanism	12.69	40.59	5.19	13.54
Ethnoculturalism	11.41	1.98	2.6	9.06
Incorporationism	3.2	0.99	4.33	3.23
Hybrid	6.61	7.92	2.16	5.91
Tax/spend	2.56	3.96	2.16	2.6
Other	0.32	0	0.87	0.39
Unclassified	22.81	17.82	14.29	20.87
No identity	26.33	25.74	65.37	33.39
Total	100 ($n = 938$)	100 ($n = 101$)	100 ($n = 231$)	100 ($n = 1270$)

Note: Thoughts include "ambivalent" and "no opinion." Pearson $\chi^2 = 225.03$ $p < .001$.

and English-only ballots, most opinionless statements referring to bilingual education involved clarification (e.g., "I don't think most people realize that there's a distinction between bilingual education and ESL"). The only difference with bilingual education is that there were, proportionally, many more statements of this nature than there were for the other two policies.

Only twelve statements explicitly stated support for bilingual education programs. A few were liberal in nature and involved speakers telling stories about people being treated unfairly without bilingual education or being put through poorly implemented programs. One thought in favor of bilingual education was civic republican and expressed the fear that minorities will continue to be excluded from public life without it. The remainder had little to

TABLE 7.3
Percentage of Thoughts for Each Policy by Direction of Opinion

	Policy			
Opinion	Official-English	English-only Ballots	Bilingual Education	Total
Support	24.09	33.66	5.19	21.42
Oppose	22.71	29.7	22.51	23.23
Ambivalent	15.03	16.83	14.72	15.12
No opinion	38.17	19.8	57.58	40.24
Total	100 ($n = 938$)	100 ($n = 101$)	100 ($n = 231$)	100 ($n = 1270$)

Note: Pearson $\chi^2 = 69.54$ $p < .001$

do with conceptions of American identity. For example, after a barrage of criticism of bilingual education from her colleagues, Anna came to its defense, saying she supports it because "I do not think it's true that [immersion is] the only way you can speak English." Her reasoning lacks any grounding in the sorts of ideals described in earlier chapters. She simply thinks that programs that work should be pursued, and she thinks that bilingual programs can meet the challenge.

More statements were made against bilingual education (fifty-two) than in favor (twelve), and 73 percent of them did not invoke any principles associated with conceptions of American identity. This high number might be an artifact of the nature of the policy and could have something to do with the clarity, or lack of clarity, among the alternatives proposed. Many respondents were unsure of what the term *bilingual education* means or what bilingual programs entail, but they knew that being against it most likely means that one thinks classes should only be in English.

It is also important to note that several of the statements against bilingual education came from Hispanic participants. For example, one of the few liberal statements against bilingual education came from Eduardo, a member of the Chicano culture club. Like many, his viewpoint is informed by personal experience. He worries that minority students will be at an economic disadvantage if they do not learn English or do not learn it well. He insists that his own experience illustrates why immersion is the most effective way to go. He says:

> I got pure Spanish in my house. My family would all speak Spanish, but when I started school, they gave me this little tutor. I didn't go to pre-K or kinder, because they gave me this teacher that taught me English so I was forced to speak English. I wasn't given the leeway to say, "Well, since you know Spanish, you're at a disadvantage so we'll teach you a little less English and some Spanish." How is that going to help? I'm supposed to be competing with the same first grader who already knows it. So you've got to educate me to the level that he's at.

He sees immersion as most effective, and pursuing the most effective policy matters because it best allows a child to have the same opportunity to pursue economic success as one who already knows English. Here we see learning English described as the instrumental goal that will enable the attainment of the American Dream, just as Schmidt's assimilationists would argue. The end is the American Dream, and Eduardo relies on personal experience to come to a conclusion about what the best means for achieving that end is.

But arguments of this nature were rare. By far, identity-free statements dominated the opposition to bilingual education. Carlos, in the same group as Eduardo, explains his opposition to bilingual education purely in terms of effectiveness. Responding to a colleague who told a bilingual education horror story, Carlos says:

I think the current system [of bilingual education] has failed also. It's like remedial education in Spanish and English, which doesn't help the kid at all. What I've seen, the best way to teach a kid a foreign language is just complete immersion in that language. So if you're trying to teach a kid who only speaks Spanish English, the best way to do it is to immerse him in English.

In a similar vein, Linda, from a community service organization, says:

When I came to this country in '87 I was eleven years old and I lived in Yardley, Pennsylvania, and I was the only—or maybe it just seemed that way—I knew I was the only Hispanic in [my] middle school. My sisters were the only Spanish girls in [their] elementary. And I think I was even the only minority. And there were no such things as bilingual classes in Pennsylvania. There is still no such thing. And it forced me to learn the language quicker.

Also speaking from experience, Ellen, a member of a hobby club, says, "I teach fourth, fifth, or sixth grade depending. And I've had kids come in from Poland, from Russia, not a word of English. By the end of the year, they've got it." None of these speakers go on to link learning English to some other goal, be it rooted in conceptions of American identity or in something else. Perhaps if the moderator had probed respondents further, they would have. On their own, however, participants talked as if learning English is the main goal. Regardless of whichever program people thought was best for doing that, the goal itself seemed to end with the educational content students acquire, and I cannot claim that they were all at root inspired by particular norms linked to ideas about American national identity.

FOCUS GROUP ARTIFACT?

One enduring concern with public opinion research is whether findings are simply an artifact of question wording. The wording used on the moderator question guide for introducing bilingual education in the focus groups was: "What do you think is the best way to educate children who do not know English?" whereas the wording for the ELA and for English-only ballots asked respondents simply to state a preference for or against (see appendix D). After finding that most bilingual education thoughts centered on the effectiveness of teaching English rather than on identity, this difference in question wording logically comes to mind as a possible cause. I returned to the transcripts to investigate further.

I focused on comparing discussions of bilingual education with discussions of English-only ballots, since the ELA was introduced in the same way in all groups at the very start of the group interview. It turns out that the moderator question guide was rarely followed in either case. The moderator's overall goal was to see that all three policies were discussed, but to let the conversation generally take its own course. The question guide was used only if certain topics did not emerge on their own or if there was a lull in the discussion. In other words, the guide was a fallback resource and was only really followed at the start and at the end of each half of the group interview (each focus group took a break halfway through). In nearly all cases, the participants themselves introduced their views of English-only ballots and bilingual education without specific prompting from the moderator. In some groups, the moderator would pick up on one participant's lead and ask other group members to jump in (e.g., "So would other people agree with Bob that at the federal level, election ballots should be in English only?"). In only two instances did the moderator use the exact wording on the moderator guide for bilingual education, and both were in Hispanic groups.

Further analysis of the bilingual education thoughts suggests, however, that relying on the guide did not result in the Hispanic groups invoking conceptions of national identity less than the other groups. As table 7.4 shows, bilingual education thoughts among the Hispanic participants were actually *more* likely to invoke conceptions of American identity than bilingual education thoughts in the remaining groups. Table 7.4 also shows that a disproportionate amount of the bilingual education thoughts are concentrated in the Hispanic groups, the one likely artifact of using the wording in the guide. Finally, table 7.4 compares the rate of identity-related bilingual education thoughts to English-only ballots and shows that ballots were far more likely to be discussed in terms of American identity across all types of groups, even though both policies were handled more or less the same way (i.e., rarely introduced by the moderator). At no time were participants encouraged to view any of the policies in terms of their relationship to conceptions of American national identity. The goal was to examine the spontaneously generated reasons for why people hold particular views on language policies and to gauge the extent to which conceptions of American identity emerge on their own. With the ELA and ballots, the link between identity and the policy was made often, without encouragement from the moderator. With bilingual education, discussions rarely got beyond debates about pedagogy.

Thus, it seems that following the wording in the guide resulted in more *attention* to bilingual education but did not result in a lower likelihood of interpreting the policy in terms of its relationship to conceptions of national identity. The high frequency of the bilingual education thoughts in the Hispanic groups could also be because many people in those groups had themselves been students in one kind of bilingual education program or another. In other words, the greater attention to bilingual education among the Latino participants is most likely due to a combination of the methodology and personal experience. In retrospect, to eliminate any uncertainty, the wording in the moderator guide should have been more parallel across all three policies. The moderator guide, however, does not appear to be the cause for why bilingual education was discussed in terms of identity less than the ELA or English-only ballots.

TABLE 7.4
Bilingual Education and English-only Ballots Thoughts by Ethnicity of the Group

Group type	% of Bilingual Education Thoughts	% Invoking American Identity	% of English-only Ballots Thoughts	% Invoking American Identity
White (n = 8)	62	8	85	52
Heterogeneous (n = 3)	7	6	7	43
Hispanic (n = 3)	32	22	9	67

BILINGUAL EDUCATION AS A "HARD" ISSUE

If this emphasis on pedagogy was not due to question wording, then what else was going on? Why does this policy seem to be an anomaly? And what lessons can we draw from it? All three of the language policies considered here are in the same issue domain, yet they show strikingly different patterns in terms of how much of the discussion did not involve identity or the statement of an explicit opinion. The work of Carmines and Stimson (1980) on the distinction between "easy" and "hard" issues is useful in helping to make sense of these patterns. Although their main task was to uncover the dynamics of issue voting, their analysis rests on the argument that some types of issues ("easy" issues) are more likely to elicit a "gut response" from voters, regardless of how informed they are about politics in general than other types of issues ("hard" issues). Easy issues are likely to (a) be symbolic rather than technical, (b) deal with ends rather than means, and (c) be "long on the political agenda" (80). They use the examples of school desegregation as an easy issue and the Vietnam War as a hard issue.

That official-English and English-only ballots are discussed by participants in largely symbolic terms while bilingual education is not suggests that official-English and ballot proposals are "easier" issues, whereas bilingual education is "harder." Other patterns confirm this perhaps fundamental difference between these types of policies and shed light on why bilingual education is such an outlier in the content analysis.

First, bilingual education is the only policy where the explicit goal is to teach English, a goal that everyone seems to support, either as an end in and of itself or as a means to promoting the liberal vision of American national identity. Just as most politicians and voters agreed that peace was the desired policy end during the Vietnam War but disagreed over how to achieve it, most participants in the focus groups agree that LEP children should know English (for a variety of reasons), but disagree over which method is most likely to accomplish that goal. Conversely, it is more difficult to determine what the exact goals of official-English and English-only ballots are, in part because of their nontechnical nature. There is more room for interpretation here regarding what the policy makers are trying to achieve, and this wiggle room allows for symbolic predispositions to come more forcefully into play. Those who fear that minorities are disliked or unwanted can read sinister motives into the debate, and any sinister motives that are actually there can rise to the surface; people who do not see minorities as true Americans or who want to keep immigrants out can use official-English as a way of communicating that sentiment. Likewise, those who fear that diversity is hurting their communities can see official-English as a way to help preserve a vibrant public life. Thus, it seems that when the goals of a policy are less clear, people's long-standing predispositions to interpret political issues in certain ways play a larger role in the opinion formation process.

Second, while the goals of bilingual education are more obvious than those of official-English or English-only ballots, the avenues for implementation are not. In fact, it is quite the opposite; while it is easy for participants to understand what having bilingual ballots means, they were more confused about what actually happens in bilingual education programs. The percentages of opinionless statements shown in table 7.3 illustrate this confusion; many opinionless thoughts involve participants hashing out what the different programs actually mean. There was some confusion about official-English, but much more about bilingual education. Although Carmines and Stimson do not investigate whether the percentage of respondents offering "no opinion" or "don't know" is higher for questions on Vietnam than for questions on desegregation, it would hardly be surprising to see that more people are unable to articulate a preference on newer, more technical issues that involve debates over how to achieve shared goals. In other words, when policy alternatives are complex or poorly understood (e.g., when the issue is "hard"), more of the conversation is devoted to untangling the different options, making symbolic predispositions a less central part of the discussion. When the goal is clear but the details of the policy are not, symbolic conceptions of American identity are eclipsed by more immediate considerations. Conversely, when the goal is vague but the details of the policy are easier to understand, symbolic predispositions seem to dominate.

An important possibility to consider is whether symbolic predispositions such as conceptions of national identity *do* shape views on "hard" issues, but during a later phase of the opinion formation process. In other words, conceptions of identity do not determine whether a person thinks all children should know English, but they may shape *which alternative* she thinks will be the most effective way to meet that goal. There are not enough identity-based statements on each education alternative in the content analysis for me to be able to study this possibility in more detail, and the few statements there are do not suggest any obvious pattern, especially regarding the ethnicity of the speaker: Latinos and Anglos alike support bilingual education if they can recount a bilingual education success story and oppose bilingual education if they can recount an immersion success story. Existing surveys are also ill equipped for testing the antecedents of perceived effectiveness because they do not ask people to evaluate whether different programs are successful at achieving various aims. Whether there is a role for national identity in determining one's preferred option for achieving the consensual end is a question that I cannot answer here but raise in the name of speculation for future analysis. The preliminary evidence in the focus group data suggests not, but it is an empirical question worthy of more in-depth investigation.

CONCLUSION

In this chapter I have addressed three aspects of this project that are not part of the direct test of how the four broad conceptions of what it means to be an American shape how people interpret and debate restrictive language policies. Each aspect represents an arena in which the symbolic politics story one might tell about ethnic change and policy preferences is not as straightforward as proponents of symbolic politics theories might hope. These complications result from a variety of sources.

Regarding hybrid thoughts, it has long been established in public opinion research that ordinary citizens are rarely as systematic, consistent, unambiguous, unambivalent, or theoretically rigorous as we would like them to be. In addition, the logical affinity between various conceptions of national identity works to encourage conceptual hybridization. It is not the case that some people are ethnoculturalists while others are incorporationists. People simultaneously accept tenets of multiple traditions and use them as tools to help them navigate debates about ethnic change. Survey research that attempts to place respondents along an identity continuum forces distinctions and a dimensionality that may not be justified. Although such attempts do not represent flaws with the underlying symbolic politics theories, they do prevent us from gaining a deeper understanding of how those theories are played out in current salient debates. Analyzing discourse involving the four conceptions of national identity under investigation here on their own *and* in combination takes us a step further in this regard than previous survey-based analyses have been able to.

One area in which survey-based analyses have been consistently strong is in repeatedly demonstrating the weakness of tangible matters to shape policy preferences, especially when compared with the power of symbolic predispositions. The analysis here confirms this general principle in addition to the more detailed expectations about how specific features of the policy in question might alter whether self-interest enters into the decision-making calculus. It supports the contention that group interest is more powerful than self-interest and that in both cases, the perception of threat is more important than actual threat.

Perhaps the most interesting complication discussed in this chapter is the case of bilingual education, for it provides the clearest and most intriguing set of findings that apply to the project as a whole. Specifically, comparing bilingual education with the other policies provides a set of expectations about how the proposed policy itself might determine whether symbolic predispositions are more or less likely to shape preferences. To date, symbolic politics research has not paid much systematic attention to this piece of the puzzle, the exception being when symbolic predispositions are pitted against measures of self-interest.

The findings presented in this chapter confirm some previous findings (e.g., that concerns about government spending are marginal), create confusion about others (e.g., that participants do not combine ascriptive and liberal beliefs as often as survey research would lead us to expect), and suggest new insights (e.g., the possibility of a "symbolic nativism" and how the nature of the policy in question affects the use of symbolic predispositions). As with many projects, it is possible that I have raised as many questions as I have tried to answer. Luckily for public opinion scholars, and perhaps unluckily for everyone else, debates about language are not likely to disappear from the political landscape anytime soon.

CHAPTER EIGHT

Conclusion

TWO MAIN QUESTIONS have guided the analysis throughout this book. The first question is why so many people express support for restrictive language policies, such as making English the official language of the United States or printing election materials only in English. The widespread support that is shown on survey after survey is curious, especially in light of a firmly entrenched incentive structure that clearly promotes the learning of English. This incentive structure, along with the continued prominence of English in public life in America (and all over the world), suggests that an official-English law would at best be superfluous and would at worst be an additional source of conflict between ethnic groups or violate civil rights and liberties. Addressing this first question leads to the second, which is whether conceptions of what being an American means determine how people think about language debates. More specifically, the goal was to examine how alternative conceptions of American identity are called forth when people are asked to explain their views. The role of symbolic predispositions like national identity in the opinion formation process has been a concern of public opinion scholars for quite some time. Centering the analysis on this particular attitudinal construct has allowed me to contribute to existing knowledge about the relationship between symbolic predispositions and opinions while also highlighting the parameters of debates about this increasingly salient public policy.

LANGUAGE AND IDENTITY

The symbolic politics approach maintains that throughout our lives, particular symbols become endowed with significant political and personal meaning and that these symbols then become powerful influences over how we interpret the world around us and our own place in it. The varied norms, values, and myths that define the content of national identities are a subset of these political symbols. They draw conceptual boundaries around membership, constrain the range of political debate, and provide guidance for acceptable action on the part of both government and individual citizens. When new situations arise—particularly new situations that call the substance of national identity into question, as is the case with rapid demographic change—attachments to the various conceptions of that identity will become salient factors that shape how we interpret the new reality. Moreover, they will influence whether we come to support or oppose policies designed to address it. Symbolic politics scholarship to date has established this much. Yet the study of the exact content of American national identity that shapes perceptions so powerfully has remained underdeveloped.

In chapter 2 I described a set of implications that the theory of symbolic politics would lead us to expect when examining the relationship between conceptions of national identity and policy preferences, and I discussed the extent to which existing empirical analyses adequately test the validity of those expectations. Symbolic politics theories suggest that symbolic predispositions that communicate information about what being American means should inform attitudes about language and ethnic change, that not all of the symbols associated with American identity will be interpreted in the same way or lead to the same policy preference even when the symbol in question is universally cherished, and that the impact of symbolic predispositions on policy preferences can vary in systematic ways depending on features of the policy itself. I then demonstrated that the first of these expectations was routinely confirmed by survey-based research, though I charged that the ways in which American identity has been measured were either too narrow or too vague, and that the remaining two expectations still required further analysis. Chapters 3 through 7 present my attempts to address these needs.

CIVIC REPUBLICANISM: THE NEGLECTED TRADITION

It is undeniable that liberalism has been and continues to be an important factor in shaping public discourse in the United States. But liberalism's central role in political life has often blinded public opinion scholars and distracted them from acknowledging that liberalism shares the stage with civic republicanism, a tradition that continues to exert a powerful role over both how Americans think about their national identity and how they interpret public policies. Scholars of American political thought have long recognized the existence of this public philosophy that emphasizes the responsibilities of citizenship. The tenets of civic republicanism regularly characterize political discourse, and public life is often structured in ways that facilitate the ability of citizens to live up to the ideal promoted by this tradition.

If there is any one finding to take away from this book, it is the important yet overlooked hold that the civic republican tradition has over the American mind. The analysis in chapters 5 and 6 shows that the civic republican tradition plays a large part in shaping how the people in my study think about being American and provides the vocabulary they use to express their views on language conflict, particularly with regard to the printing of government materials in other languages. Public opinion scholars would do well to incorporate ideas about "community," the need and ability to communicate with one's fellow citizens, and the duty to be informed about and involved in public life into their analyses. Recall Ernie, who said, "For everybody to get along and communicate, everyone should learn English at least," or Dave, who argued, "I'd say it's better to have citizens make an informed choice and to participate in the voting process. And if the price we have to pay to do that is to provide the ballots in multiple languages, than I would say we should." Sentiments like these are common, and their role in shaping how people think about language conflict needs to be acknowledged. People may not always do an admirable job of being good civic republicans themselves, but the ideal still wields normative force and sustains an image of the American way of life that people do not want to erode.

Including civic republicanism in symbolic politics research becomes even more important when we recognize that concerns about all citizens being able to be a part of public life in the community lead to divergent policy preferences, as is the case with the examples provided by Ernie and Dave. Whether the civic republican tradition exerts the same type of influence over other issue areas as it does over language policy remains to be seen. I have shown that it is a hypothesis certainly worth pursuing. More explicit attention to civic republicanism is also needed to confirm the extent to which the findings from these focus groups can be generalized to the broader American population. What little survey data there is on civic republican values is encouraging. The work presented here, combined with the rapidly growing body of work on civic engagement, will hopefully continue to inspire further explorations into the role of the civic republican tradition in twenty-first-century America.

One must proceed with caution, however, before proclaiming civic republicanism's dominance over opinion formation in the realm of language policy or ethnic change more broadly. One drawback of relying entirely on the language of the participants without additional statistical controls is that one can never be entirely certain that people are not simply using civic republican discourse to express implicitly their prejudicial attitudes about racial and ethnic minorities. As I showed in chapter 3, American history has no shortage of examples when it comes to exclusive policies being justified in the name of the public good. The use of innocuous language or appeals to universally accepted norms instead of racist rhetoric can be a conscious effort, but it can be beyond the level of self-awareness as well (Mendelberg and Oleske 2000). People can appeal to seemingly collective goods, such as local control or community cohesion, to express opposition to policies designed to promote racial equality without being aware of the ethnocultural meaning underlying their arguments. Studies have shown, for example, that people often draw upon their attitudes about race when offering opinions on seemingly race-neutral issues, such as crime or welfare (Gilens 1999; Mendelberg 1997). Further, people can simply choose to remain silent rather than express views that might be deemed inappropriate (Berinsky 1999).

How much of the focus group discourse represents implicit ethnocultural concerns of this nature is difficult, if not impossible, to say. On the one hand, it would be naïve for me to insist that such coded dialogue played no role during the discussions or that the few participants who kept quiet throughout the discussions were just shy. On the other hand, the lack of self-censorship that I saw in some of the groups suggests that participants did not need to rely on coded language to express their views. In nearly every white non-Hispanic group, at least one participant was quite willing to appeal to narrow and ascriptive definitions of what makes someone American, which paved the way for others to do so as well. Once one participant goes down the ethnocultural road, others become free to follow and, presumably, fears of appearing racist diminish. I also went to great lengths when coordinating the focus groups to create a setting that made people feel comfortable expressing their views (see appendix C). Moreover, the coding procedure allows for subtle expressions of ethnoculturalism to be captured. For example, it is unlikely that any participant would openly say, or agree, that only white people can be truly American. Yet several people referred to minorities in general as not being American and assumed that having an accent or poor English skills means one is a foreigner. This sort of subtle, automatic, and "inadvertent" ethnoculturalism did not slip through the coding cracks. Furthermore, civic republican discourse was not confined to the white non-Hispanic participants. Hispanic participants routinely voiced desires for policies that promote an active and informed citizenry and expressed an aversion to divisiveness. Finally, the quantitative analysis in chapter 4 shows that an adherence to a rough scale of civic republican concerns does not make one more likely to harbor negative perceptions of immigrants.

Still, fearing the "balkanization of America" or wanting all voters to understand political debates and be informed about important issues before casting their votes could, for some people, be covers for prejudice against minorities. My finding in chapter 7 that hybrid statements involving both ethnoculturalism and civic republicanism are used more often than hybrid statements involving ethnoculturalism and liberalism to justify support for restrictive policies suggests it is worth investigating whether the civic republican tradition indeed provides vocabulary that makes modern expressions of anti-immigrant views—"symbolic nativism"—possible. Research on symbolic racism has shown that liberal beliefs on their own are not indicative of racial resentment. The modern expression of antiblack views entails the simultaneous support for liberal principles and the belief that blacks fail to live up to them. Based on that work and on the findings presented here, I suspect that symbolic nativism operates in a similar fashion. I suspect that civic republicanism can be combined with the belief that today's immigrants fail to emulate the civic republican ideal, which would generate resentment, which in turn would lead to opposition to ethnicity-related policies. Support for the civic republican tradition on its own, however, does not constitute resentment.

INCORPORATIONISM: THE NEW(ER) KID ON THE BLOCK

Though liberalism, civic republicanism, and ethnoculturalism have shaped the American mind for years, I have also shown that American identity is not a static concept. Change may be slow, but it would be a mistake to identify a set of ideological traditions and use them as measures without investigating whether the content and meaning of those traditions change over time or whether other clusters of ideals enter the scene. A case in point is the tradition of immigration and the civic myth of cultural diversity that participants in the focus groups invoked repeatedly when discussing what they think it means to be an American. As Smith points out, calls for a multicultural understanding of American identity have traditionally been voiced from below, not above. It is not clear whether this is still the case, and there are signs that it is not. The needs and concerns of ethnic groups have come to receive ever more formal and genuine governmental attention thanks to the social movements of the sixties and seventies. Smith's work ends with the Progressive Era, yet an analysis of citizenship laws and judicial decisions through the present would probably reveal that the immigrant tradition in America and the ethnic diversity it continues to bring have come to exert more of an influence over elite discourse and behavior.

But even if attachments to the immigrant tradition are still more from below than from above, the analysis here and the research tradition from which it grows are more concerned with the former than with the latter. My analysis suggests that any study of opinions on conceptions of American identity should address whether incorporationism is a relevant component. In this case, a four-part model is a more accurate one to use than Smith's three-part approach when studying mass opinion and language policy. For some, this tradition emphasizes the dynamic and assimilative powers of American society; for others, it calls for efforts to sustain diversity. An understanding of the balance and the boundaries within this tradition as American citizens understand it is something most observers of ethnic change are still struggling to achieve.

What we can say at this point is that scholars such as Walzer, Glazer, Higham, and others theorize about the role this immigrant tradition plays as a conception of American identity and that the focus group participants identify with it, routinely describing the joys and wonders of living in a diverse society and lamenting when they become out of touch with the culture of their ancestors. They see cultural diversity as distinctly American, and they are wary of too much assimilation, though a certain degree of assimilation is deemed both necessary and good. Although some versions of incorporationism may blend with other concerns, such as liberal calls for tolerance or economic opportunity, the tradition is distinct in its emphasis on cultural diversity and should be recognized as a separate guiding philosophy of American political culture.

It is also important to note that nowhere in the focus groups was support for group rights or cultural separatism voiced. And at no point did anyone argue for placing their ethnic identity prior to their national identity. If participants had been asked directly to prioritize their identities, perhaps a few of them would have chosen their ethnic identity. But the purpose of the focus groups was to study how issues surrounding ethnic and linguistic change are understood by ordinary citizens without much guidance from the moderator. It would be interesting to see the product of a discussion in which people were asked to choose one identity over another, but that was not the aim here. When left to their own devices, no one advocated removing themselves emotionally and cognitively from the national community.

Some people did lament that they don't view themselves as American, but they placed the blame on the dominant society that continuously treats them as foreigners, and they certainly did not say that alienation was their preferred state of affairs. Rather, most people in the focus groups, regardless of age, ethnicity, class, or gender, seemed to genuinely want both diversity and unity. They struggled against each other and within themselves over how to find a balance between the two. On a deep level, they sense that diversity and unity need not be mutually exclusive, and they subscribe to an image of American identity that allows for both. On the ground, however, policies that enable that image to become reality remain elusive. Scholars of public opinion are only now just beginning to explore these struggles and the role they play as people try to make sense of ethnic change.

AMERICAN IDENTITIES

My research also confirms that there is no single American identity but rather multiple American identities. Some, like liberalism and civic republicanism, are widely accepted and can reasonably be said to form a universal American public philosophy. Ethnoculturalism, on the other hand, is contested and is only accepted by certain portions of society. For those who reject ethnoculturalism, however, its narrow and ascriptive vision still provides the framework they use to discuss their views. People experiencing reactive ethnicity, for example, do not think of themselves as American because the ethnocultural norm does not allow them to. They acknowledge that ethnoculturalism is a part of American identity, but unlike their views toward liberalism, civic republicanism, or incorporationism, they see it as something to regret and condemn. Findings such as these point to the need for us to highlight the difference between consensual and conflictual civic myths.

Through documenting the multiple identities, I have also demonstrated the value that insights from scholarship in political theory can bring to public opinion research. To design our studies well, whether they are quantitative or qualitative, we need to look not only to prior public opinion research, but also to more abstract, philosophical, and elite-centered treatments of the issue at hand.

CONSENSUAL MYTHS BUT CONFLICTUAL IMPLICATIONS

In addition to making the case for expanding the range of norms and traditions that should be included in public opinion analyses of the relationship between identity and attitudes, I have shown that it is not enough to simply add measures of civic republicanism and incorporationism to our models. Rather, as Elder and Cobb argue, it is necessary to recognize that a widely cherished value can be interpreted in different ways and have different meanings for members within a society. For instance, people can agree on the importance of having an informed and involved citizenry but disagree quite strongly on how such a citizenry can be created. For some, making English the official language will promote the vibrant and stable communities they think America is supposed to have and will ensure that those participating in the political process are able to understand mainstream political discourse. For others, that same legislative act will divide communities and limit the ability to be informed and involved to those who belong to the cultural majority.

Such patterns underscore the dangers I describe in chapters 2 through 4 of relying on monolithic scale measures of "Americanism." It is not the case that believing that a broad range of values defines being American leads to support for official-English while an absence of such beliefs leads to opposition. Both supporters *and* opponents use conceptions of American identity to justify their position. Determining the individual-level factors that influence divergent uses of consensual civic myths is beyond the scope of this analysis, though doing so should clearly be one of the next steps in this ongoing research agenda.

POLICY GOALS AND IMPLEMENTATION

I have also shown that even though ideas about American identity dominated discussions of language policy, the extent to which participants relied on it seemed to be affected by the specifics of the policy in question. That the influence of American identity might vary across issue areas and matter less on issues unrelated to language and ethnicity would not be surprising. But that discussions about official-English and bilingual ballots on the one hand and bilingual education on the other differed greatly in the extent to which they were characterized by conceptions of national identity is striking. Recall that official-English and English-only ballots, two policies presented as having limited alternatives for implementation and ambiguous goals, were discussed using the language of American identity much more than bilingual education, a policy presented as having several avenues for implementation and the clear goal of having students learn English. Most participants agreed that LEP children should learn English and supported whichever method they felt would best achieve that end. Occasionally, people argued that their preferred way of dealing with LEP students was necessary in order to advance other goals. But for the most part, whether one's favored method was seen as promoting or violating a particular conception of what being American means was rarely considered. Whether certain independent variables can have a different impact on attitudes within a single policy realm due to factors such as the number of proposed alternatives or the clarity of potential outcomes has not received much explicit academic attention, a notable exception being the work of Carmines and Stimson on "easy" and "hard" issues (1980). More systematic study of how the specific proposal in question affects which attitudinal predispositions will influence policy preferences is called for, both in this specific issue area and as well as in other areas of public opinion research.[1]

My finding on bilingual education also speaks to the virtue of using focus groups in political science research. The pattern that emerged from the discussions on this topic was not one that I anticipated and would not have been something I would have thought to look for had I instead relied on a survey with a closed-ended question design. Allowing participants to debate the merits and drawbacks of policy proposals in their own vocabulary and on their own terms permits such discoveries. My initial reading of the focus group transcripts led me to sense that there was something different about the way bilingual education was factoring into the discussions. My approach to the content analysis, which incorporates every thought into the data set, allowed me to show that there was indeed a systematic pattern driving my impressions. As Hibbing and Theiss-Morse (1996) write, and as I have shown here, focus groups "can be real eye-openers" (19).

WHY IDENTITY?

A legitimate question one can raise at this point is whether yet another attitudinal construct needs to be added to the tool kit of causal variables in public opinion research. What does including measures of American identity in our models get us that we did not already have with measures of partisan identification, economic self-interest, and prejudice? My answer to this question is twofold.

First, as I demonstrated in chapter 2, scholars have included ideas about

---

[1] Dennis Chong, Jack Citrin, and Patricia Conley (1999) have presented work that uses experiments embedded within surveys to examine how policy presentation affects whether measures of self-interest will determine preferences. Paul Sniderman has also presented work in this area (1999). Greg Huber and I have also examined how perceived policy outcomes might shape whether and how conceptions of American identity influence attitudes (Huber and Schildkraut 1999).

American identity in their analyses for years and have long recognized the importance of identity in determining how people interpret the social and political world. Over and over, scholars have shown that conceptions of national identity influence attitudes toward immigration and language policies, even when other traditionally strong influences, such as education or anti-minority affect, are included in the model. The surveys used to produce such findings do not just ask if one thinks people should pull themselves up by their bootstraps or if people from all backgrounds should be treated equally. They also ask if such beliefs are important in making someone an American. They link the value to national identity, and analyses show that policy preferences are influenced by whether people accept those linkages. The value itself may indeed have an independent role to play in the opinion formation process, but so does one's acceptance of the political culture that promotes such values. The relationship between the two—the value and the belief that the value constitutes American-ness—may not be one that is fully understood. But survey research suggests that people use particular beliefs to demarcate national identity and that the resulting construct influences attitudes. Conceptions of national identity are a part of one's worldview, and learning more about it is a task worth pursuing. Given the consistent and strong evidence that American identity is a powerful attitudinal dimension, it is worth our while to investigate further.

Second, the concept of national identity has become an important feature of political discourse all over the world during the latter half of the twentieth century, and its importance shows no signs of abating. One cannot read a newspaper without finding an article about a place where differences in ethnicity, religion, or race are causing internal conflict. Whether these conflicts are a backlash against globalization, the reemergence of "primordial" tendencies, or an extension of liberal beliefs grounded in the notion of self-determination is debated fiercely and not a question I seek to answer here (e.g., Hobsbawm 1990; Huntington 1996; and Anderson 1991). What is clear, however, is that these tensions affect the domestic politics of the United States as they do anywhere else. Though we do not see calls for national boundaries to coincide with the territorial distribution of ethnic groups as is so common elsewhere, we have seen great changes in the ethnic makeup of the country, and the state finds itself repeatedly challenged to find solutions to problems that arise from such change. How ordinary citizens react to these changes and to the government's responses is something that political leaders have to contend with and social scientists rightly seek to understand. Asking who does and does not belong to the society and what determines the yardstick has become a regular exercise. The unyielding quest to define boundaries, both territorially and conceptually, is an important enterprise with serious consequences. These consequences cannot be adequately explained by the traditional variables in the public opinion tool kit. I hope that my investigation into attitudes toward restrictive language policies, an issue area that is particularly relevant to identity politics, convinces the reader to agree.

The Future of Language Policy and Language Conflict in the United States

If the census projections for the next few decades are correct, then both language and immigration issues will continue to be on the front burner. Debates about how to educate children who do not know English, whether to fortify a wall along the border with Mexico, or whether to provide government services only in English are so pressing and so animated because they arise from real population shifts, but also because these issues tap into people's very sense of who they are and what they think their national identity means. As the United States tries to both incorporate new residents into the polity and deal with issues that arise from demographic change, the question of what being American means is going to be more prominent and in flux. Ethnoculturalism is not as universally accepted as civic republicanism or liberalism, and over the next several decades, more and more of the American population will be excluded by ethnoculturalism's narrow vision of who is and is not truly American. Perhaps ethnoculturalism will eventually fade from the radar screen as a viable notion of American identity. In the meantime, however, conceptions of identity, including ethnoculturalism, are going to be prominent players in how policy issues like language and immigration are interpreted and in how preferences are voiced.

The increased importance of debates about language in recent years can be seen in the extent to which people have become aware that English is not the official language of the United States. To be sure, many Americans, some focus group participants included, are still surprised to hear that it is not, but the number of people unaware that the United States lacks an official language has decreased quite a bit, at least according to two national surveys. In 1986, the Hearst Corporation commissioned a survey called "Knowledge of the U.S. Constitution," which asked a national adult sample a series of true-or-false questions. One question was: "The U.S. Constitution establishes English as the national language, requiring that it be used in schools and government." Sixty-four percent incorrectly answered "true," 34 percent correctly answered "false," and 3 percent said they did not know. Eleven years later, the National Constitution Center commissioned a similar survey that asked whether "the Constitution states that the first language of the United States is English." This time, only 35 percent of the respondents incorrectly answered "true," while 58 percent correctly answered "false," and 8 percent said they did not know.[2] Question wording across the surveys differs, but the increase in the per-

---

[2] Poll data accessed through LexisNexis.

centage of respondents with the factually correct information is still striking. It would be interesting to know whether the increase in knowledge is primarily located in states that experienced loud and messy battles over whether to make English the official state language or whether the issue has sparked knowledge on a wider scale. Regardless, the evidence suggests a learning process, one that has most likely resulted from an increased occurrence of language conflict.

THE DIVERSITY OF CONFLICT

This conflict is taking on forms beyond simply whether to make English the official language at the state level. Local language ordinances, such as the one in Georgia that mandates signs be 75 percent English, are becoming more common. Citizens in Massachusetts and Arizona have followed California and voted to eliminate bilingual education. English for the Children, Ron Unz's organization that spearheaded the campaigns in all three states, says on its website that its goal is to get rid of bilingual education in the entire country. They still have many states to go, and these initial victories surely provide motivation to continue their efforts. In states such as New York that do not allow for initiatives, English for the Children has sought to put the issue on local and city ballots (Tierney 1999).

The courts are also receiving their share of the language-related action. In addition to ruling whether particular official-English laws are constitutional, they have handled cases like the one involving Wayland Cooley, the tax assessor in Alabama who refused to grant the homesteaders tax credit to non-English speakers, and one involving Carl and Mary Lindow, landlords in San Jose who refused to lease their properties to non-English-speaking tenants (Mintz 1998). In November of 2000, the Ninth Circuit Court of Appeals upheld the original jury ruling that the Lindows' policy did not discriminate based on national origin (Egelko 2000).

Not all newsworthy developments reflect actions taken to enshrine the place of English in the United States. For instance, the New Mexico Supreme Court ruled that jurors could not be excused or excluded from serving because they do not speak English (Fecteau 2000). And in an attempt to connect with minority communities, police officers in Nashville and Oakland have been experimenting with hand-held language translators. The technology still has a way to go; it is not yet capable of facilitating a meaningful conversation. But the machines can ask for one's driver's license, and an officer can say "Miranda" into the device and it will produce "You have the right to remain silent . . ." in the programmed language (Lite 1999; Manuel 1999). And in perhaps the most interesting case of all, the city of El Cenizo, Texas, declared Spanish to be the official language for all local government affairs (McLemore 1999).

ALIENATION AND IDENTIFICATION

An important trend in the focus groups, and one that anyone concerned about ethnic change should consider, is the tendency of the nonwhite Americans who participated in my study to discuss readily that they do not see themselves as Americans. The reason offered for the lack of attachment to the United States was the continued hold that ethnoculturalism has over how minorities are treated and received by whites and the cast that it puts over how they navigate their relationship with American politics and society. More studies of the extent and dynamics of this reactive ethnicity are needed. As long as it exists, we won't be in the clear. As long as it exists, ethnoculturalism, though formally denounced, will still shape what being American means and have real consequences. Recall Paloma, who said, "I was born here, but I don't feel that America includes me at all. I live here, but that's it." Important questions to consider are whether members of minority groups are going to continue to feel this way as their numbers increase, and what it means for American society if they do. These questions speak to a more abstract debate about why it matters for members of a political community to self-identify as members of that community and what the political consequences are when they do not. They also speak to a more concrete and immediate debate about what, if anything, political leaders and institutions can do to prevent a scenario in which a large percentage of American citizens feel that they do not belong to the political community. Should that scenario occur, using Spanish on a sign for a supermarket would surely be the least of our problems. Implementing sensible, effective, and humane language policies can be one part of the larger project of finding that elusive balance between unity and diversity and of finding a way to minimize reactive ethnicity while enabling positive attachments to one's national and ethnic identities.

Although it might be counterproductive to legislate an official language or dictate how much of a sign in a store window needs to be in English, there are virtues to having everyone in the country speak the same language, as many of the focus group participants so eloquently articulated. These virtues mostly relate to our ability to emulate the civic republican ideal of having citizens who take part in common public enterprises, who can communicate and debate with one another, and who can work together to promote the common good. But since there are also virtues in avoiding discrimination and unnecessary conflict, we need to be cautious in our approaches to achieving these aims.

The United States has always been a society in which a multiplicity of languages are spoken, and the incentives to learn English are probably as strong as, if not stronger than, they ever have been. Declaring English the official language will not render the incentives more compelling. And evidence suggests that the incentives, for the most part, work quite well and that the generations that succeed immigrants know English. For example, in their panel study of second generation adolescents in southern Florida and southern California, Portes and Rumbaut (2001) found that the children of immigrants learn English, generally learn it quickly, come to prefer using English rather than their native language, and eventually lose fluency in that native language. More than 98 percent of their sample reported being able to speak and understand English well or very well in the second wave of the survey. The preference for English was strongest among those adolescents who had been born in the United States, as opposed to those who immigrated as children with their parents (aka "the 1.5 generation").

Perhaps those in most need of resources beyond the existing incentives are the ones who are immigrants themselves, adults as well as children. For instance, over 70 percent of the parents in the sample studied by Portes and Rumbaut used a foreign language in the home. If adult immigrants are slower to learn English than their children, it is likely due to the inordinate demands on one's time, energy, and resources that establishing a new life requires, to the cognitive challenges of learning a new language as an adult, and to the fact that many new immigrants are not highly educated in their own native language. However, declaring English the official language or printing government documents only in English does nothing to overcome these obstacles. Perhaps many Americans feel as if the incentives to learn English are no longer working because so many immigrants in the United States today face obstacles that make learning English difficult. For their children, and for their children's children, however, lack of English fluency is unlikely to be a problem.

Refining our ability to truly promote the learning of English for immigrants of all ages would perhaps be a wiser (and, judging from the focus groups, a more broadly popular) approach to making sure that all American citizens and U.S. residents know English. As with bilingual education programs in the schools, it is likely that for adults, good programs work and bad programs do not. Determining what factors make for a good program is beyond my expertise. But as Hochschild and Scovronick (2003) observe, ensuring that facilities have qualified teachers along with the resources and flexibility that best suit the particular needs of the community in question is probably a pretty good place to start. Additionally, I suspect that when the students are themselves adults with families and full-time jobs (or multiple jobs), good programs are also marked by convenience and affordability.

Schmidt's (2000) advocacy of pluralistic integration lays out what seems to be a very reasonable set of proposals that takes the concerns of people on both sides of language debates seriously. And their concerns *should* be taken seriously. It would be a mistake to dismiss all support for official-English policies as racist. Some of it is, but a nontrivial amount stems from legitimate desires to see that people know English. The reasoning for such desires is rooted in universally accepted beliefs about the norms and values that constitute American identity. Schmidt's program of pluralistic integration acknowledges this.

It seeks to guarantee English instruction to all that desire it while also providing resources to preserve America's rich cultural diversity—a diversity that we should all celebrate regardless of our own specific heritage. The final chapter of his book should be required reading for activists on both sides of language policy battles and for anyone else concerned about the future of language policy in the United States.

As a student of public opinion, I am driven to understand the determinants of attitudes toward restrictive language policies and what effects such attitudes will have over future policy-making efforts. As a member of the society in which these conflicts and developments are taking place, I am concerned about the effects they will have in both the short and long run. So far, the only impact of official-English and English-only policies appears to be that of fostering further conflict. How concerned should we be if a policy's only noticeable impact is to create tension? Is that result any worse than a policy that robs people of a tax credit worth several hundred dollars because they do not know English or one that flatly eliminates a potentially effective means of teaching English? It's a tough call, though I'm sure that none of these is anything a stable democracy with an ethnically diverse citizenry should want. The diverse character of the American population is not going to diminish, nor should it. Once our diversity is recognized as fact, it becomes clear that we cannot ignore the concerns people have as they see so much change taking place around them in such a short period of time and as they see how public institutions respond to such change. People have strong attachments to what they think being American means, and with good reason: there's a lot to like. Ethnic change, and proposals for dealing with it, makes people on all sides fear that the nation's identity is threatened. As we move ahead and address the reality of ethnic change, we need to take those fears seriously. Doing so will be one of the best ways to ensure that we avoid policies that bring out the nation's worst traditions and aim for policies that strengthen its best.

Appendix A: Exploratory Factor Analysis of American Identity Items (1996 GSS)

EXPLORATORY factor analysis is an appropriate tool for developing insights about relationships among variables, such as whether those variables can convincingly be argued to result from a common underlying factor (Kim and Mueller 1978a, 1978b). In this case, an exploratory factor analysis of the six identity items does not yield results that are as conclusive as one might hope. By convention, factors are generally retained if they have eigenvalues greater than 1 (Spector 1992; Zeller and Carmines 1980), and the eigenvalues for the first two factors in this analysis are 2.31 and 0.41, suggesting a one-factor structure.[1] But Zeller and Carmines advise that "after rotation, specific items should have higher factor loadings on the hypothesized relevant component than on other components" (61), and as table A.1 shows, the pattern of factor loadings here supports a two-factor model.[2] Citrin and Duff (1998) performed

TABLE A.1
Factor Analysis of American Identity Items

	Rotated Factor Matrix (Varimax Rotation)	
	Factor 1 (Ethnoculturalism)	Factor 2 (Assimilationism)
Born in America	0.76	0.25
Lived in America	0.76	0.31
Be a Christian	0.53	0.31
Have U.S. citizenship	0.38	0.46
Respect U.S. government	0.05	0.54
Feel American	0.21	0.57
Eigenvalue	2.31	0.41

Note: N = 1144.

[1] An eigenvalue is the sum of the squared factor loadings for each item and is used to gauge how much variance in the correlation matrix can be attributed to the unobserved factor(s) (Spector 1992; Zeller and Carmines 1980).

[2] A factor loading is a measure of correlation between the item and the underlying factor (Kline 1994).

a more rigorous confirmatory factor analysis on the same data set, and their analysis provided "stronger evidence for two factors underlying the American identity items than for either one or three factors" (12).[3] In light of the support provided by their more advanced approach, I adopt the two-factor model that corresponds to my theoretical expectations and move on to creating variables for these factors by using summated rating scales.

[3] In the end, Citrin and Duff drop the item that asks about respecting American political institutions and laws because they concluded that it does not fit as well with the others.

Appendix B: Question Wording and Coding for 1996 GSS Data Analyzed in Chapter 4

AMERICAN IDENTITY ITEMS

Some people say the following things are important for being truly American. Others say they are not important. How important do you think each of the following is?

a. To have been born in America
b. To have American citizenship
c. To have lived in America for most of one's life
d. To be able to speak English
e. To be a Christian
f. To respect America's institutions and laws
g. To feel American

1 = not important at all; 2 = not very important; 3 = fairly important; 4 = very important

(re-coded to range from 0 to 1)

AGE: Respondent's age in years is recorded (re-coded to have a range of 1 and a mean of 0)

EDUCATION

0 = no schooling
1–12 = number of years of primary and secondary education
13–20 = up to eight years of post–high school education

(re-coded to have a range of 1 and a mean of 0)

GENDER ("MALE" IN TABLES): 0 = FEMALE; 1 = MALE

NATIVITY ("BORN IN U.S." IN TABLES)

Were you born in this country?

0 = no; 1 = yes

PARTISAN AFFILIATION ("REPUBLICAN" IN TABLES)

Generally speaking, do you usually think of yourself as a Republican, Democrat, Independent, or what?

0 = strong Democrat
1 = not very strong Democrat
2 = Independent, close to Democrats
3 = Independent

4 = Independent, close to
Republican
5 = not very strong Republican
6 = Republican

(re-coded to have a range of 1 and a mean of 0)

POLITICAL IDEOLOGY ("CONSERVATIVE" IN TABLES)

We hear a lot of talk these days about liberals and conservatives. I'm going to show you a seven-point scale on which the political views that people might hold are arranged from extremely liberal—point 1—to extremely conservative—point 7. Where would you place yourself on this scale?

0 = extremely liberal
1 = liberal
2 = slightly liberal
3 = middle of the road

4 = slightly conservative
5 = conservative
6 = extremely conservative

(re-coded to have a range of 1 and a mean of 0)

FAMILY INCOME

In which of these groups did your total family income, from all sources, fall last year before taxes, that is?

1 = under $1,000
2 = 1,000–2,999
3 = 3,000–3,999
4 = 4,000–4,999
5 = 5,000–5,999
6 = 6,000–6,999
7 = 7,000–7,999
8 = 8,000–9,999
9 = 10,000–12,4999
10 = 12,500–14,999
11 = 15,000–17,499

12 = 17,500–19,999
13 = 20,000–22,499
14 = 22,500–24,999
15 = 25,000–29,999
16 = 30,000–34,999
17 = 35,000–39,999
18 = 40,000–49,999
19 = 50,000–59,999
20 = 60,000–74,999
21 = 75,000 or over
22 = refused

(re-coded to have a range of 1 and a mean of 0)

ECONOMIC PERCEPTIONS

During the past few years, has your financial situation been getting better, worse, or has it stayed the same?

0 = getting better
1 = stayed the same
2 = getting worse

(re-coded to have a range of 1 and a mean of 0)

LANGUAGE SPOKEN AT HOME

What language(s) do you speak at home? [open-ended] Coded such that:

0 = speaks at least one other language in the home
1 = speaks only English in the home

ETHNICITY

From what part of the world did your ancestors come? [open-ended] Respondents are allowed up to two mentions. Answers are re-coded into four dummy variables for white (non-Hispanic), black, Hispanic, and Asian. A person is categorized as Hispanic if he is classified as "white" or "other" on the race item (where the only categories are white, black, and other), *and* if he says he has ancestors from Mexico, Spain, Puerto Rico, or "other Spanish." A person is categorized as Asian if she is classified as either "white" or "other" on the race item *and* if she says she has ancestors from China, Japan, the Philippines, or "other Asian." Respondents who are both black and who say they have ancestors from Asian or Hispanic countries remain categorized as black (only six respondents fit this description).

PERCEPTIONS OF IMMIGRANTS

There are different opinions about immigrants from other countries living in America. How much do you agree or disagree with each of the following statements? (c and d are coded such that a higher number signifies a less immigrant-friendly response)

a. immigrants increase crime rates
b. immigrants take jobs away from people who are born in America
c. immigrants are generally good for America's economy
d. immigrants make America open to new ideas and cultures

1 = disagree strongly
2 = disagree
3 = neither agree nor disagree
4 = agree
5 = agree strongly

(re-coded to range from 0 to 1)

IMMIGRATION POLICY

Do you think the number of immigrants into America nowadays should be . . .

1 = increased a lot
2 = increased a little
3 = remain the same as it is
4 = reduced a little
5 = reduced a lot

Appendix C: Focus Group Procedures

THIS APPENDIX expands upon the methodological discussion in chapter 5. In it, I discuss focus groups as a methodological tool for public opinion research, explain the specific procedures used in this study, provide a profile of the participants, and explain how the transcripts were analyzed.

GENERAL ISSUES

WHAT ARE FOCUS GROUPS AND WHEN ARE THEY USED?

Focus groups are often used as an alternative to both surveys and one-on-one interviews. Each group typically involves five to ten people, and analysis consists of content analysis and/or rigorous observation of transcripts, conversational patterns, and group dynamics. Focus groups have recently become more common as an academic data-gathering tool. Given their relative novelty to the discipline, there are few standards in terms of research design and analysis, and several different approaches have been used. The use of focus groups is grounded in the beliefs that (a) surveys often fail to evoke the many considerations that people have regarding complex issues, (b) attitudes and ideas are formed in relation to others, and (c) people will be more comfortable and less inhibited about vocalizing their ideas in a group with their peers than they are with anonymous pollsters (Delli Carpini and Williams 1994; Sigel 1996).

Focus group research may not be the most appropriate way to study opinions. When starting a project, scholars need to decide if their topic warrants their use. Hibbing and Theiss-Morse (1995) have used focus groups in their studies of public opinion toward political institutions like Congress and the Supreme Court, and in justifying their approach, write that "survey questions on political institutions have usually been superficial, poorly worded, posed sporadically, or accompanied by inadequate or nonexistent background questions" (4). Even when appropriate survey items are asked, they add, focus groups are valuable because

> if we have learned nothing else from survey research it is that we must be very careful to avoid asking respondents to provide more than they are capable of providing. . . . Extended sessions with ordinary citizens will allow us to learn more about what they do and do not know and about what real attitudes happen to lie behind snap responses to key words. (39)

If these two quotes can be thought of as advice for when focus groups might be an appropriate methodology, then the topic under investigation here meets the criteria. First, appropriate survey questions on language policy or on alternative conceptions of national identity either do not exist or are rarely asked. Second, even if the appropriate questions were asked, closed-ended items about abstract attachments tend to be vague and difficult for both respondents and analysts to interpret. For example, what does it mean when 87 percent of the 1996 GSS respondents say that "feeling American" is important in making someone a true American?

Another approach one might take is to use in-depth interviews instead of either focus groups or telephone surveys. Again, the goals of the study can determine which method is more appropriate. Although there is no consensus or solid empirical evidence about how the findings or the data differ when one uses interviews instead of focus groups, there are some differences to take into account (Morgan 1997). Focus groups allow for a larger sample size, which in turn allows for comparisons across groups or across different types of people to an extent that interview samples do not. On the other hand, interviews are better at providing information for individual-level analyses. Focus groups are typically less structured or controlled than interviews, making them an appropriate tool for exploration.

STRENGTHS AND WEAKNESSES OF FOCUS GROUPS

As with any research method, focus group research has both strengths and weaknesses. Morgan (1997) writes that these strengths and weaknesses come from a reliance on two factors: the discretion of the researcher and group interaction (13). On the one hand, these factors make focus groups a useful method in social science because they let the participants voice their own understandings of the issues. Gamson (1992) explains that focus groups allow us "to observe the process of people constructing and negotiating shared meaning, using their natural vocabulary" (17). Delli Carpini and Williams (1994) point out that focus groups are unique in their ability to reveal "the *process* of opinion formation, in providing glimpses of usually *latent* aspects of this process, and in demonstrating the *social* nature of public opinion" (64; emphasis in original). Focus groups provide more detail and insight than telephone surveys are able to deliver. They allow the researcher to recognize that opinions are often socially constructed through interpersonal interactions and permit that interaction to be a part of the analysis.

Relying on the discretion of the researcher and on group interaction also makes focus groups advantageous when the researcher does not have a clear hypothesis about a particular aspect of the project or is interested in allowing for unanticipated patterns to emerge. In my study, for instance, the focus group method allowed me to discover the unanticipated yet powerful relationship between the importance of economic self-sufficiency and support for restrictive language laws (see chapter 6). If I had decided only to conduct a survey, I would not have thought to create questions to test for this relationship between liberalism and official-English, and my understanding of how conceptions of national identity shape preferences would have suffered.[1]

PROCEDURES

RECRUITMENT

There are many ways to recruit participants for focus groups. One method is to post notices in public spaces and wait for volunteers (Hibbing and Theiss-Morse 1996). Another is to set up tables at malls or local fairs to make contacts (Gamson 1992). Some researchers have recruited from lists of people who previously participated in telephone surveys (Delli Carpini and Keeter 1993; Sigel 1996). In some cases, everyone who is to participate is contacted personally, while other times one participant is asked to bring friends or family members—a procedure known as "snowball sampling" (Gamson 1992; Liebes and Katz 1990). As this brief list indicates, there are few recruiting standards in focus group research. My recruitment strategy was to approach members of local community groups and ask if their members would participate. This technique is similar to snowballing in that all participants within each group know one another. An advantage it has over snowballing is that the universe of potential participants is constrained to the members of his or her organization. It also reduces self-selection issues because I initiated contact in all cases.

I compiled a list of active community groups in the greater Mercer County area in New Jersey from a community group clipping file at the Mercer County Public Library. The list covered a wide range of groups, including community service organizations, business-related groups, and hobby clubs, like gardening or stamp collecting. All eligible groups in the clipping file were put on the list, and I attempted to contact all groups on the list multiple times. Groups were considered *ineligible* if they had what Gamson calls "political atypicality," if they were likely to promote a heightened sense of ethnic identity, or if personal tragedies or hardships brought their members together. Thus, I avoided contacting specifically political groups (e.g., the local chapters of a pro-choice organization), ethnic organizations (with the exception of some Hispanic groups), and self-help and support groups (e.g., groups for cancer survivors).

I called each contact person and asked if the group's members would consider participating in a focus group in exchange for a donation to the group of three hundred dollars.[2] All phone calls were followed up with a letter, and some were followed up with my attendance at a meeting to make a direct ap-

---

[1] See chapter 5 for a discussion of how to offset the weaknesses of focus groups.

[2] Incentives were funded by the National Science Foundation, grant SB-9807968.

peal to the group's members. I told potential participants they would be discussing local and national political issues. If pressed for more details, I said that the research was about the role of the English language in American society and the political issues that go along with it. In the end, I conducted seventeen focus groups throughout central New Jersey from April to December of 1998, fourteen of which were included in the final analysis.[3] Participants within each group were already acquainted with one another. In some cases, they knew each other quite well; in others, they had only met once or twice before. The following groups were involved in the study:

- five hobby clubs (e.g., cars, gardening, dance)
- three community service or charity organizations (one is church-affiliated and one serves a local Hispanic community)
- three career-related organizations
- one public-speaking group
- one historical society
- one Chicano culture organization

GROUP COMPOSITION

Recruiting is often conducted with the aim of forming groups in which participants share certain characteristics. Some might have separate groups for men and women; others might control for education or income. Whatever the control may be, the decision to keep certain characteristics homogeneous within groups is usually driven by the research question or expectations regarding small group dynamics. My aim was to have groups that were homogeneous with respect to two characteristics. First, I wanted all participants to be American citizens. Since my goal was to examine how Americans define being American and how those definitions influence preferences, it would not have made sense for me to interview people who were not citizens.[4] Second, I wanted the groups to be relatively homogeneous in terms of ethnicity. More specifically, I tried to conduct some focus groups in which the participants were all white Americans, not of Hispanic descent, and others in which the participants were all Hispanic. Given the nature of the topic under discussion, I hoped that ethnic homogeneity would minimize pressures for social desirability. Getting focus groups of non-Hispanic whites was relatively simple and often occurred without any effort on my part. However, it was more of a challenge to select Hispanic groups that were not political or ethnic in nature. In the end, the study includes eight white, non-Hispanic groups, three Hispanic

[3] One group was discarded because one participant dominated the discussion and the other group members did not pay attention. A second group was discarded because the participants were uncooperative. A third group was discarded because over fifteen people showed up and most of them were not U.S. citizens.

[4] All but two participants were citizens. The two noncitizens were in the same group. One said she is trying to become a citizen; the other said she is planning to move to Spain.

groups, and three groups that were ethnically heterogeneous. I was the moderator for the non-Hispanic and heterogeneous focus groups, and a colleague from Puerto Rico conducted the Hispanic ones.[5]

THE INTERVIEW SETTING

Conducting successful focus groups requires creating an environment in which people are at ease and willing to share their personal thoughts and experiences. Choosing the interview setting is an important component of the data-gathering process. For my purposes, the ideal setting was wherever the group normally holds its own meetings because that is where participants are used to seeing each other and it would likely be an informal and welcoming environment. Further, making inordinate demands in terms of travel time would discourage people from attending, and presumably the group's meeting place is not too far from the members' homes. I conducted five of the fourteen sessions on the group's own turf. Six of the remaining groups were held in rooms at Princeton University. Of the remaining three groups, two were held in the contact person's home, and one was held in a meeting room at the contact person's place of work.

CONDUCTING THE INTERVIEW

Ten of the fourteen sessions were held with all participants sitting around a table. In the remaining groups, everyone sat in a circle, either on chairs, couches, or on the floor. All discussions were audiotaped. Upon arrival, participants were asked to complete a pre-discussion questionnaire to obtain background information (partisan identification, education, etc.), as well as to gauge pre-discussion opinions about official-English legislation, bilingual education, and bilingual ballots. The interviews began with the moderator reviewing the topic to be discussed and laying out the "rules" of the discussion (e.g., only one speaker at a time, etc.). Then the moderator asked participants to say how they and their families came to be American. The moderator always went first to give an idea of how much information was necessary. The icebreaker in one of the career-related groups went like this:

> MODERATOR: My first question is to ask each of you to go around and share with
> everyone else how you and your family came to be Americans. I will start, to give
> you an idea of what I'm looking for. My family came to the United States around
> the turn of the century from mainly Eastern Europe—Austria, Russia, and
> Poland—and settled in the New York area. And as far as I know, we've been here
> ever since. I don't know any relatives who are still over there, so we've been Americans since around 1910.

[5] Most discussions were in English, although participants in the Hispanic groups were asked to use the language with which they were most comfortable; only a handful of participants opted to use only Spanish, and several used both English and Spanish.

LISA: I'll start with my mother, because her family's been here the longest. She's sort of Mayflower stock, I think. [They] came over very early. That's the WASP side. And my father is a first generation Italian-American. His parents came here around the turn of the century also, from Italy. And that's how long we've been here.

PAULA: My name is Paula. I'm 100 percent Italian descent, three-quarters Sicilian. All four of my grandparents were born in Italy. However, my family is a little bizarre because my children are adopted from India, and they got here just within the last few years. We're kind of an international family.

Next, the moderator read the text of HJ Res 37, aka the English language amendment, a proposed amendment to the United States Constitution to declare English the official language, and asked participants how they would want their representatives to vote if and when the resolution came to the floor of the House (see chapter 5 for the amendment wording). The remainder of the discussion was rather free-form. The moderator had a question guide and tried to cover all topics on the list. Topics included opinions on bilingual voting ballots, bilingual education, and characteristics that Americans should have. Many of the issues on the list came up without the moderator's introduction. Other times, more moderator involvement was needed.[6] At the end of the interview, participants filled out a post-discussion questionnaire that contained questions about the policies discussed during the interview and included other questions about American identity. It also had an open-ended section where participants could add any thoughts they either did not get a chance to say or did not feel like sharing with the rest of the group.

PARTICIPANTS

Table C.1 compares the focus group sample with more representative information about New Jersey and the United States as a whole. The first column contains the data from the focus group sample. The next two columns contain 1997 census estimates for New Jersey and data from a 1998 telephone survey of 296 New Jersey residents (NJPOLL).[7] The last two columns show 1997 census estimates for the United States and data from the 1998 GSS, which uses a national random sample. The table shows that the focus group sample has more women and higher means for both income and education than the rest of New Jersey and the nation. The sample is also more Democratic and less conservative than the NJPOLL and GSS samples.[8] The percentage of white,

[6] See appendix D for question guide.

[7] The 1998 NJPOLL was conducted by Gregory Huber and myself at the Survey Research Center at Princeton University in the fall of 1998.

[8] The 1996 and 1998 NES data sets have nearly identical partisan and ideological breakdowns as the 1998 GSS (see "The NES Guide to Public Opinion and Electoral Behavior" at www.umich.edu/~nes/).

TABLE C.1

Comparison of Focus Group Sample, New Jersey, and the United States

Characteristic	Focus Groups 1998	New Jersey Census[a]	New Jersey 1998 NJPOLL	United States Census[a]	United States 1998 GSS
% Female	69	52	60	51	57
Mean age	47	n.a.	46	36	46
Mean education	B.A.	High school diploma[b]	Some college	High school diploma[b]	Some college
Mean household income[c]	$55,000	$47,468	$40,000	$47,123	$21,250
% White[d]	75	70	81	72	77
% Black[d]	1	15	7	12	14
% Hispanic origin[d]	20	12	3	11	6
% Asian[d]	0	5	3	4	2
% Foreign-born	9	15[e]	7	9[f]	9
% Democrat	42	n.a.	35	n.a.	34
% Republican	27	n.a.	33	n.a.	26
% Liberal	18	n.a.	25	n.a.	27
% Conservative	25	n.a.	35	n.a.	33
% Favors official-English	51[g]	n.a.	80	n.a.	60[h]
% Favors English-only ballots	36[g]	n.a.	47	n.a.	36[h]
N	108	7 million	296	268 million	2832

Note: n.a. = "not available."

[a] 1997 estimates. Source: U.S. Bureau of the Census, Statistical Abstract of the United States: 1998.

[b] In New Jersey, 85 percent completed high school, 29 percent have B.A. or more. In United States, 82 percent completed high school, 24 percent have B.A. or more.

[c] Median income, before taxes, for New Jersey. Mean income, before taxes, for United States.

[d] In focus groups, NJPOLL, and GSS, race measures are exclusive. In census, "white" is non-Hispanic, and "Hispanic origin" may be any race.

[e] Source: March Current Population Survey.

[f] 1998 estimate.

[g] From pre-discussion survey.

[h] From 1994 GSS; n = 1474.

non-Hispanic participants in my study closely mirrors the rest of New Jersey and the nation. Hispanics are overrepresented, while blacks and Asians are underrepresented. Table C.1 also shows that support for official-English among focus group participants is much lower than in the NJPOLL sample and is nine percentage points lower than in the GSS sample, due in part to the Hispanic oversample in the focus groups. Among whites only, support for official-English in the focus groups is 61 percent. Finally, support for English-only ballots is quite similar to both the NJPOLL sample and the GSS sample.

I suspect the discrepancies between the focus group sample and the larger, more representative ones are due to the concerns that drove my recruiting procedures. My sample is biased toward people who are involved in any type of community organization, and Hispanic members of the community are overrepresented. A simple probit analysis of the GSS data from 1990 to 1994 confirms that, as one might expect, older and wealthier respondents are more likely to belong to at least one community group and that people who call themselves conservative are more likely to join organizations (results not shown). In their influential study of citizen participation, Verba, Schlozman, and Brady (1995) found that whites and people with higher levels of education are more likely to be affiliated with nonpolitical organizations than minorities and people of a lower socioeconomic status. They did not find noticeable differences in terms of class or gender. Given these results, it is not surprising that the focus group sample, in which 100 percent of the people belong to at least one local organization, would be wealthier and more educated that the rest of the state and nation.

Analysis

As with recruiting, there is no single approach to analyzing focus group data. And as with recruiting, the strategy a researcher chooses to adopt is largely driven by theoretical concerns. One common strategy is content analysis, which consists of developing a coding scheme and counting how often the topic of interest appears in the transcripts. As I explain in chapter 5, I decided that content analysis was an appropriate tool for this project. With that decision made, the next step was to develop the code and decide on the unit of analysis. A discussion of the code appears in chapter 5, and so I will use this space only to explain the unit of analysis. My unit of analysis is the "completed thought," which I define as (a) the dialogue of one speaker at one time or (b) the minimum amount of dialogue necessary to communicate the speaker's main point. Definition (a) was used when a speaker said little, and definition (b) was used when a speaker said a lot at once.

An example of definition (a) comes from one of the community service groups:

> MODERATOR: So knowing English then presents you in a way towards everyone else that will make it easier . . .
> EILEEN: It's a common denominator.
> ANNE: It's a balancing of who you are.
> KATHERINE: I like that—common denominator.

Here, each comment by Eileen, Anne, and Katherine is counted as one completed thought. The following is an example of definition (b), from a member of the same group. This excerpt was said all at once, without interruption, but contains a handful of completed thoughts, each one marked by hard brackets:

[My thoughts on that are, you know, if I want to go . . . if I want to hear and see everything Spanish, such as in Miami, I can go to Spain or Puerto Rico.] [I'm not putting that down, but I'm just saying this is supposed to be one nation.] [And I think if you diversify it through language. . . . We have. . . . We are just a really rich nation in differences in people, but there's got to be some kind of unification.] [I want to go to Miami in America. I don't want to go to Miami and be in Spain, basically. Have you seen Miami lately? Sections of it?] [I think what you had read, that is in law in twenty-six states, I think you had mentioned . . . as far as the public aspects of it . . . I think that if people want to speak their native language in the privacy of their home or in a social gathering or what have you, that would be fine. But as far as anything public, yeah, I think it should be unified in English and English only.]

In these cases, the decision rule for what constitutes a completed thought was, "If she stopped speaking now, would she have made her point?" Once all completed thoughts were demarcated and numbered, three transcripts, selected at random, were read to guide the development of the coding scheme.

APPENDIX D

Appendix D: Question Guide for Focus Groups

1. Please share with the rest of the group how you and your family came to be Americans.
2. More than twenty states have declared English to be the official language of the state. Some have done so through voter initiatives, others have amended their state constitutions, and still others have simply passed laws making this declaration. Currently, there is a proposed amendment to the U.S. Constitution that would declare English the official language of the United States. I am going to read the text of that amendment to you and then ask you a question about it. The amendment as it is currently written states: "The English language shall be the official language of the United States. As the official language, the English language shall be used for all public acts, including every order, resolution, vote or election, and for all records and judicial proceedings of the government of the United States and the governments of the several states." If this amendment were to make it to the floor of the House of Representatives, how would you want for your representative to vote?
3. Who do you think would support this amendment and why?
4. Who do you think would oppose this amendment and why?
5. What arguments would you expect to hear being made in favor of this amendment?
6. What arguments would you expect to hear being made against this amendment?
7. What do you think the effects of this amendment might be?
8. Would it surprise you to hear that in public opinion polls, many Hispanic-Americans consistently support it?
9. If the country were gradually to become 60 percent Hispanic, should we then declare Spanish the official language?
10. What about election materials? Should we provide voting ballots in languages other than English?
11. What do you think is the best way to educate children who do not know English?
12. Now I have a question about the communities where you live. Have you seen much change over the past few years in terms of the number of languages you hear?
13. Is the concept of the melting pot an appropriate way to think about American identity?
14. What is it that makes us American?

15. What, if anything, does the government have a right to expect from its citizens?
16. The Constitution says that the president must be a native-born citizen. Do you think this makes sense?
17. Should we allow for dual citizenship?
18. Now imagine that after we've been sitting around and talking about this for two hours, Senator Toricelli knows that we're the local experts on the matter. Before going back to Washington, he wants to spend five minutes with us. What would you tell him to think about as he decides how to vote on the proposal to declare English the official language?
19. What do you think the most important thing you heard us discussing today was?

Appendix E: Coding Ambivalent and Opinionless Policy-related Thoughts

CLAIMS OF SUPPORT for or opposition to the English language amendment were usually rather obvious and represent the type of sentiment that scholars who work with survey data are accustomed to thinking about. Statements expressing ambivalence or no opinion, however, are more unique to the focus group approach because surveys are designed to minimize the opportunity to offer these types of thoughts. Although most of my analysis is confined to those thoughts that express a clear preference, I use this space to explain the treatment of ambivalent and opinionless comments in the coding process.

Thoughts were considered to be ambivalent if the person speaking indicated that his or her opinion was conditional on the potential effects of the policy in question. Given the vague language of the proposed amendment, some people were reluctant to offer a preference. Others indicated that they would support the amendment if it meant one outcome but not if it meant another. An example of ambivalence comes from a woman who said:

> I don't know the intent of the law and I don't know how I would want my representative to vote at this time because it seems to me, from the opposition, that there is an underlying motive there, that I wouldn't normally see just from reading that law, probably because I'm not that familiar with it.

Another example is from a woman who said, "You would like our opinion on yes or no, although we don't know what [the law] means. That's where I'm having a problem." In the ambivalent thoughts, the speaker is usually in the process of sorting out his or her ideas and attempting to arrive at an opinion.

Thoughts were considered to be unclear in their policy preference or without an opinion if they referred to the policy but did not offer an explicit opinion or reveal any attempt to sort out preferences conditional on potential implications. An example of a policy-related thought without opinion content comes from a man who said, "To most of us, it makes no difference, because it is all English." A final example is from a participant who said:

> Well, I think part of the impetus behind this amendment probably is the fact that we get a lot of people coming into the United States who really are not skilled in a

job, or do not have skills and so therefore they either wind up on say unemployment or welfare or they wind up in a low-paying job.

These thoughts make direct reference to the language law but do not indicate support, opposition, or ambivalence. One hundred ninety-two policy-related thoughts expressed ambivalence and 511 did not involve the statement of an opinion.

References

Appleby, J. 1986. Republicanism in old and new contexts. *William and Mary Quarterly* 43: 20–34.

Anderson, B. 1991. *Imagined communities: Reflections on the spread of nationalism.* London: Verso.

Associated Press. 1999. Tax assessor loses English-only battle. November 27.

Ayers, C. 1997. English it is—in Carbon. *Morning Call* (Allentown), June 5, B1.

———. 1998. Carbon to house 29 illegal aliens. *Morning Call* (Allentown), April 10, B1.

Bailyn, B. 1967. *The ideological origins of the American Revolution.* Cambridge: Harvard University Press.

Banks, A., A. Day, T. Muller, and S. Phelan. 1997. *The 1997 political handbook of the world.* Binghamton: CSA Publications.

Banning, L. 1986. Jeffersonian ideology revisited: Liberal and classical ideas in the New American Republic. *William and Mary Quarterly* 43: 3–19.

Barber, B. 1984. *Strong democracy: Participatory politics for a new age.* Berkeley: University of California Press.

Baron, D. 1990. *The English-only question: An official language for Americans?* New Haven: Yale University Press.

Baumgartner, F., and B. Jones. 1993. *Agendas and instability in American politics.* Chicago: University of Chicago Press.

Bellah, R., R. Madsen, W. Sullivan, A. Swidler, and S. Tipton. 1985. *Habits of the heart: Individualism and commitment in American life.* Berkeley: University of California Press.

Belsie, L. 1999. America's hot new melting pot. *Christian Science Monitor,* March 5, 1.

Berinsky, A. 1999. The two faces of public opinion. *American Journal of Political Science* 43: 1209–30.

Berry, M. 1998. Civic ideals: Conflicting visions of citizenship in U.S. history (book review). *American Historical Review* 103: 1677–78.

Bobo, L. 2000. Race and beliefs about affirmative action. In *Racialized Politics: The Debate about racism in America,* edited by D. Sears, J. Sidanius, and L. Bobo. Chicago: University of Chicago Press.

Branigin, W. 1999. Spread of Spanish greeted by some unwelcome signs: Businesses facing language restrictions. *Washington Post,* February 2, A4.

Brubaker, R. 1996. *Nationalism reframed: Nationhood and the national question in the new Europe.* New York: Cambridge University Press.

Camarota, S. 1999. Impact of immigration on a different America. *San Diego Union-Tribune,* February 2, B7.

Campbell, A., P. Converse, W. Miller, and D. Stokes. 1960. *The American voter.* Chicago: University of Chicago Press.

Carmines, E., and J. Stimson. 1980. The two faces of issue voting. *American Political Science Review* 74: 78–91.

Chavez, L. 2001. *Covering immigration: Popular images and the politics of the nation.* Berkeley: University of California Press.

Chong, D. 1993. How people think, reason, and feel about rights and liberties. *American Journal of Political Science* 37: 867–99.

Chong, D., J. Citrin, and P. Conley. 1999. When self interest matters. Paper presented at the annual meeting of the International Society of Political Psychology, Amsterdam, the Netherlands, July.

Citrin, J. 1990. Language politics and American identity. *Public Interest* 99: 96–109.

Citrin, J., and B. Duff. 1998. Alternative symbolic meanings of American national identity. Paper presented at the annual meeting of the International Society for Political Psychology, Montreal, Canada, July.

Citrin, J., D. Green, C. Muste, and C. Wong. 1997. Public opinion toward immigration reform: The role of economic motivations. *Journal of Politics* 59: 858–81.

Citrin, J., B. Reingold, and D. Green. 1990. American identity and the politics of ethnic change. *Journal of Politics* 52: 1124–54.

Citrin, J., B. Reingold, E. Walters, and D. Green. 1990. The "Official English" movement and the symbolic politics of language in the United States. *Western Political Quarterly* 43: 536–59.

Citrin, J., C. Wong, and B. Duff. 2001. The meaning of American national identity. In *Social identity, intergroup conflict, and conflict reduction*, edited by R. Ashmore, L. Jussum, and D. Wilder. New York: Oxford University Press.

Citrin, J., E. Haas, C. Muste, and B. Reingold. 1994. Is American nationalism changing? Implications for foreign policy. *International Studies Quarterly* 38: 1–31.

Citrin, J., D. Sears, C. Muste, and C. Wong. 2001. Multiculturalism in American public opinion. *British Journal of Political Science* 31: 247–75.

Clark, M. 1998. Voters make English the state's official language. *Associated Press State and Local Wire*, Anchorage.

Cohn, D. 2000. 2100 Census forecast: 2000 × 2; Minorities expected to account for 60 percent of U.S. population. *Washington Post*, January 13, A5.

Conover, P. 1988. Feminists and the gender gap. *Journal of Politics* 50: 985–1010.

Conover, P., D. Searing, and I. Crewe. 1999. Cultural tolerance: Dilemmas of membership in the liberal state. Paper presented at the annual meeting of the American Political Science Association, Atlanta, Georgia, September.

Conover, P., I. Crewe, and D. Searing. 1991. The nature of citizenship in the United States and Great Britain: Empirical comments on theoretical themes. *Journal of Politics* 53: 800–832.

Cotliar, S. 1996. Towns make English official; 4 suburbs deny discrimination. *Chicago Sun-Times*, August 25, 15.

Crawford, J. 1992. The debate over Official English. In *Language loyalties: A source book on the Official English controversy*, edited by J. Crawford. Chicago: University of Chicago Press.

———. 2001. Proposition 227: A new phase of the English Only movement. In *Language ideologies: Critical perspectives on the Official English movement*. Vol. 1. Edited by R. D. González, 28–61. Mahwah, NJ: Lawrence Erlbaum Associates.

Davis, J., and T. Smith. 1997. *The General Social Survey codebook.* Chicago: National Opinion Research Center.

Davis, J., T. Smith, and P. Mardsen. 1998. *General Social Surveys, 1972–1998: Cumulative codebook.* Chicago: National Opinion Research Center.

de la Garza, R., L. DeSipio, F. C. Garcia, J. Garcia, and A. Falcon. 1992. *Latino voices: Mexican, Puerto Rican, and Cuban perspectives on American politics.* Boulder: Westview Press.

Delli Carpini, M., and S. Keeter. 1993. Measuring political knowledge: Putting first things first. *American Journal of Political Science* 37: 1179–1206.

Delli Carpini, M., and B. Williams. 1994. The method is the message: Focus groups as a method of social, psychological, and political inquiry. *Research in Micropolitics* 4: 57–85. Greenwich: JAI Press.

Edelman, M. 1971. *Politics as symbolic action: Mass arousal and quiescence.* New York: Academic Press.

———. 1985 (1964). *The symbolic uses of politics.* Urbana: University of Illinois Press.

Edmonston, B., and J. Passel, eds. 1994. *Immigration and ethnicity: The integration of America's newest arrivals.* Washington, DC: Urban Institute Press.

Edwards, J. 1985. *Language, society, and identity.* Oxford: Basil Blackwell.

Egelko, B. 2000. Court upholds landlords' right to require fluent English. *San Francisco Examiner*, November 3, A5.

Elder, C., and R. Cobb. 1983. *The political uses of symbols.* New York: Longman.

Ellis, R. 1993. *American political cultures.* New York: Oxford University Press.

Epstein, D. 1984. *The political theory of "the Federalist."* Chicago: University of Chicago Press.

Erikson, B., and T. A. Nosanchuk. 1990. How an apolitical association politicizes. *Canadian Review of Sociology and Anthropology* 27: 206–19.

Espenshade, T., and C. Calhoun. 1993. An analysis of public opinion toward undocumented immigration. *Population Research and Policy Review* 12: 189–224.

Espenshade, T., and K. Hempstead. 1996. Contemporary American attitudes toward U.S. immigration. *International Migration Review* 30: 535–70.

Espinosa-Aguilar, A. 2001. Analyzing the rhetoric of the English Only movement. In *Language ideologies: Critical perspectives on the Official English movement*, Vol. 2. Edited by R. D. González, 268–88. Mahwah, NJ: Lawrence Erlbaum Associates.

Fecteau, L. 2000. Justices: Language no barrier for jury duty. *Albuquerque Journal*, January 20, A1.

Feldman, S. 1982. Economic self-interest and political behavior. *American Journal of Political Science* 26: 446–66.

Feldman, S., and J. Zaller. 1992. The political culture of ambivalence: Ideological responses to the welfare state. *American Journal of Political Science* 36: 268–307.

Fetzer, J. 2000. *Public attitudes toward immigration in the United States, France, and Germany.* New York: Cambridge University Press.

Firth, R. 1973. *Symbols: Public and private.* London: George Allen and Unwin.

Fishkin, J. 1995. *Voice of the people.* New Haven: Yale University Press.

Fiske, S., and S. Taylor. 1991. *Social cognition.* 2d ed. New York: McGraw-Hill.

Foote, L. 1942. *Bibliography of the official publications of Louisiana, 1803–1934* (noncirculating volume at the State Library of Louisiana).

Forbes, H. D. 1997. *Ethnic conflict: Commerce, culture, and the contact hypothesis.* New Haven: Yale University Press.

Frendreis, J., and R. Tatalovich. 1997. Who supports English-Only laws? Evidence from the 1992 National Election Study. *Social Science Quarterly* 78: 354–68.

Frolik, J. 1997. Powell relishes role touting volunteerism. *Plain Dealer*, May 4, 25A.

Gamble, B. 1997. Putting civil rights to a popular vote. *American Journal of Political Science* 41: 245–69.

Gamson, W. 1992. *Talking politics*. New York: Cambridge University Press.

Garreau, J. 1992. Columbus and the sailing-the-ocean blues; Hero to zero: Why the quincentenary went bust. *Washington Post*, October 12, D1.

Geller, A. 1997. Signs of change: Fearful of legal lashing, towns back off English-also ordinances. *Record* (Bergen Co, NJ), July 10, L1.

Gellner, E. 1983. *Nations and nationalism*. Ithaca: Cornell University Press.

Gilens, M. 1999. *Why Americans hate welfare*. Chicago: University of Chicago Press.

Gimpel, J., and J. Edwards. 1999. *The congressional politics of immigration reform*. Boston: Allyn and Bacon.

Glaser, J. 1994. Back to the black belt: Racial environment and white racial attitudes in the south. *Journal of Politics* 56: 21–41.

Glazer, N. 1997. *We are all multiculturalists now*. Cambridge: Harvard University Press.

Gleason, P. 1980. American identity and Americanization. In *The Harvard encyclopedia of American ethnic groups*, edited by S. Thernstrom. Cambridge: Harvard University Press.

González, R. D., ed. 2001. Introduction to *Language ideologies: Critical perspectives on the Official English movement*, Vol. 1. Edited by R. D. González, ix–xviii. Mahwah, NJ: Lawrence Erlbaum Associates.

Green, D., and A. Gerken. 1989. Self-interest and public opinion toward smoking restrictions and cigarette taxes. *Public Opinion Quarterly* 53: 1–16.

Greenhouse, L. 1999. Appeal to save English-only law fails. *New York Times*, January 12, A16.

Hamilton, A., J. Madison, and J. Jay. 1961 (1787–1788). *The Federalist papers*, edited by C. Rossiter. New York: Penguin.

Hartz, L. 1991 (1955). *The liberal tradition in America*. New York: Harcourt Brace.

Heath, S. B. 1992. Why no official tongue? In *Language loyalties: A source book on the Official English controversy*, edited by J. Crawford. Chicago: University of Chicago Press.

Held, D. 1996. *Models of democracy*. 2nd ed. Stanford: Stanford University Press.

Hero, R. 1998. *Faces of inequality: Social diversity in American politics*. New York: Oxford University Press.

Hibbing, J., and E. Theiss-Morse. 1995. *Congress as public enemy: Public attitudes toward American political institutions*. Cambridge: Cambridge University Press.

———. 1996. The public side of public opinion: Focus groups in political science research. Unpublished manuscript.

———. 2002. *Stealth democracy: American's beliefs about how government should work*. New York: Cambridge University Press.

Higham, J. 1963. *Strangers in the land: Patterns of American nativism, 1860–1925*. New York: Atheneum.

———. 1993. Multiculturalism and universalism: A history and critique. *American Quarterly* 45: 195–220.

Hill, K. Q., and A. Hinton-Andersson. 1995. Pathways of representation: A causal analysis of public opinion-policy linkages. *American Journal of Political Science* 39: 24–35.

Hobsbawm, E. J. 1990. *Nations and nationalism since 1780: Programme, myth, reality*. Cambridge: Cambridge University Press.

Hochschild, J. 1981. *What's fair? American beliefs about distributive justice*. Cambridge: Harvard University Press.

———. 1984. *The new American dilemma: Liberal democracy and school desegregation*. New Haven: Yale University Press.

———. 1995. *Facing up to the American dream: Race, class, and the soul of the nation*. Princeton: Princeton University Press.

———. 1998. Civic ideals: Conflicting visions of citizenship in U.S. history (book review). *Political Science Quarterly* 113: 321–23.

———. 2000. Lumpers and splitters, individuals and structures. In *Racialized politics: The debate about racism in America*, edited by D. Sears, J. Sidanius, and L. Bobo. Chicago: University of Chicago Press.

———. 2001. Where you stand depends on what you see: Connections among values, perceptions of fact, and political prescriptions. In *Citizens and politics: Perspectives from political psychology*, edited by J. Kuklinski, 313–40. New York: Cambridge University Press.

Hochschild, J., and N. Scovronick. 2003. *The American dream and the public schools*. New York: Oxford University Press.

Honig, B. 2001. *Democracy and the foreigner*. Princeton: Princeton University Press.

Hood, M. V. III, I. Morris, and K. Shirkey. 1997. "¡Quédate o vente!": Uncovering the determinants of Hispanic public opinion toward immigration. *Political Research Quarterly* 50: 627–47.

Hood, M. V. III, and I. Morris. 1997. ¿Amigo o enemigo?: Context, attitudes, and Anglo public opinion toward immigration. *Social Science Quarterly* 78: 309–23.

Hollinger, D. 1995. *Postethnic America*. New York: Basic Books.

Huber, G., and D. Schildkraut. 1999. Values and policy outcomes as determinants of support for English-only ballots: Evidence from a New Jersey Poll. Paper presented at the annual meeting of the American Political Science Association, Atlanta, Georgia, September.

Huddy, L., and D. Sears. 1995. Opposition to bilingual education: Prejudice or the defense of realistic interests? *Social Psychology Quarterly* 58: 133–43.

Huntington, S. 1981. *American politics: The promise of disharmony*. Cambridge: Belknap Press.

———. 1996. *The clash of civilizations and the remaking of world order*. New York: Simon and Schuster.

Hutchinson, J., and A. Smith. 1994. *Nationalism*. New York: Oxford University Press.

Ingram, D. 2000. *Group rights: Reconciling equality and difference*. Lawrence: University Press of Kansas.

Johnson, K. 1997. The new nativism: Something old, something new, something borrowed, something blue. In *Immigrants out! The new nativism and the anti-immigrant impulse in the United States*, edited by J. Perea, 165–89. New York: New York University Press.

Kallen, H. 1924. *Culture and democracy in the United States*. New Brunswick: Transaction Publishers.

Kammen, M. 1972. *People of paradox: An inquiry concerning the origins of American civilization*. New York: Alfred A. Knopf.

Kellstedt, P. 2000. Media framing and the dynamics of racial policy preferences. *American Journal of Political Science* 44: 239–55.

Key, V. O. 1949. *Southern politics in state and nation*. New York: Random House.

———. 1963. *Public opinion and American democracy*. New York: Alfred A. Knopf.

Kim, J., and C. Mueller. 1978a. *Introduction to factor analysis: What it is and how to do it*. Beverly Hills: Sage Publications.

———. 1978b. *Factor analysis: Statistical methods and practical issues*. Beverly Hills: Sage Publications.

Kinder, D., and L. Sanders. 1996. *Divided by color: Racial politics and democratic ideals*. Chicago: University of Chicago Press.

Kinder, D., and D. Sears. 1981. Prejudice and politics: Symbolic racism versus racial threats to the good life. *Journal of Personality and Social Psychology* 40: 414–31.

King, R. 1997. English as the official language: The problem of multiple cultures. *Current*, no. 394 (July–August): 3–8.

Kingdon, J. 1999. *America the unusual*. New York: St. Martin's Worth.

Kline, P. 1994. *An easy guide to factor analysis*. New York: Routledge.

Klinkner, P., and R. Smith. 1999. *The unsteady march: The rise and decline of racial equality in America*. Chicago: University of Chicago Press.

Krasno, J. 1994. *Challengers, competition, and reelection: Comparing Senate and House elections*. New Haven: Yale University Press.

Krueger, R. 1998. *Focus groups: A practical guide for applied research*. Newbury Park: Sage Publications.

Kymlicka, W. 1989. *Liberalism, community, and culture*. Oxford: Oxford University Press.

———. 1994. Return of the citizen: A survey of recent work on citizenship theory. *Ethics* 104: 352–81.

Lapinski, J., P. Peltola, G. Shaw, and A. Yang. 1997. The polls—trends: Immigrants and immigration. *Public Opinion Quarterly* 61: 356–83.

Lezin, S. 1999a. Fines anger Latino merchants; Municipal ordinances requiring English in commercial signs galvanize Hispanics. *Atlanta Journal-Constitution*, May 7, 1E.

———. 1999b. Latino merchant files suit in Norcross sign dispute. *Atlanta Journal-Constitution*, May 10, 3C.

Lictblau, E. 2003. Bush issues racial profiling ban but exempts security inquiries. *New York Times*, June 18, A1.

Liebes, T., and E. Katz. 1990. *The export of meaning*. Oxford: Oxford University Press.

Lind, M. 1995. *The next American nation: The new nationalism and the fourth American revolution*. New York: Free Press.

Lipset, S. 1963. *The first new nation: The United States in historical and comparative perspective*. New York: Basic Books.

Lite, J. 1999. Police looking to voice-activated interpreter to talk with non-English speakers. *Associated Press State and Local Wire*, December 3.

Luker, K. 1984. *Abortion and the politics of motherhood*. Berkeley: University of California Press.

Manuel, M. 1999. Nashville police to test electronic translator. *Atlanta Journal-Constitution*, December 3, 4B.

Marshall, D. 1986. The question of an official language: Language rights and the English language amendment. *International Journal of the Sociology of Language* 60: 7–75.

McConahay, J. 1982. Self-interest versus racial attitudes as correlates of anti-busing attitudes in Louisville. *Journal of Politics* 44: 692–720.

McClosky, H., and J. Zaller. 1984. *The American ethos: Public attitudes toward capitalism and democracy.* Cambridge: Harvard University Press.

McGrory, B. 1997. A new call to action: Political heavyweights gather to urge a spirit of volunteerism. *Boston Globe*, April 28, A1.

McLemore, D. 1999. Hot in any language: S. Texas town stirs things up by adopting Spanish, banning cooperation with INS. *Dallas Morning News*, August 14, A1.

Mead, L. 1986. *Beyond entitlement: The social obligations of citizenship.* London: Trentham.

Mendelberg, T. 1997. Executing Hortons: Racial crime in the 1988 presidential campaign. *Public Opinion Quarterly* 61: 134–57.

———. 2001. *The race card: Campaign strategy, implicit messages, and the norm of equality.* Princeton: Princeton University Press.

Mendelberg, T., and J. Oleske. 2000. Race and public deliberation. *Political Communication* 17: 169–91.

Merriam, C. 1966 (1931). *The making of citizens.* New York: Teachers College Press.

Miller, D. 1995. *On nationality.* Oxford: Oxford University Press.

Miller, W., and J. M. Shanks. 1996. *The new American voter.* Cambridge: Harvard University Press.

Mills, C. 1997. *The racial contract.* Ithaca: Cornell University Press.

Mills, N. 1994. Introduction: In the era of the *Golden Venture.* In *Arguing immigration: The debate over the changing face of America,* edited by N. Mills. New York: Touchstone.

Mintz, H. 1998. Jury rules for landlord in housing discrimination case. *San Jose Mercury News,* December 10.

Morgan, D. 1993. *Successful focus groups: Advancing the state of the art.* Newbury Park: Sage Publications.

———. 1997. *Focus groups as qualitative research.* 2d ed. Newbury Park: Sage Publications.

Morgan, E. 1975. *American slavery, American freedom: The ordeal of colonial Virginia.* New York: W. W. Norton.

Mutz, D. 1998. *Impersonal influence: How perceptions of mass collectives affect political attitudes.* New York: Cambridge University Press.

Myrdal, G. 1944. *An American dilemma: The Negro problem and modern democracy.* New York: Harper.

Newman, A. 1999. Court upholds extensive stops of black men after a crime. *New York Times,* October 27, B5.

Oliver, J. E., and T. Mendelberg. 2000. Reconsidering the environmental determinants of racial attitudes. *American Journal of Political Science* 44: 574–89.

Page, B., and R. Shapiro. 1983. Effects of public opinion on policy. *American Political Science Review* 77: 175–90.

Pemberton, M. 2003. Alaska Supreme Court hears English-only arguments. AP Wire, June 17.

Perea, J. 1997. Introduction to *Immigrants out! The new nativism and the anti-immigrant impulse in the United States,* edited by J. Perea, 1–10. New York: New York University Press.

Piatt, B. 1990. *Only English? Law and language policy in the United States.* Albuquerque: University of New Mexico Press.

Pocock, J.G.A. 1975. *The Machiavellian moment*. Princeton: Princeton University Press.

Popkin, S. 1991. *The reasoning voter: Communication and persuasion in presidential campaigns*. Chicago: University of Chicago Press.

Portes, A., and R. Rumbaut. 2001. *Legacies: The story of the immigrant second generation*. Berkeley: University of California Press.

Public Agenda. 2003. *Now that I'm here: What America's immigrants have to say about life in the U.S. today*. Report available from Public Agenda.

Putnam, R. 1995. Tuning in, tuning out: The strange disappearance of social capital in America. *PS: Political Science and Politics* 28: 664–83.

———. 2000. *Bowling alone: The collapse and revival of American community*. New York: Simon and Schuster.

Ratcliffe, R. G. 2002. Democrat fires back; Party leader assails Texas GOP platform. *Houston Chronicle*, June 11, A15.

Rather, D. 2001. *The American dream: Stories from the heart of our nation*. New York: William Morrow.

Rein, L. 2002. Ten Commandments bill advances. *Washington Post*, February 8, B9.

Ricento, T. 1998. Partitioning by language: Whose rights are threatened? In *Language and politics in the United States and Canada*, edited by T. Ricento and B. Burnaby. London: Lawrence Erlbaum Associates.

Rodgers, D. 1992. Republicanism: The career of a concept. *Journal of American History* 79: 11–37.

Sack, K. 1999. Don't speak English? No tax break, Alabama official declares. *New York Times*, June 4, A24.

Sanders, L. 1997. Against deliberation. *Political Theory* 25: 347–76.

Sapiro, V., and J. Soss. 1999. Spectacular politics, dramatic interpretations: Multiple meanings in the Thomas/Hill hearings. *Political Communication* 16: 285–314.

Schildkraut, D. 2001. Official-English and the states: Influences on declaring English the official language in the United States. *Political Research Quarterly* 54: 445–57.

Schmid, C. 2001. *The politics of language: Conflict, identity, and cultural pluralism in comparative perspective*. New York: Oxford University Press.

Schmidley, D. 2003. *The foreign-born population in the United States: March 2002*. Current Population Reports, P20-539, Bureau of the Census, Washington, DC.

Schmidt, R. 2000. *Language policy and identity politics in the United States*. Philadelphia: Temple University Press.

Schudson, M. 1998. *The good citizen: A history of American civic life*. New York: Free Press.

Schuman, H., C. Steeh, L. Bobo, and M. Krysan. 1997. *Racial attitudes in America: Trends and interpretations*. Cambridge: Harvard University Press.

Sears, D. 1993. Symbolic politics: A socio-psychological theory. In *Explorations in Political Psychology*, edited by S. Iyengar and W. McGuire. Durham, NC: Duke University Press.

Sears, D., and C. Funk. 1990. Self-interest in Americans' political opinions. In *Beyond Self-Interest*, edited by J. Mansbridge, 147–70. Chicago: University of Chicago Press.

Sears, D., J. Hetts, J. Sidanius, and L. Bobo. 2000. Race in American politics: Framing the debates. In *Racialized politics: The debate about racism in America*, edited by D. Sears, J. Sidanius, and L. Bobo. Chicago: University of Chicago Press.

Sigel, R. 1996. *Ambition and accommodation: How women view gender relations*. Chicago: University of Chicago Press.

Simon, H. 1985. Human nature in politics: The dialogue of psychology with political science. *American Political Science Review* 79: 293–304.

Simpson, D. 1986. *The politics of American English, 1776–1850*. New York: Oxford University Press.

Simpson, K. 2000. Religion in the schools: Nation searches its soul on whether faith has a place in its classrooms. *Denver Post*, February 20, A1.

Skocpol, T. 1999. How Americans became civic. In *Civic Engagement in American Democracy*, edited by T. Skocpol and M. Fiorina. Washington, DC: Brookings.

Smith, R. 1988. The "American Creed" and American identity: The limits of liberal citizenship in the United States. *Western Political Quarterly* 41: 225–51.

———. 1993. Beyond Tocqueville, Myrdal, and Hartz: The multiple traditions in America. *American Political Science Review* 87: 549–66.

———. 1997. *Civic Ideals: Conflicting visions of citizenship in U.S. history*. New Haven: Yale University Press.

Sniderman, P. 1999. The hollowed-out citizen: Political argument and political judgement. Invited address presented at the annual meeting of the International Society of Political Psychology, Amsterdam, the Netherlands, July.

Sniderman, P., and R. Brody. 1977. Coping: The ethic of self-reliance. *American Journal of Political Science* 21: 501–21.

Snyder, J., and K. Ballentine. 1996. Nationalism and the marketplace of ideas. *International Security* 21, no. 2: 5–40.

Spector, P. 1992. *Summated rating scale construction: An introduction*. Newbury Park: Sage Publications.

Stevens, G. 1994. Immigration, emigration, language acquisition, and the English language proficiency of immigrants in the United States. In *Immigration and ethnicity: The integration of America's newest arrivals*, edited by B. Edmonston and J. Passel. Washington, DC: Urban Institute Press.

Stevens, J. 1995. Beyond Tocqueville, please! *American Political Science Review* 89: 987–97.

Sullivan, W. 1982. *Reconstructing public philosophy*. Berkeley: University of California Press.

Tajfel, H., and J. Turner. 1986. The social identity theory of intergroup behavior. In *Psychology of intergroup relations*, edited by S. Worchel and W. Austin. Chicago: Nelson-Hall.

Tatalovich, R. 1995. *Nativism reborn? The Official English language movement and the American states*. Lexington: University Press of Kentucky.

Terry, D. 1998. The reply, it turned out, was bilingual: No. *New York Times*, June 5, A12.

Thernstrom, A. 1980. Language: Issues and legislation. In *The Harvard encyclopedia of American ethnic groups*, edited by S. Thernstrom. Cambridge: Belknap Press.

Theiss-Morse, E. 2003a. Characterizations and consequences: How Americans envision the American people. Paper presented at the annual meeting of the Midwest Political Science Association, Chicago, Illinois, April.

———. 2003b. Identification and disidentification: Americans' commitment to the national collective and its consequences. Paper presented at the annual meeting of the American Political Science Association, Philadelphia, Pennsylvania, September.

Thompson, S. 1997. The year of the volunteer. *Tampa Tribune*, December 29, 1.

Tierney, J. 1999. Polyglot city raises a cry for English. *New York Times*, August 16, B1.

Tocqueville, A. 1990 (1835). *Democracy in America*. New York: Vintage Books.

U.S. Bureau of the Census. 1997. *Statistical abstract of the United States: 1997.* 117th ed. Washington, DC: U.S. Government Printing Office.

———. 1998. *Statistical abstract of the United States: 1998.* 118th ed. Washington, DC: U.S. Government Printing Office.

U.S. Department of Justice, Immigration and Naturalization Service. 1999. *Annual report: Legal immigration 1998 fiscal year.* Can also be found at: www.uscis.gov/graphics/publicaffairs/newsrels/98Legal.pdf.

U.S. General Accounting Office. 1997. *GAO/GGD-97-81 Bilingual voting assistance provided and costs.* Can also be found at: www.gao.gov/archive/1997/gg97081.pdf.

U.S. Immigration and Naturalization Service. 1999. *Statistical yearbook of the Immigration and Naturalization Service: 1997.* Washington, DC: U.S. Government Printing Office.

Vecoli, R. 1994. The lady and the huddled masses: The Statue of Liberty as a symbol of immigration. In *The Statue of Liberty revisited,* edited by W. Dillon and N. Kotler. Washington, DC: Smithsonian Institution Press.

Verba, S., K. Schlozman, and H. Brady. 1995. *Voice and equality: Civic voluntarism in American politics.* Cambridge: Harvard University Press.

Vidanage, S., and D. Sears. 1995. The foundations of public opinion toward immigration policy: Group conflict or symbolic politics? Paper presented at the annual meeting of the Midwest Political Science Association, Chicago, Illinois, April.

Vobejda, B. 1992. Columbus: Which legacy? Explorer's image changes with the times. *Washington Post*, October 11, A1.

Volkan, V. 1994. *The need to have enemies and allies: From clinical practice to international relationships.* Northvale: Aronson.

Walzer, M. 1983. *Spheres of justice: A defense of pluralism and equality.* New York: Basic Books.

———. 1996. *What it means to be an American: Essays on the American experience.* New York: Marsilio.

Waters, M. 1990. *Ethnic options: Choosing identities in America.* Berkeley: University of California Press.

Wilson, J., and J. DiIulio. 1998. *American government: Institutions and policies.* 7th ed. Boston: Houghton Mifflin.

Wolpert, R., and J. Gimpel. 1998. Self-interest, symbolic politics, and public attitudes toward gun control. *Political Behavior* 20: 241–62.

Wood, G. 1969. *The creation of the American Republic.* Chapel Hill: University of North Carolina Press.

Zaller, J. 1992. *The nature and origins of mass opinion.* New York: Cambridge University Press.

Zeller, R., and E. Carmines. 1980. *Measurement in the social sciences: The link between theory and data.* New York: Cambridge University Press.

Zolberg, A., and L. Woon. 1999. Why Islam is like Spanish: Cultural incorporation in Europe and the United States. *Politics and Society* 27: 5–38.

Index

Page references followed by *fig* indicate an illustrated figure; followed by *t* indicates a table.